PUB PADDLES

The Best Short Paddling Trips in the South of England

"Nice? It's the ONLY thing," said the Water Rat solemnly, "Believe me, my young friend, there is NOTHING - absolute nothing - half so much worth doing as simply messing about in boats. Simply messing," he went on dreamily: "messing - about - in - boats…"

*The Wind In The Willows
by Kenneth Grahame*

PETER KNOWLES

Chris Wheeler

"The guidebook never said anything about getting wet!"

Copyright: Rivers Publishing UK.

ISBN: 978-0-9957513-5-4.

Second Edition 2025. First edition 2010.

The author Peter Knowles asserts the moral right to be identified as the author of this work.

All rights reserved. No part of this publication may be reproduced, stored in a computer system, or transmitted, in any form or by any means - electronic, mechanical, photocopying, recording or otherwise, without the prior written permission of the publishers.

A CIP catalogue record for this book is available from the British Library.

Photographs and illustrations are as credited.

Back cover: Peter Knowles, Norman Teasdale, Richard Ash.

Cartoons by Alan Fox.

Graphic Design by Leon Reichel Design.

Layouts by Stuart Fisher.

Maps by Bute Cartographics.

Contains Ordnance Survey data © Crown copyright & database right 2022.

Printed in Scotland by Bell & Bain Ltd.

Distributed throughout the UK by:

Cordee Outdoor Books & Maps,

11 Jacknell Road, Hinckley, Leicester, LE10 3BS

www.cordee.co.uk

Disclaimer

This book is only a guide - it was written in good faith, but rivers and features change, so that information may be out of date or misleading. Note that all journeys on water can be hazardous (just like road journeys!) especially in high water or extreme weather conditions.

If you decide to undertake a journey by water then the risk assessment is yours, the decision to make that journey is yours, and the consequences arising from that decision are yours and yours alone. The publishers, editors and contributors can accept no responsibility for any loss or injury sustained by any person as a result of ideas expressed in this book.

Contents

The Trips

1. Kingston to Richmond
2. Hampton Court
3. Thames at Shepperton
4. River Mole
5. Wey at Guildford
6. Basingstoke Canal
7. Odiham Castle
8. Marlow to Maidenhead
9. Henley upon Thames
10. St Patrick's Stream
11. Goring Gap
12. Wolvercote Circuit
13. Oxford Cherwell
14. Grand Union at Tring
15. Stort
16. Cam
17. Houghton Mill
18. Chelmer
19. Contstable's Stour
20. Medway
21. Canterbury Stour
22. Bodiam Castle
23. Cuckmere
24. Arun
25. Hamble
26. Itchen

- Very easy
- Easy
- Experience needed

Other Contents and Page numbers

- 4 Summary table
- 6 Using this book
- 8 Best Trips
- 10 Safe paddling
- 11 Acknowledgements
- 12 The Pub Paddles story
- 13 Author
- 14 The Trips
- 208 London
- 212 Where next?
- 213 River Access Notes
- 214 Index

Green = very easy   Blue = easy   Red = experience needed

No	Best	Trip	Scenic	4 Kids?	Water	Type	Hr	km
1	***	Kingston to Richmond	☻☻	☺☺	Wide river	One way	3	7
2	***	Hampton Court	☻☻	☺☺☺	Wide river	Return	2	6
3	**	Shepperton	☻☻	☺☺	Wide river +	Return	3	8
4	***	River Mole	☻☻☻	☺☺☺	Small river	One way	3	8
5	***	Wey at Guildford	☻☻☻	☺☺☺	Canalised river	Return	3	8
6	**	Basingstoke Canal	☻☻☻	☺	Canal	Return	3	8
7	**	Odiham Castle	☻☻	☺☺	Canal	Return	2	6
8	**	Marlow to Maidenhead	☻☻☻	☺	Wide river	One way	4	14
9	**	Henley upon Thames	☻☻☻	☺	Wide river +	One way	5	18
10	***	St Patrick's Stream	☻☻☻	☺☺	Small stream +	Circular	2	8
11	**	Goring Gap	☻☻☻	☺☺	Wide river	One way	2	7
12	**	Wolvercote Circuit	☻☻		River + canal	Circular	3	10
13	***	Oxford Cherwell	☻☻	☺☺☺	Small river	Return	4	13
14	**	Grand Union at Tring	☻☻	☺☺	Canal	One way	2	7
15	*	Stort	☻	☺☺	Canalised river	One way	2	7
16	***	Cam	☻☻	☺☺☺	Small river	Return	2	6
17	***	Houghton Mill	☻☻☻	☺☺☺	River & stream	Return	2	6
18	**	Chelmer	☻☻	☺☺	Canalised river	One way	2	8
19	***	Constable's Stour	☻☻☻	☺☺	Small river	Return	4	13
20	**	Medway	☻☻	☺☺	Canalised river	Return	3	12
21	**	Canterbury Stour	☻☻	☺☺	Tidal river	Return	4	16
22	**	Bodiam Castle	☻☻	☺☺☺	Placid river	Return	3	12
23	***	Cuckmere	☻☻☻	☺☺	Tidal river	Return	3	13
24	**	Arun	☻☻☻	☺	Tidal river	Return	3	13
25	***	Hamble	☻☻	☺☺	Wide tidal river	Return	3	11
26	**	Itchen	☻	☺☺☺	Small river	Return	1	3

Summary table

Parking	Launch	Portage	Quiet	Permit?	Hire	Notes
**	***	1 rollers	*	Yes	**	A classic 'must do'.
***	***	2 rollers	*	Yes	***	Entertaining & historic trip.
***	***	None	*	Yes	***	Fine selection of Thames pubs.
***	*	1 weir	***	Free	None	Natural flowing chalk stream.
***	***	3 locks +	**	Yes	***	Surrey at its best!
***	***	None	***	Yes	***	Friendly, winding, ideal beginner's trip.
***	***	None	***	Yes	***	Head to a castle or a fine country pub?
*	***	2 locks	*	Yes	**	Cruise past Cliveden Country House.
***	***	4 locks	**	Yes	**	Quintessential River Thames day trip.
*	**	1 lock	**	Yes	*	Fast flowing backwater + Thames.
*	**	None	*	Yes	***	Beautiful short River Thames trip.
***	***	4 (or 1)	**	Yes	None	Thames meadows & suburban gardens.
*	***	1 rollers	**	Yes	**	Classic Oxford punting trip.
**	**	None	**	Yes	None	Interesting summit stretch.
**	**	4 locks	**	Yes	*	Surprisingly rural yet close to London.
**	**	None	**	Yes	**	Two diverse & excellent trips to choose.
**	**	1-4	**	Yes	***	Scenic river plus backwater.
**	***	4 locks	***	Special	***	Escape to peaceful rural Essex.
***	***	1 lock	***	Yes	***	A picture of idyllic English countryside.
**	***	1 lock	**	Yes	**	Paddle through the 'Garden of England'.
***	**	None	**	Free	***	Beautiful, secret, rural paddle.
**	**	None	***	Free	***	A stealthy assault on this famous castle.
***	***	1	***	Free	*	Cruise through the scenic South Downs.
**	*	None	***	Free	*	Paddle the spectacular Arun Gap.
**	***	None	**	Free	***	From yachts to unspoilt woodland.
***	**	None	**	Free	***	Ideal venue for beginners.

Using this book

Doug Dew

Steve Douch

Selection of trips

Some purist, old school canoeists will throw their hands up in horror because this is a **selective guide book** designed to highlight what we consider to be the most interesting and convenient **short trips**. However that being said, if you read the descriptions carefully, the sections on 'Extending the trip' and 'Other paddling trips nearby' you should get lots of ideas for putting longer trips together and we have tried to help by "opening the door" to other information sources.

Star Ratings – 1 to 3 stars.

These are **subjective** – if you don't agree, then put your own rating in the notes section.

 **Scenery**. Entirely our subjective view.

 4 Kids. Is this a good family trip? This depends on the age of the children and how adventurous they feel.

✱✱ "**Best Trips**" A rating taking all factors into account.

Length of trip

This is a very rough guide of how long a trip might take allowing for a few stops – a fast paddler could probably do some of these trips in a third of our suggested time.

How Easy?

Very Easy Trips

These are suitable for beginners. They are often canals or similar waterways with no current and few boats or other hazards.

Easy Trips

These require some experience and common sense – typically these might be a river with minor hazards like current, weirs, wind, and other boats. Obviously factors like high winds or fast currents can make any river dangerous.

Experience needed

This means a more adventurous trip where all of the group should have suitable previous experience.

Parking

*** Means that normally you should have no difficulty parking at the start point.
** Parking is more limited and/or less convenient.
* You may need to unload and then park some distance away.

Brian Biffin

Launching

*** Easy launching from a slipway, low stage or concrete bank, and close to where you can unload or park.

** You may have to carry your boat some way, or launch from a grassy bank or beach.

* You probably have to carry your boat some way and launching is difficult.

Fiona Firth

Portages

Note that you may be able to cut down the number of portages by varying the start point or the length of the trip. On the River Thames and some other navigations it may be possible to travel through the locks if portaging is a problem for you.

Special Points

These are normally negative points and potential hazards that you should take note of.

Alan Tilling

Permits

Most of the trips in this book are on statutory navigations where the navigation authority makes a charge. If you belong to Paddle UK (formerly "British Canoeing") then your membership fee covers you for trips on the Thames and many other waterways. You may need to produce your membership card if asked – usually by lock keepers . We recommend membership as it has many benefits including third party liability insurance.

Canoe & Paddleboard hire

*** A choice of canoes, kayaks and SUPs are available at, or near, the Start point.

** Canoe, kayaks &/or SUP hire is available at a point somewhere on the trip.

* Canoes, kayaks, &/or SUPs are available for collection in the local area – or for delivery to the Start Point.

Pubs and Tea Shops

Sadly these change! If you are looking forward to a pub lunch then it is worth a quick phone call beforehand.

Dan Knowles

Best trips

Peter Knowles

Phil Arnold

Chris Wheeler

Best Trips for Paddle Boards

No.	Trip
2.	Hampton Court
3.	Shepperton
6.	Basingstoke Canal
10.	St Patrick's Stream
11.	Goring Gap
12.	Wolvercote Circuit
15.	Stort
17.	Houghton Mill
19.	Constable's Stour
21.	Canterbury Stour
26.	Itchen

Best Trips with Stations

If you live in central London, then taking a train to one of these paddling trips may be easier than you think, and much pleasanter than fighting traffic.

No.	Trip	Station
2.	Hampton Court	Hampton Court
4.	Mole	West Humble and Leatherhead
5.	Wey at Guildford	Guildford
6.	Basingstoke Canal	Ash Vale
9.	Henley upon Thames	Henley
10.	St Patrick's Stream	Wargrave or Shiplake
11.	Goring Gap	Goring and Pangbourne
12.	Wolvercote circuit	Oxford
14.	Grand Union	Tring
15.	Stort	Harlow and Sawbridgeworth.
20.	Medway	Yalding
21.	Canterbury Stour	Sturry
24.	Arun	Amberley
25.	Hamble	Burlesdon

Best Trips for Castles & NT Properties

No.	Trip	Castle or property
1.	Kingston to Richmond	Ham House N.T.
2.	Hampton Court	Hampton Court Palace
5.	Wey at Guildford	Dapdune Wharf N.T.
7.	Odiham Castle	Odiham Castle
8.	Marlow to Maidenhead	Cliveden House N.T.
17.	Houghton Mill	Houghton Water Mill N.T.
19.	Constable's Stour	Flatford Mill N.T.
22.	Bodiam Castle	Bodiam Castle N.T.
23.	Cuckmere	Alfriston Clergy House N.T.

Fiona Firth

Best Trips for the Physically Challenged

Many physically challenged people tell us that canoeing is a wonderful sport that gives them real freedom to explore the outdoors. They also say that the big problem is carrying the boat, launching and portages. Everyone has their own limitations so rather than use some broad brush wheel chair emblem this guide book tries to give you the information so that you can make your own decisions about which trip is likely to be suitable for you. We have especially tried to be informative about the suggested Start point and where possible we show a photograph.

Are you on your own, fancy doing a canoe trip, but are hesitant about all the hassles of carrying and launching a boat? - our top tip is to consider hiring a canoe from one of the locations we list – this means there will be someone to launch the boat and give you a hand. Just give them a phone call ahead of time to check availability.

We suggest the following trips to consider

- 2. Hampton Court
- 6. Basingstoke Canal
- 9. Henley upon Thames
- 14. Oxford Cherwell
- 19. Constable's Stour
- 21. Canterbury Stour
- 3. Thames at Shepperton
- 7. Odiham Castle
- 11. Goring Gap
- 17. Cam
- 20. Medway
- 26. Itchen

More information

We recommend the following -

www.gopaddling.info

This is the information website run by PaddleUK.

It also hosts **PaddlePoints** interactive map of where to paddle.

www.paddleuk.org

Wider information on our sport including training and competition.

www.canoedaysout.com

Details of over 200 day trips.

www.songofthepaddle.co.uk

A great website for open boaters.

www.ukriversguidebook.co.uk

A popular website for all aspects of paddlesports.

Safe paddling

Weil's Disease (Leptospirosis)

This is a bacterial infection which contaminates water and river banks. It is occasionally caught by paddlers and can be a mild, flu-like illness with fever, muscle aches, conjunctivitis and sometimes vomiting. However, very occasionally it can lead to a more serious illness called Weil's disease with jaundice and kidney failure.

Symptoms usually develop 7-12 days after paddling so if you then feel ill, you should see your doctor ASAP (or if out of hours contact NHS24) and stress that because or your paddling then Weil's disease is a strong possibility. The disease can escalate fast and so recommended treatment is an early course of antibiotics whilst awaiting the results of blood tests (which can take ages). Doctors are rightly reluctant to prescribe antibiotics, however we know several paddlers who have ended up on life support systems when the first doctor had delayed prescribing antibiotics whilst awaiting the results of the blood tests.

For more information see www.hpa.org.uk/ and search on Weil's.

More information

PaddleUK and BCU Awards have some excellent videos and e-learning courses on their websites.

Safe and Enjoyable Paddling

If you are new to paddle sports then we recommend that you join a local paddling club and/or take a course with a PaddleUK provider. We advise -

1. Always wear a buoyancy aid.
2. Paddle with a buddy.
3. Tell someone where you are going.
4. Carry a mobile phone.
5. Check the Weather forecast and avoid offshore winds..
6. Keep away from weirs and sluices which can be very dangerous.
7. Avoid paddling when rivers are high, or in extreme weather.

On Navigations like the River Thames -

- Keep together as a group.
- Keep to the right hand side where it is safe and practical to do so.
- Do not get in the way of other craft by suddenly changing course.
- Look out behind you for fast rowing boats – silent and deadly!

Health

Most of the rivers in this guide book are surprisingly clean, however all rivers receive some sort of dirty water so use common sense and

1. Cover minor cuts with waterproof plasters.
2. Wash hands before eating – or use antiseptic hand gel.
3. We personally try to avoid paddling after the first heavy rain following a dry period as this washes a lot of 'nasties' into the river.

Responsible Paddling

1. Park considerately and change discretely.
2. Be friendly to local residents and those you meet.
3. Be kind to nature, minimise noise and disturbance.
4. Leave a clean river and collect plastic rubbish if safe to do so.
5. Watch for anglers - avoid their lines & pass by quickly & quietly.
6. Stop the spread of alien species - check, clean and dry your gear.

Paddle Board Leashes?

We advise against wearing a paddleboard leash on the trips in this book due to a low risk of entrapment. If you do decide to wear one then please make sure that it is a quick release waist leash. See up to date advice from PaddleUK.

Sunset paddle on the Thames. *SUP life*

Acknowledgements

The first edition of this book was the sum of a flattering amount of help from literally hundreds of people – individuals, clubs, local experts, photographers, etc. THANK YOU again everyone.

We would like to say thank you to the many people who helped update this Second Edition and especially -

Phil Arnold	Nick Grenside	David Savage
Richard Ash	Peter Hennessy	Peter Scutt
David Crosson	Mike Hewlett	Mike Shaw
Richard Davies	Craig Hill	Dave Surman
Steve Douch	Dave Hillier	Chris Taylor
Fiona Firth	Bill Lockton	Julian & Cathie Taylor
Alan Fox	Paul Mackenzie	Norman Teasdale
Dave & Sheryl Francis	Lesley Montague	Alan & Claire Tilling
Clive & Martha Goadby	Matt Oseman	Tony Ward
Jane Goldsmith	Peter Nash	
Mal Grey	Frank Ryan	

Thank you and Happy Paddling!   Peter Knowles, Rivers Publishing, May 2025.

Pub Paddles story

At the Station. *Nick Grenside.*

On the River. *Nick Grenside.*

Who needs a car?

Nick and his family lived in Central London. Inspired by Pub Paddles, they purchased a couple of folding Pakcanoes and used public transport to pursue their dreams. Lack of storage space and car were no impediment to paddling adventure!

Nick says that if you live in central London, then taking a train out to one of these paddling trips is simpler than you think, and much pleasanter than fighting traffic.

The story behind the guidebook

The idea for this guidebook came from my friend George Wood. We were sitting in the "Magpie" pub after a paddle on the Thames and he said to me "Pete, your guidebook to Nepal is fabulous but what we really need is a guidebook to our local rivers around London". I did a bit of research and realized how right he was - there seemed to be a real need for an inspiring, high quality, guidebook that answered the question "Where in the South East of England can I go paddling?"

The South East of England posed a different kind of challenge from our other guide books as there were some 2000km of possible waterways however paddling information was incredibly scarce. We worked on a long list of suggested trips to research, check out and paddle and these were then eventually whittled down to 26 selected "Best Short Trips" – each then carefully checked out for things like best parking and launching spots. Over a hundred volunteers, clubs, and local experts contributed to the first edition - suggesting possible trips, writing trip descriptions, checking the route details, contributing photographs, and then test paddling the final descriptions. Thank you everyone!

The First Edition of this book was published in 2010 and it proved to be huge success with reviewers consistently calling it "Brilliant" and giving it five stars. Sandi Toksvig (a keen leisure paddler) interviewed Pete about it for her regular travel program on Radio Four. Pub Paddles became a paddling best seller and has had to be reprinted several times since. We were heartened when readers got in touch to share their paddling stories.

The team at Rivers Publishing had originally planned a new edition for 2020 but these plans had to be delayed because of the Covid epidemic. Thankfully most of the team who had helped produce the first edition were still paddling and volunteered to update the trip descriptions for the new edition. The other good news was that almost all the pubs in the first edition are still thriving and welcome paddlers! We hope you enjoy them.

The author

The Author

Peter Knowles was first introduced to canoeing and learnt early survival skills in the Second Wallasey Sea Scouts. It took a lot of years and some epic swims before he learnt to eskimo roll, just in time for a kayak trip down the Grand Canyon in 1973. This ability to roll didn't help when he was run over by a 35ft motorised rubber raft in one of the rapids!

This trip was a life-changing experience that gave him a love for big water, multi-day trips and started 50 years of exploring the great whitewater rivers of the World. He has led over 40 expeditions and first descents and in 1994 he was selected by the Royal Geographical Society as one of "20 modern day explorers". More recently he was one of a few Brits to be elected to the International Whitewater Hall of Fame.

Of all the countries he has paddled, Nepal is his favourite. He first went there in 1983, has returned there numerous times and feels privileged to have helped the development of kayaking in that country. He has also explored other Himalayan rivers in Pakistan, India, Bhutan, and Tibet. His guide book, "White Water Nepal" is now in its third edition and was described by the Alpine Kayak Club as "the best guidebook ever". The success of the book led to a new career as a guidebook and map publisher.

Peter spent some 35 years living in Surrey so he was very well qualified to produce the first edition of this guidebook. He now lives in the English Lake District and should rightly be retired but couldn't resist the opportunity of this second edition to revisit some favourite pubs and rivers in the South of England!

The Author on arduous research in the Himalayas.
Mark Nichols

The author recovering from arduous research nearer home.

Author's Note

Despite a lifetime exploring wonderful rivers all over the World I was pleasantly surprised when I had to research the rivers in the South of England for the first edition of this book. This research re-confirmed to me how lucky I was to be living in Great Britain - it is such a fascinating and lovely country for the diversity of its scenery, culture, people and history - and what better way to explore it than by water?

Kingston to Richmond 1

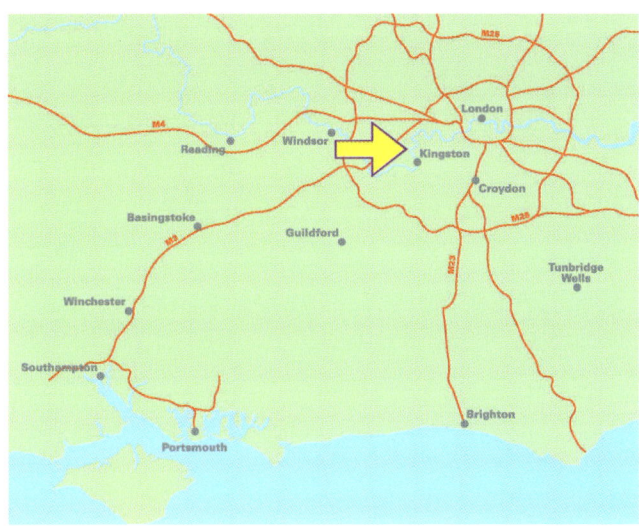

Wide river – partly tidal
One way trip
3 hours - 7km
Easy

Parking	★★
Launching	★★★
Portages?	Rollers at the lock
Quiet?	A busy but wide river

Special points

1. Beware current and wind in bad conditions.
2. Membership of Paddle UK or Thames permit required

Why do this trip?
Our closest trip to London and a classic "Must Do"!

Tell me more
One of the most interesting and scenic stretches of the river Thames with iconic views of famous Richmond Hill – and easily accessible to London. This is a great paddle if you want to stop off and take your time as there are so many interesting things to see. Of course nothing could be cooler than arriving at Richmond riverside by SUP, canoe or kayak!

Canoe & SUP Hire

Paddle Richmond Tel:0203 488 1785
Offers Paddle board, Kayak hire, and tuition from bases at Richmond and Teddington.

Back of Beyond Adventures
Tel: 020 8050 4051
Offers Canoe, kayak and SUP hire, from River Lane, upstream of Richmond.

Start
Kingston upon Thames
GR TQ179703   Post code: KT2 5AZ

The best option for launching and parking is on Lower Ham Road at the apex of Canbury Gardens where it meets the Thames. There is **free parking on a Sunday** and no time restriction - however on other days there is only **four-hour** parking. To reach the parking take the Richmond Road out of central Kingston, turn left down Woodside Road and then right at the end onto Lower Ham Road.

River Thames at Richmond Hill.   *Paddle Richmond*

1 Kingston to Richmond

Finish

Richmond Riverside
GR TO177747   Post code: TW9 1NL

We recommend taking out at Bambers steps just downstream of the **White Cross Pub** or at the nearby slipway. This is downstream of the Turks Launches pier and beyond the very busy main stretch of riverbank. You can bring a car right down to the water front here to load up (albeit on double yellow lines).

To reach this point by car, on entering Richmond Town Centre from the Richmond Bridge end go over the roundabout and head straight on. As the town centre traffic turns right you keep straight on down a one way road towards Richmond Green, a little past the shops turn left onto **Friar's Lane** and then continue on to reach the river. Limited car parking is available in Friars Lane Car Park - 4 hour limit.

Trip description by Fiona Firth

Paddling down towards Richmond Hill. *Andrew Jackson*

The Shuttle

1. **The number 65 bus.** The easiest shuttle for most people is for the drivers to catch the bus back to Kingston whilst the rest of the team are enjoying tea and cakes in one of the riverside cafes. The buses are every ten minutes from Petersham road (access from the towpath across a small area of grass just before 'Stein's' Bavarian restaurant), the bus stop is on the far side of the road. Alight at the Latchmere Road stop.

2. It is possible to return by **river boat** to Kingston - check the internet for the time table.

3. If you can fit a bike in the car and drop this in Richmond first, you can have a very pleasant cycle ride back on the towpath.

Alternative Start Point

Ham House GR 171732   Post Code: TW10 7RS
If you want a 'there and back' paddle then we recommend starting from the riverside near Ham House where there is easy launching and a huge free car park next to the river - but with a **height restriction**. N.b. If you stay downstream of Teddington Lock then you do not need a Thames Permit. An option if you have a high vehicle is to park and launch from River Lane, Petersham Meadows.

Tidal planning

Whilst not essential, a bit of tidal planning will make your journey easier. The ideal is to set off from Kingston some time after high tide so that any tidal current will then help push you along – however normally you will have few problems as long as you avoid going downstream in the 3 hours before high water when the tide is flooding gently up the river.

Teddington is the limit of the tidal Thames, however the 5km between Teddington and Richmond are only truly tidal for about 2 hours before and 2 hours after high tide. This is because at all other times, the river is dammed up just downstream of Richmond to maintain a minimum depth for navigation. High water at Teddington lock is about an hour after high tide at London Bridge - see the Port of London web site. www.portoflondon.co.uk

1 Kingston to Richmond

Pubs and tea shops

If you fail to show restraint on this trip it can very easily take all day! You could start with a swift one in the **Boaters Inn** in Canbury Gardens, they have a large outside area in the park and serve good pub food. Tel: 020 85414672. Perhaps it is better to start off and then treat yourselves enroute? Just after Teddington Lock is **The Anglers** riverside pub - once you have completed the portage paddle upstream to the weir and the pub is on your right. They have a huge riverside garden, and serve a wide range of good food. It can, however, get very busy. Tel: 0208 9777475.

Further on at Twickenham, on the left bank, and tucked behind the far end of Eel Pie Island is The **White Swan** Pub. This has a large beach for easy access, lots of outdoor seating, and serves good food. Tel: 0208 744 2951. A little bit further on and also on the left bank is **Orleans Gardens** where there is a children's playground and café.

As you approach Richmond Riverside the options for refreshments are numerous. If you are in search of a calm retreat then seek out **Hollyhock Café** in Terrace Gardens (entrance through a grotto, in the small park before the first set of boathouses). Tel: 0208 948 6555. There is also the **Tide Tables Café** under an arch of Richmond Bridge. Tel: 020 8948 8285. If you are after a pub head for the really busy section of the riverside downstream of Richmond Bridge and near the **White Cross Inn** and the take out – this is a great place to people watch!

More information

River conditions
www.gov.uk/guidance/river-thames-current-river-conditions

River Thames
www.visitthames.co.uk

Kingston upon Thames
www.kingstonuponthames.info

Richmond tourist information
www.visitrichmond.co.uk

Thames Young Mariners
www.surreyoutdoorlearning.uk/centres/thames-young-mariners

The Finish Point near Richmond Bridge in 2006. *Fiona Firth*

The Finish Point near Richmond Bridge in 1906. *Sutton Palmer*

The journey

If you are paddling on a Sunday, immediately after setting off you will be confronted by the sight of tall white sails skidding across the water. These beautiful yachts are Tamesis club's Thames 'A' rated boats which race each week. Paddle on, cross to the left bank, and you will find Trowlock Island which is worth paddling round (be careful to avoid the chain ferry). The Island is home to **Royal Canoe Club** and many quaint wooden bungalows. Back on the main flow (river left) you will come to Broom Water. Large attractive houses back onto this sheltered, quiet back water and we have seen a pair of Herons hopping from boat to boat. Continuing on, you will next come to the Lensbury sports club, whose grounds lead you up to **Teddington Lock**.

Look carefully at the posts in front of the weir, there are often Cormorants fishing from these vantage points. Follow signs for the lock to the right of the river, at the end of the weir you will find a ramp and a set of **boat rollers** which can easily be used to portage the lock. The challenge is to portage without exiting your boat! Teddington Lock is worth exploring, and you may wish to re-enact the Monty Python 'Fish-Slapping Dance' filmed here in 1969.

If you intend visiting **The Anglers** pub then turn left after the portage, otherwise keep right and carry on down the river - you will now have Ham riverside lands to your right, and lots of very desirable and expensive houses and gardens dropping to the river on your left. Looking up river the rather elegant building of Radnpr House Independent School for boys will come into view. The main building dates from 1844, and was built by Thomas Young a Tea

Other trips nearby

For a full day trip, you might like to consider combining this paddle with the next journey upstream - trip no. 2 Hampton Court. You would then start at Molesey and finish at Richmond.

Other trips are possible on the tidal Thames downstream but require experience and may be hazardous – see 'Thames Tideway' notes. Trip no. 27.

Places of interest nearby

Richmond Park is one of the largest royal parks and a wonderful open space for cycling, walking and roller blading - www.royalparks.org.uk

Ham House and **Marble Hill House** are both magnificent riverside historic houses -www.nationaltrust.org.uk/hamhouse and www.english-heritage.org.

The famous **Royal Botanical Kew Gardens** are 5km to the north - www.kew.org.

1 Kingston to Richmond

The Royal Canoe Club

The Royal Canoe Club is the oldest and probably the most distinguished Canoe Club in the world.

John MacGregor launched canoeing as a recognised sport in the late 1800's with tours in his famous 'Rob Roy' canoe. Through his books and lectures, which he gave on his return, he formed a group of interested gentleman who met in the Star and Garter Hotel in Richmond on the 25th July 1866 to form this, the first Canoe Club in the world.

Membership quickly grew and in 1873, by command of Queen Victoria, it became the "ROYAL CANOE CLUB" this was a significant honour for a club devoted to small craft at a time when larger yachts were a status symbol. Club members competed at the Berlin Olympics in 1936, and 72 years later Club member Tim Brabant won Britain's first Canoeing Olympic Gold Medal at the 2008 Beijing Olympics.

Royal Canoe Club has grown to have many varied interests and even sections for Dragon boats and Hawaian Outrigger Canoes. It has many family members, has an active social and training programme, and welcomes new members.

Peter Wells

John MacGregor in 'Rob Rob'. *From an old print*

Merchant; it is intended to look reminiscent of a tea caddy. Just prior to the school you will come to Nesmans Boat Repairs on Swan Island. On the right bank at this point is Ham Riverside local nature reserve - look out for grebes and herons which frequent this stretch of the river. Thames Young Mariners Base is then on the right bank based on a small lake separated from the river – this is a very active outdoor centre offering canoeing and sailing courses.

Eel Pie Island is the next landmark on the left bank and we suggest keeping left of the Island so that you get some fine views of the old riverside village of **Twickenham**. Eel Pie Island has a footbridge to it, there are 50 houses and 120 inhabitants. Each end of the island is a nature reserve. The Island was the site of the legendary Eel Pie Hotel, a genteel 19th C. building that hosted ballroom dancing up to the 1950's before becoming a venue for Jazz and then in the 1960's for Rock and R&B. Many famous names performed at the hotel in its heyday, including The Rolling Stones, The Who, and Pink Floyd. .

Beyond the Island you come to **Orleans Gardens** on the left bank with a children's playground, toilets and café. On the opposite bank is the large free car park that we recommend as an alternative start point if you want a 'there and back' trip. Just downstream is Hammertons foot ferry – one of the very few ferries that survive on the Thames. The river now passes between the grounds of two famous old houses. To the right you will get a glimpse of **Ham House** (NT) whilst **Marble Hill House** is then to the left. Both are the last complete survivors of the elegant villas and gardens which bordered the Thames between Richmond and Hampton Court in the 18th century

Everyone likes canoeing! *Fiona Firth*

Teddington Lock - the boat roller.   *Andrew Jackson*

Looking ahead on your right you should be able to spot the surprising sight of cows grazing on Petersham Meadows below the steep rise of **Richmond Hill**. The cows retain their pasture due to the Richmond Ham and Petersham Open Spaces Act of 1902, intended to preserve this iconic view of the Thames, surrounding heath and woodland from Richmond Hill. This view had been immortalised by Turner, and is supposed to be the only view in the country protected by a special Act of Parliament. The imposing building on the top of the hill was formerly the Star and Garter Home for wounded war veterans (now converted to flats).

Once you have passed Glover's Island, you are on the approach to Richmond and at this point you may well see racing paddlers in kayaks and canoes out training from **Richmond Canoe Club** which you will pass on the right hand bank. Pull up before the first set of boathouses if you want to visit the **Hollyhock café** in Terrace Gardens, otherwise paddle on under Richmond Bridge past the crowds to the take out at "Bambers Steps" after the **White Cross Pub**.

Special thanks to Andrew, Dominic and Clare.

Extending the trip

Downstream is not very inspiring and brings you to Richmond Lock in just under a kilometre.

Upstream is much more interesting. If you paddle up and through Kingston Bridge you will see the old and new buildings of Kingston's riverside on the river right bank, whilst on the left bank is the start of Hampton Court Deer Park. If you are feeling adventurous then look out for the **Hogsmill Stream** which comes in on the river right 200m upstream of Kingston Bridge - you can explore a short way up this as far as the ancient 'Clattern Bridge' – the oldest bridge in Surrey.

Hampton Court 2

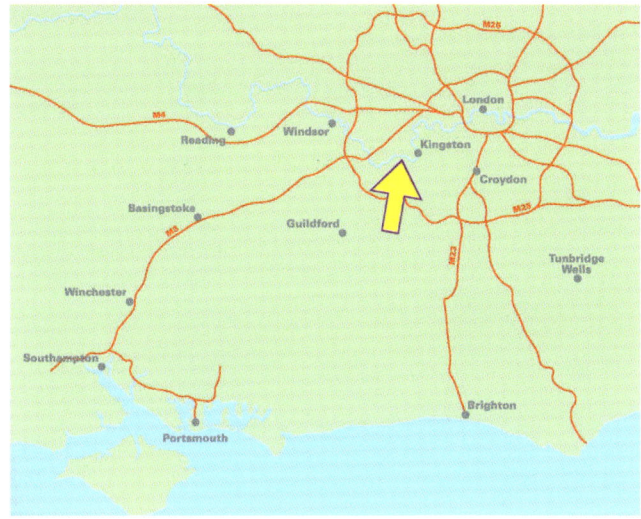

Wide river
There and back
2 hours - 6km
Easy paddling

Parking	★★★
Launching	★★★
Portages?	Rollers at lock
Quiet?	Busy river traffic

Why do this trip?
This is easily accessible, close to London and full of interest – a trip that is sure to entertain all the family.

Tell me more
This is a great short paddle for an evening or afternoon. What better way to arrive at Hampton Court Palace than by water – just as King Henry and the court entourage did some four centuries ago! On fine summer days there are many picnic spots, whilst on chilly Autumn days there are several riverside pubs which offer a warm welcome to the patron arriving by river. Although this is a 'there and back' journey, there are many islands en route so you can avoid seeing the same section of river twice.

Start and Finish
Hurst Park   GR TQ141692   Post code: KT8 1SU
Sadlers Ride Car Park provides exceptional access to the river with free easy parking, a slipway for launching, **toilets**, and also a large open space with a children's play park nearby – the area was formerly Hurst Park Race course until the early 1960's. The car park closes at

Special points
1. Beware of rowing eights – fast and quiet!
2. Membership of Paddle UK or Thames permit required.

Canoe & SUP Hire

Canoe & Kayak the Thames is based at Shepperton Marina some 7km upstream and offers a range of quality canoes and kayaks for hire – www.wwtcc.com –
Tel: 01932 247 978

Hampton Court Paddle Sports offers SUP hire at West Molesey riverside.
Tel: 07730 898802.

"Prithy kind sir, wouldst thou guard my paddle whilst I seek audience with the King?"
Paul Mackenzie

2 Hampton Court

9pm and frequently has a 2.1 meter height restriction barrier in place – if you are over-height then there is an alternative launch point close to Molesey Boat Club (GR TO148689) with parking in the lay-by near by. Sadlers Ride car park is sign posted as 'Riverside space' off the A3050 and at busy times is best approached from the direction of Hampton Court.

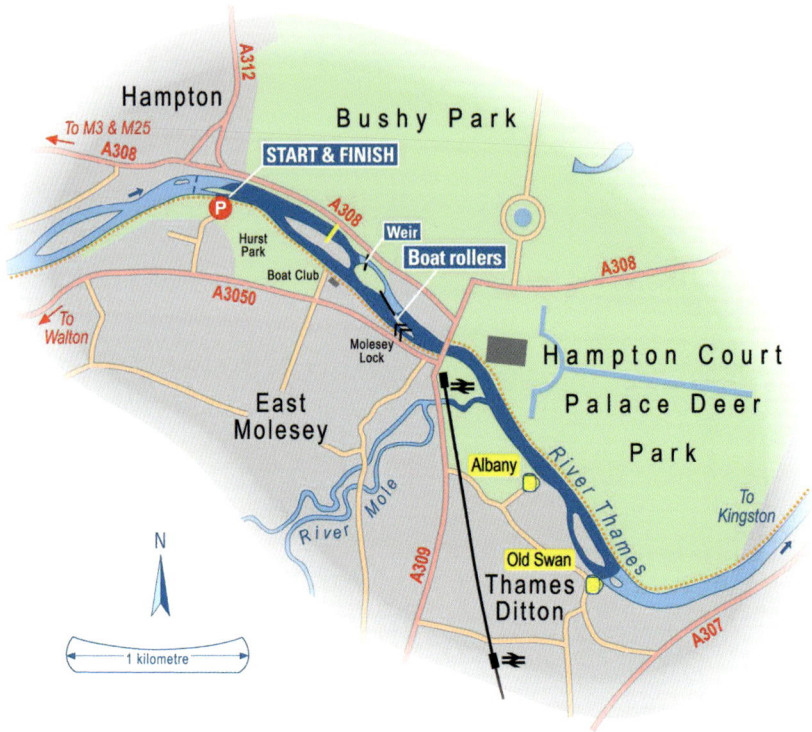

Trip description by Paul Mackenzie

More information

O.S. Map 1:50,000 sheet 176

Hampton Court Palace
www.hrp.org.uk

River Thames
www.thames.me.uk

River conditions...www.gov.uk/guidance/river-thames-current-river-conditions

Dittons Skiff and Punt club
www.dittons.org.uk/

Pubs and tea shops

The route has many refreshment opportunities - ice cream vans (in season) are at the suggested launch site, Molesey Boat club and Molesey Lock. Café and coffee shops are at Molesey Cricket club, (although this is a difficult spot to land at), Bridge Street at Hampton Court, and in Hampton Court Palace itself. Our favorite pub is the **Albany** close to the turnaround point – we like to sit outside and watch the passing craft - often you can see the beginners from the local skiff and punting club getting to grips (or not) with poling along the Thames! www.the–albany.co.uk. Tel: 0208 972 9163. King Henry VIII is said to have given his seal of approval to **Ye Olde Swan Inn** on the riverside at Thames Ditton. This historic 13th century Inn is in a great location.

Hampton Court Palace. *Andreas Tille*

The journey

Take care when you launch as one of the country's largest (and friendliest?) colonies of swans live on this stretch of the Thames. We suggest that once afloat you remain close to the South bank and paddle East (right) downstream with the usually gently flowing current towards Molesey Lock.

You will initially pass Swan Island, a small uninhabited outcrop followed by Taggs Island. The second and much larger island supports some of the most luxurious and amazing houseboats as well as some in need of a facelift. In a few moments you will pass the cricket club (& café) and then **Molesey Boat Club**. Look out for the sculpture of a rowing boat emerging from the ground some 30 feet into the air. The Molesey regatta used to be the second biggest in the country, behind only Henley, and still takes place each summer.

Keep to the right as you approach **Molesey Lock** – beware of the weir which is on the left. Then look out for the small boat rollers signed 'portage' on the left, immediately before the lock gates. This series of metal rollers allow boats to be slid and guided down to the lower river level and used with caution they make a fine introduction to seal launching – the air is often filled with excited squeals and splashes! Note there are toilets available at the lock if required, and often in the summer there is an ice-cream van.

Other trips nearby

Further downstream Kingston to Richmond, trip no. 1 is a fine half day trip and can be combined with this one to make a fine full day excursion. Our next suggested trip upstream is trip no. 3 at Shepperton and this could also be combined easily with this trip if wanted.

Public Transport

This journey is well served by Hampton Court train station for those with folding or inflatable craft.

2 Hampton Court

Hampton Court Palace Astronomical Clock. *Daniel Mitsui*

Places of interest nearby

Bushy Park offers a huge area of green 'wilderness' to explore. It has free parking or you can take the foot ferry across the river from our suggested start point at Hurst Park.

Passing through Molesey Lock *Paul Mackenzie*

After the lock the river widens dramatically and the grandeur of your setting becomes clear. We suggest you keep right as you paddle downstream towards the new Hampton Court Bridge (the old bridge was replaced in 1930). On the left bank you will see the Mitre Hotel – an up market riverside bar and café. Once through the bridge on your left is the historic **Hampton Court Palace** and formal gardens, designed by Sir Christopher Wren. This was Henry VIII's favorite palace and can form an extension to any day out with many hours of exploring. Take a look at the chimneys as you drift by, they say that every one has a different brickwork design! The land between the river and the palace is known as the Boardwalk, this was restored to its more natural features in 2007 with the removal of several small sheds, landings and storage buildings.

There is easy landing if you want to visit Hampton Court Palace - land on the river left downstream of the bridge and before the landing stages. Across the tow path a metal gate leads to the front of the Palace. We suggest you tie up and walk into the well kept lawns at the front of the Palace to admire the grandeur of the setting. The scale and detail, along with the staff in costume all add to the experience. There is no charge to admire the front of the palace and you can also usually walk through part of the Gardens towards the Lion Gate and the Maze. This short taster will probably inspire you to come for a longer guided tour of the Palace, Chapel, Tudor Tennis Court, and Gardens – a visit that really needs a whole day and can be well recommended!

Opposite the Palace, on the right bank there is a nice grassy area for a quiet picnic. Just after this the **River Mole** joins and more active members of your group can explore up this – see 'Extending the trip' - whilst more mellow members sit back on the grass and take in the fine panorama of the palace and all the passing river boats and people. Depending upon the time of year you may see the many visitors, or contractors working on the Hampton Court Flower Show (Usually early June), the biggest flower show in the UK.

Continuing downstream you get another fine view of the palace and the Knot Garden through the tall ornate wrought iron gates. This stretch is very green with lovely open vistas of water, sky and trees. Soon there is another opportunity to top up on refreshments with the **Albany** pub on the river right. Just downstream is Dittons Skiff and Punt Club – a sociable and recreational club. Further downstream is **Thames Ditton Island** - we recommend that you pass with the island on your left so that you can enjoy the quiet channel away from the other river users. The little bungalows on this island probably cost a lot more than most large detached houses elsewhere – and yet the islanders have to carry all their goods and baggage across the footbridge in a wheel barrow!

You are now approaching our suggested turn around point at the bottom of these two islands, marked by **'Ye Olde Swan Inn'** – another

The First Hampton Court Bridge *From an old print*

possible lunch stop. Here the river is quite wide, so we suggest crossing over to the North bank. This provides landing opportunities and picnic spots – you can go through a gate into **Home Park** which was popular with Henry VIII for hunting – look out for the deer that still live in the park.

From here you are on your return journey. Once through the bridge at Hampton Court, and as you approach the lock there is an interesting channel to the right that is worth exploring – but stay away from the weirs! You will have to return back to the rollers (or possibly, if it is not too busy you may be able to pass through the lock). Once above the lock we suggest that you remain close to the North bank so that you will get a different view. Once back close to the car park you will see an old, very large riverboat, the **Astoria** - this was a Victorian party boat – can you imagine the dancers waltzing away on the ballroom floor on the upper deck? More recently, Pink Floyd guitarist Dave Gilmour bought it in 1986 and turned it into a recording studio.

Before you return to your start point, there is one further point of interest - **Garrick Temple**, open to the public most Sundays. This sits on the North bank almost opposite the car park in what was the grounds of Garrick House. David Garrick was a local and famous playwright. The temple was originally built as a homage to Shakespeare. It was restored with lottery funding, has an interesting display inside, and is well worth a visit.

Extending the trip

The trip can be extended by traveling further **upstream** past Hampton Sailing Club and paddling around Platts Island. Although the island now looks rather dilapidated it played a critical part in our war efforts with the construction of float planes and plywood torpedo boats. You can also of course extend the trip downstream towards Kingston upon Thames, but in our opinion this stretch is not as interesting or as scenic.

Deviant paddlers might like to think about exploring up the **River Mole** – approx 300m up from the Thames you come to a weir. Hidden away in an underground passage is a long set of rollers that allow you to portage your boat up above the weir for further exploration upstream.

If you are looking for a longer day trip, then we recommend that you consider a one way trip starting at Hurst Park and paddling past Kingston upon Thames to finish at Richmond – see trip no. 1.

Thames at Shepperton 3

Wide river & Backwater
Circular there and back
3 hours – 8km
Easy paddling

Parking	★★★
Launching	★★★
Portages?	None
Quiet?	Busy at weekends

Why do this trip?
A short circular tour which gives you a brilliant snap shot of everything that is typical of this famous river and offers a fine selection of riverside pubs and cafés.

Tell me more
This trip is unusual for the River Thames in that it offers a circular tour with much of interest to explore en route - locks, weirs, islands, quaint riverside bungalows, sailing and rowing clubs, marinas, meadows, willow trees and swans. Tree lined avenues open up into grassy meadows with bright green parakeets flying over head.

Start and Finish
Walton Bridge   GR TO093665   Post code KT12 1QW
Our suggested start point is just upstream of Walton Bridge. Parking is free here and there are public toilets close by. There is easy launching from a slipway at the far end of the car park or a quieter but slightly more awkward put in from the river bank.

From junction one on the M3 (Sunbury) head west on the A308 signed 'Staines', then turn south after 1km on the A244 signed 'Walton'. This brings you to Walton Bridge. Immediately after the bridge, turn right, signed Weybridge, and you will see a large public car park on your right and left signposted Cowey Sale car park. There is a 2.1m height barrier.

Special points
1. Beware of rowing eights – fast and quiet!
2. Membership of Paddle UK or permit required

Canoe and SUP Hire
Canoe & Kayak the Thames based at Shepperton Marina.
www.canoeandkayakthethames.com
Tel: 01932 247978

Paddle Up is a friendly paddle board club based at Shepperton.

Summer day at Shepperton.   *Leon Reichel*

3 Thames at Shepperton

More information

O.S. Map 1:50,000   sheet 176

River Thames   www.thames.me.uk

River conditions...www.gov.uk/guidance/river-thames-current-river-conditions

Tourist information
www.thamesvalleyguide.co.uk

Shepperton Slalom Canoe Club
www.sheppertonscc.co.uk

Elm Bridge Canoe Club
www.elmbridgecanoeclub.org.uk

Trip description by Pete Scutt

Youth slalom training – Shepperton Front Weir at full flow. *Vivian Mugford*

Pubs and tea shops

This section of the river has a plethora of pubs, tea shops and cafes to choose from. **The Wild Brunch Cafe** at the put in is renowned for its sausage & bacon rolls. At Shepperton lock there is a quaint **River Cafe** only open in the summer which sells a great cream tea at a very reasonable price - on the opposite bank is the **Ferry Coffee Shop**, excellent cake (tel: 01932 221094). There is also a large lawn area on which to relax and watch the world drift by. Just above Shepperton Lock is the legendary **Thames Court pub** (tel: 01932 221 957) – a super pub where it's possible to sit in or outside, however it can get busy. The food is good - the steak and ale pie or whale and chips would be our personal recommendations! The **Red lion** (tel: 01932 244 526) is an alternative choice and has a good menu which is continually updated. Another option, the new D'Oyly's Café. Located on the riverside D'Oyly Carte Island this new spot sells excellent crêpes and has a good selection of beer and cocktails and excellent coffee! (tel: 07850 686017).

Over on the other side of the river at Weybridge, there is the **Minnow** (tel: 01932 831672) which also has a good reputation for its food (it's owned by the same people who run the St George and Dragon at Wargrave). Close by, and with a riverside garden, is the **Old Crown** (tel: 01932 842 844) which is a traditional family run pub, dating back to the 17th century that has a reputation for good pub food and real ale.

3 Thames at Shepperton

Other trips nearby

Only a few km downstream is trip no. 2 'Hampton Court.

The **Abbey Stream at Chertsey** is an interesting circuit involving paddling down the Thames and then up one of its old channels. This is part of the Thames navigation and is done regularly by local paddlers but we judged it a bit too much of an expedition through fallen trees to warrant a full write up. If you plan to do it we suggest you park at Laleham Meadows GR TO052678 – paddle down to Chertsey Lock and then paddle up the Abbey Stream. Information can often be found on the Song of the paddle website.

The journey

After launching, head upstream towards your left. After some 500m the old river curves away to your right – keep straight on here under the bridge - you will now be paddling along the Desborough Cut - this artificial cut was dug in 1935 and was named after Lord Desborough who was the chairman of the Thames conservancy (1904 – 1937). This tree lined corridor is about a km long and then after another bridge, you pass two important clubs on your left hand side. First is **Elmbridge Canoe Club**, started in 1984 with the aim of promoting the sport of flat water racing (Marathon and sprint) to all age groups, and it has produced several World Champions. The Kayaks they use are known as K1's, they are very fast in a straight line but quite unstable! Secondly a 100m upstream is **Weybridge Ladies Amateur Rowing Club** – one of the few women's only rowing clubs in the UK. The rowing boats and sculls they use are very fast and the rowers face the wrong way! It's always a good idea to have a peak over your shoulder just to check nothing is coming!

On your right is a small Island known **as D'Oyly Carte Island** which is named after Richard D'Oyly Carte, Who produced the Gilbert and Sullivan Operas from 1871 to 1896. Then on your right you will see Shepperton lock. We recommend that you continue past the

Start point at Walton Bridge. *Jon Wood*

Open day at White Water the Canoe Centre. *Jon Best*

lock, keep left and hug the south bank. Next to the lock you will see the mooring for the river police launch, and then to the right you will see **Shepperton Front weir**. In winter high flows, the river roars over this and forms a dramatic 'stopper' wave, in the right conditions this can be one of the best inland waves in Europe. This is a great training spot for white water paddlers and is the base for Shepperton Slalom Canoe Club – one of the foremost Slalom clubs in the U.K. and the base for several Olympic slalom competitors. Take care and stay close to the bank when passing Shepperton Front Weir as there is often a powerful current here.

We suggest that if you have time, you keep to the left (south) bank and explore the **furthest left channel** which is the old channel of the river Wey, it firstly goes past a small boat yard and then there is a public slip way. You can land here to visit the **Minnow** pub which is just over the road – this does excellent food and has a good beer garden. A great alternative is to continue up the old river for a hundred metres and land at the riverside garden of the **Old Crown** – a traditional, family run pub with good value food and a reputation for well kept real ale – small boats have been landing here for refreshment since about 1720!

Continuing on, you can explore up the old river Wey for nearly a km – the channel is shallow and gets tighter and tighter before opening up into a delightful weir pool with a sandy bay (after heavy rain

Terrapins in the River Thames?

Whilst out paddling out on the Thames early one morning we saw what we thought was the end of a stick above the water - then as I got nearer, it swam off! Upon closer inspection it was what I assumed was a turtle, with a shell the size of a dinner plate. It appears that fresh water terrapins are occasionally spotted in the Thames. The source? Do you remember the Teenage Mutant Ninja Turtle's popularity in the late 1990's? A trend in terrapins as a cute household pet emerged at this time and as they grew too big for people's houses, they are thought to have been released into the river (even though this is illegal). The experts thought at first that the river water was too cold for them to survive, however they seem to have been proved wrong and perhaps they are now breeding.

Paul Mackenzie

3 Thames at Shepperton

Places of interest nearby

Hampton court palace - don't get lost in the maze!

Thorpe Park – a large family adventure Park.

Richmound Park - a great area of wilderness on the outskirts of London.

Chertsey Museum - a great "Little" museum that tells the storey of the local area very well!

Trying out a canoe sail at WWTCC. *Mike Scutt*

the water flow through here is very fast - so be careful as the river is tight and tree lined). In the summer this is a great little stretch of river with houses backing down onto the river - the narrowness makes it an exciting channel to paddle up and down!.

Back at the main river, the next narrow channel to your left takes you almost immediately to a lock and marks the start of the **River Wey Navigation** which continues all the way up to Guildford and Godalming. This historic canal has been in use for over 200 years and there is an excellent visitors centre opposite the lock house detailing the canals history – you may want to stretch your legs and explore and in the summer this is a great spot for a picnic.

The third channel is the widest, and is also worth exploring as it bends round and continues to Shepperton Back weir – this channel is lined with attractive houses backing onto the river. In 2007 the back weir was renovated by the Environment Agency, at a cost of £550,000 and it now has a fish ladder to try to encourage migrating salmon to swim up the Thames.

When you have finished exploring and want to return downstream, we suggest that you pass over to the left bank downstream of the lock and just before D'Oyly Carte Island. Then keep to the left so that you paddle down the old course of the river Thames which skirts the old village of Shepperton. You will see **Desborough Sailing Club** on your left and may meet a few colorful dinghies racing around the buoys – sailing on the Thames is a deviant branch of the sport – with trees, quirky wind shifts, and river traffic to contend with. Apart from sailing dinghies, this old course of the river is relatively peaceful - most river traffic uses the Desborough Cut that you used for your upstream journey. As you continue down river there are plenty of landing spots and sandy beaches that are perfect to stop and play - Desborough Island, to your Right, is mainly left to grass and is ideal for a game of football or Cricket.

Continuing down river you will pass several grand houses backing onto the river, and Gibbs chandlery is to your left. Most of this stretch is private landing however there is a small slip way 100m downstream behind a small island – land here and cross the road to find another pub the **Red Lion**, there is a small beer garden over looking the river and this is a cracking spot to spend an hour with a Pimms.

Paddling down along the old river channel section there is more bird life than you can shake a stick at - ducks, swans, moorhens, herons, kingfishers, coots, grebes and geese are plentiful as are the ever increasing number of colourful and noisy bright green parakeets that live along this part of the river – some 15 years ago a breeding pair escaped from captivity and now there are several flocks living and thriving along this section of the river Thames. As you carry on down this meandering old river it will eventually bring you back to the bottom of Desborough Island near where you started and you will see your launch point and ice cream van beckoning.

River Thames at Shepperton. *Paddleup.co.uk*

Extending the trip

You can conveniently extend your trip 2km **downstream to Sunbury Lock** and weir. On the way, 500m downstream of Walton Bridge, you get Walton Marina on the right, whilst on the left of the river is the entrance to Shepperton marina and the home of **Whitewater the Canoe Centre** – the largest canoe shop in the South East. A km further on the right brings you to pub heaven! There are 3 pubs here all within 400m of each other - the **Anglers** is set right on the river bank and has great food and good local Ale; the **Swan** is literally 10 seconds up the road, and then the **Old Manor Inn**, another 10 seconds round to your right! All can be recommended. A further km, close to Sunbury weir, is the **Weir pub**, which has a very wide selection of ales and a good size beer garden. This makes a good turning point.

If you choose to extend your trip **upstream** then you will need to go through Shepperton lock or portage around it - there is a canoe landing stage just downstream of the lock. After putting back on the river, 100m round the bend and on the right is the **Thames Court pub**, a favourite with local paddlers that does hearty food, real beer and it has a warm crackling fire in the winter. Continuing upstream, the next island you come to is called Pharaoh's island and was given to Lord Nelson as a fishing retreat after his victory at the battle of the Nile. Two km further will bring you to the lovely old **Chertsey Bridge** – just beyond are two welcoming riverside pubs, the lock, a large weir pool and a riverside campsite belonging to the Camping Club of G.B. The pubs are the **Bridge** and my favourite, the **Kingfisher** - both have good sized family beer gardens.

Notes

Mole 4

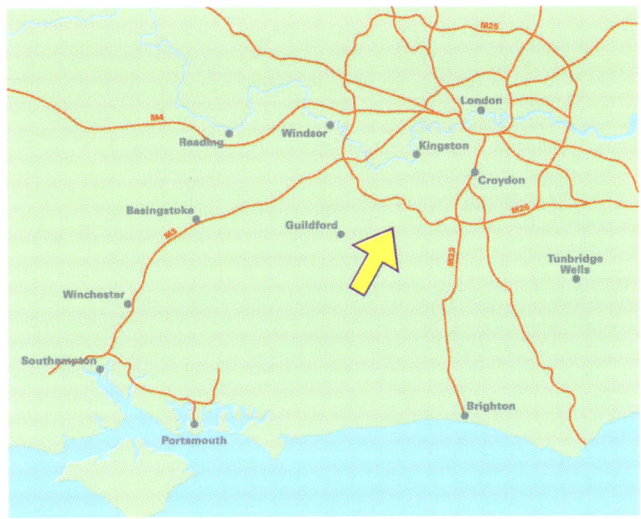

Small swift river

One way

3 hours – 8km

Experience needed

Parking	★★★
Launching	★
Portages?	1 small weir
Quiet?	Few if any other boats

Why do this trip?

This is a trip for the more experienced paddler - a natural flowing river which cuts through the prettiest part of the North Downs. Frequent kingfishers and herons join you on your journey.

Special points

Fallen trees and strainers

Fast current in places

Tell me more

Most of the river Mole can be paddled – the stretch we suggest here is probably the most beautiful and interesting. It has one weir (easily portaged) and a few gentle rapids for excitement, grade 1 or 2 on the international scale of difficulty. However the main hazard is large fallen trees which at times can completely block the river, so caution is needed and the river can be **dangerous in high water conditions**. Even in low water you need to make sure that you have the experience so that you can stop in good time and can maneuver or portage around these 'strainers' – we have heard of several paddlers who have had scary incidents where their boats have been trapped and capsized. This trip is **unsuitable for beginners**.

Our suggested trip is in an area of outstanding natural beauty. The river is flanked on both sides by steep wooded hillsides and it winds along the valley floor with an abundance of flora and fauna. The start is only ten minutes from junction 9 of the M25 and less than an hour's drive from central London, but you are in the heart of some beautiful countryside.

Canoe Hire

The nearest canoe hire is **Canoe & Kayak the Thames** some 16 miles away at Shepperton Marina.
Tel: 01932 247 978.

Fluffy and friends on the River Mole. *Norman Teasdale*

4 Mole

Start

Box Hill Stepping Stones
GR TQ172513
Post code RH5 6AE

The Stepping Stones at the bottom of Box Hill make a convenient, interesting, and scenic start point. From the M25 take exit 9, Leatherhead. Then follow the A243/A24 towards Dorking. This drops you down to the valley of the river Mole and then you drive upstream, parallel but hidden from the river, on a dual carriageway until you arrive at a large roundabout with the Burford Bridge Hotel on your left, continue straight on towards Dorking for about 500m and on the left at the start of the trees is a turn in to the Stepping Stones car park - easily missed and not signposted. From this car park but you will have to carry your boats about 150m to the river.

It's a fun place to start for the younger members of the crew as there are 17 stepping stones where the North Downs Way crosses the river at the bottom of Box Hill. Please take care as they can be quite slippery when wet. The river provides a scrape free paddle for SUPs or canoes even when the level is several centimetres below the tops of the stepping stones – if it is more than 10cm below the stepping stones then it is going to bump and scrape – if the river is above the stepping stones then the river is in high water and you need to be suitably experienced to cope with a fast current and potential 'strainers'. If in doubt, we suggest you walk downstream to inspect the river a bit more.

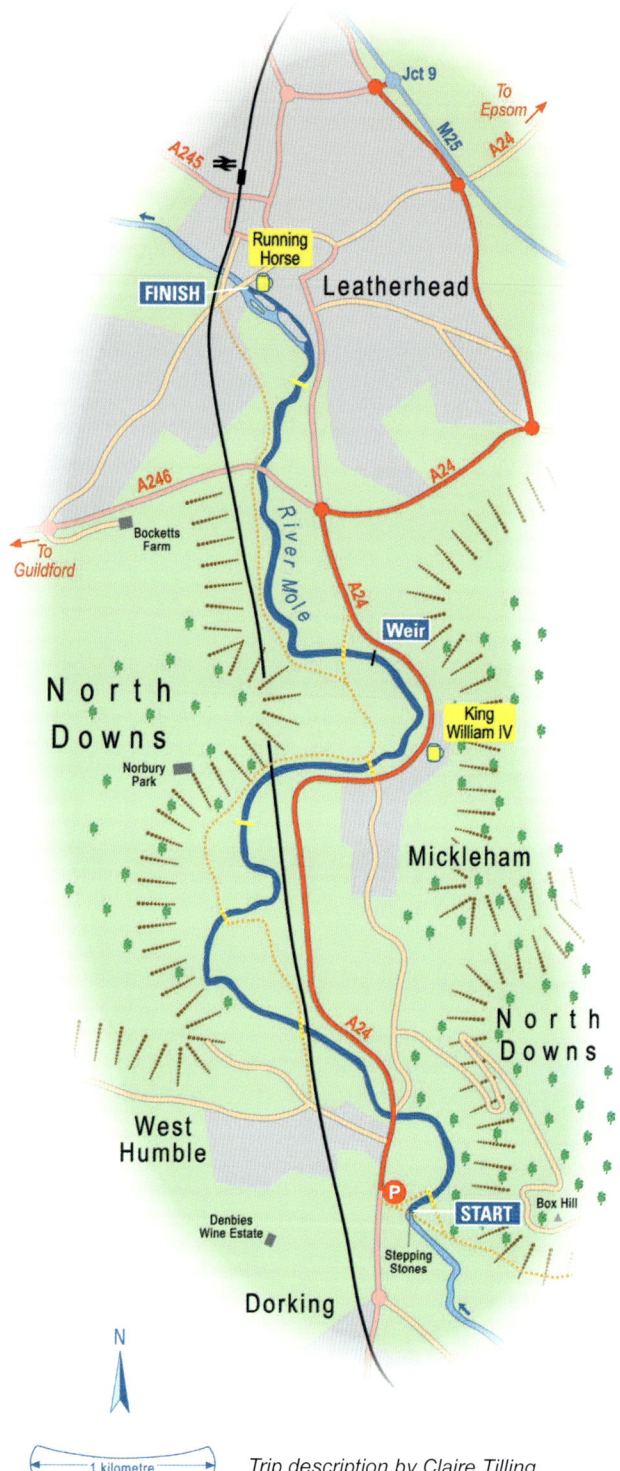

Trip description by Claire Tilling

River Mole and Box Hill. *Wendy Smit*

This stretch of the river has been paddled regularly since before the war, mostly outside the Coarse fishing season. Water levels in the summer months are often insufficient for paddling so you need to inspect the river level - either at the Start or Finish point – see below.

Finish

Leatherhead   GR TQ164563   Post code   KT22 8BZ
We suggest you finish this trip in Leatherhead town centre, just upstream of the old bridge and close to the Running Horse Pub where there is a Pay and Display car park. This car park can be busy on Saturdays however there is a road opposite which can be used for unloading. There are both cycle and footpaths that follow the valley of the Mole back to your start point so these could make a pleasant way back if you don't have a second car for a shuttle. There is also a regular bus service from Dorking to Leatherhead that leaves from near the Bull Hotel.

Portaging the weir on the Mole. *Norman Teasdale*

4 Mole

Can't think why the shuttle is taking so long.
Norman Teasdale

The River Mole

The river Mole has its headwaters near Gatwick Airport and then flows North West for some 80km to join the river Thames at Hampton Court. According to one train of thought the river is so named because in very dry summers parts of the river become completely dry, (most recently in 1978) and it appears to burrow underground like its animal namesake. The underlying rock is chalk and there are supposed to be around 25 'Swallow Holes' which allow the river to run underground – however these holes are no bigger than a few centimetres so there is no fear of your boat being sucked under! In most of the Autumn, winter and spring months there is enough water to paddle, but this just depends on how much rain has fallen in the previous few days.

Other trips nearby

The River Wey at Guildford offers a safe and scenic paddle – see trip no. 5.

A short alternative trip on the river Mole is to start further upstream at **Betchworth** for a 5km paddle downstream. This section seems to hold its water well and is navigable for much of the year. The river is small and meanders through pretty countryside with open pastures and clear views of wooded hills and the North Downs. There are only a couple of places requiring a little care with willows so this may be an option for less experienced paddlers.

From the A25, enter **Betchworth** and turn left at the **Dolphin pub** (which we recommend) - the village church was featured in the film "Four weddings and a funeral". There is space for several cars to park for free on the side of the road and the Mole is just 20m from a left hand bend (GR TQ212497). A Second World War pill box is clearly visible at the access point. For the energetic, it's possible to explore upstream of the start point for a km or two.

Setting off downstream, the Mole meanders under a bridge and then after a km the river splits with weirs on both river left and right - neither are runnable. Keep right and portage above or immediately below the iron railings on river right. Put in again at a series of concrete steps 20m below the weir. Another km brings you to an arched brick bridge and you may find it a bit of a bump and scrape through here. This bridge marks **Brockham** village where one of the largest bonfire nights in Surrey is held. The next big road bridge is the A25 and then 300m later we suggest you take out on the right just before the next bridge (disused) – downstream is another high weir and the river is then shallow. Note that you cannot take out here on the left bank, or cross the disused bridge, however there is parking in the lane on the North bank which you can get to from the East along the 'Old Reigate Road' – turn off the A25 just after the Garden Centre.

Special thanks to Wendy Smitt

Fallen trees can be a major hazard. *Norman Teasdale*

Starting out from the Stepping Stones. *Norman Teasdale*

Pubs and tea shops

The **Running Horse Pub** is adjacent to the take out in Leatherhead. It is six hundred years old and history has it that Elizabeth I spent a night at the Inn due to floods making the river Mole impossible to cross. Food is served at lunchtimes and evenings - along with a fine selection of real ales. Tel: 01372 372081.

There are no other riverside pubs that we can recommend - however a little away from the river is one of our favorite pubs - the **King William IV** in Mickleham – it is hidden on the hillside behind 51 Degrees North café on the A24 which you pass going south. It is a past winner of Surreys best pub food award and from the garden it has great views across the valley of the Mole.   Tel: 01372 372590.

Another idea for refreshments after your trip is **Denbies Wine Estate** which is the largest vineyard in England. It is a fascinating place to visit for all wine buffs as it gives an insight into all aspects of the wine producing process, with indoor and outdoor tours and tasting sessions. The Visitor Centre is home to the popular Conservatory Restaurant serving a wide range of options from light lunches, teas, to Sunday Roasts. www.denbiesvineyard.co.uk. Tel: 01306 876616.

More information

O.S. Map 1:50,000   sheet 187

Norbury Park
www.surreywildlifetrust.co.uk

Leatherhead
www.visitleatherhead.com

The 16th century Running Horse Inn. *Running Horse*

4 Mole

Places of interest nearby

Polesden Lacey is a famous National Trust property which was home of the legendary Edwardian hostess the Hon Mrs Greville. The house has an opulent interior with a collection of Old Master paintings. There are a variety of walks in landscaped gardens and a tea shop in a pretty courtyard. www.nationaltrust.org.uk

Box Hill guards the Southern entrance to the valley of the Mole. The views from the summit towards the South Downs are quite superb however it is a strenuous walk up the hill from the stepping stones to the viewpoint. Alternatively, for the softees amongst us, there is a wiggly drive up the zig-zag road and at the top there is ample parking, an information centre, refreshment kiosk and gift shop. www.nationaltrust.org.uk

Bocketts Farm is a working family farm set in beautiful countryside near the river Mole. It has lots of old and modern breeds of animals and many other attractions for all the family both inside and out. www.bocketts-farm.co.uk/

The journey

There is a small pool at the **stepping stones** where you can practice breaklng in and out of the gentle current whilst you wait for everyone to get afloat. Setting off, the current whooshes you round the corner and under a graceful wooden footbridge. Then the river carves a big bend into the scarp face of Box Hill – this steep right bank rises up for about 130m and is densely covered in trees, shrubs and undergrowth – but predominantly box trees and so hence the name 'Box Hill'. Look out for little slides down the chalky banks where creatures, presumably otters, have been at play. If you are lucky enough you will see many species of bird including the beautiful Kingfisher and majestic Heron, both of which tend to fly downstream when disturbed meaning you are likely to see them time and time again on your descent. The river's habitat is so diverse as it flows over a variety of different rock types: alluviums and gravel, chalk and clay which help to support so many different species of bird, mammal, butterfly and dragonfly. On nearby Box Hill there are several species of orchid to be found in the summer months.

The steep slope and soft chalk rock means that small land slides and **fallen trees are common**. After about 1km you come to the gardens of the Burford Bridge Hotel on your right and civilization intrudes with the sound of traffic from the A24. There is a little rapid where the river twists and ducks under the A24 but then you soon leave the temporary noise of traffic behind as you float off into a relative wilderness. A further 600m and the railway crosses the river for the first time with a small footbridge adjacent to it. From here on there is little to mark mans' presence other than the occasional distant view of a big house up in the hills or an old farm bridge with gargoyles staring at you as you float under.

The river continues to meander its way through the eastern part of **Norbury Park** which was first mentioned in the Domesday Survey of 1086. Thomas Grissell, owner of the estate and a railway engineer, used his influence to put the new railway into a tunnel to ensure that the views from the Manor House were uninterrupted. This tunnel is just by where the second railway bridge crosses the river.

Warming up by the Stepping Stones. *Norman Teasdale*

Note the gargoyle on the bridge. *Norman Teasdale*

The river curves back towards the A24 and you pass under a pretty bridge with wrought iron railings. The **weir** is about 800m past this bridge - the river bends round and is close but hidden from the main road. Look out for a horizon line and the concrete abutments. You can land on either bank to inspect and portage. After the weir it's a further kilometre to the next road bridge - along this stretch there are usually a few pairs of swans so watch out for the cygnets if paddling in spring.

You are now approaching the outskirts of **Leatherhead** and It is about 1.5km to our suggested finish point. The river winds gently with meadows on both banks then you will see some houses on the right bank with beautiful gardens running down to the river (see if you can spot the 'spooky monk' in one of the gardens). Here the river splits around a number of islands - take the right hand channel each time and then the river speeds up as it is squeezed between the islands. This final flurry of a rapid makes a fine climax to the trip - there is no big eddy, but be ready to land after the rapid and take out just before the bridge on the right bank by some benches. This lovely old 14 arch Shell Bridge at Leatherhead was built in 1784 to replace an earlier medieval bridge. The **Running Horse** pub is just over the road, alternatively you could send your scurvy crew on an expedition to buy ice creams – just a few minutes walk up the road.

Extending the trip

Beyond Leatherhead the river may be conveniently run to 'Fetcham Splash' (GR TQ148571) a further 2km downstream, but there is only limited parking here. After this the river slows down and winds its way through flatter lands for 30km to join the River Thames at Molesey (see trip no. 2.). This is a less interesting but still worthwhile journey for the more adventurous – note that there are several weirs that need portaging.

The river immediately **upstream** of the Stepping Stones is shallow and this is the stretch that sometimes dries out, so it needs plenty of water if you want to start the trip further upstream.

Wey at Guildford 5

Canalised river

There and back

3 hours – 8km

Easy paddling

Parking	★★★
Launching	★★★
Portages?	4 easy ones
Quiet?	A few other boats

Special points

Membership of Paddle UK or N.T. permit required – available from Dapdune Wharf or online.

Canoe & SUP Hire

Roar Outdoor offer paddleboard and Sit on top hire from Dapdune Wharf in Guildford and also at Godalming

Why do this trip?

Explore the most scenic stretch of the River Wey, through historic Guildford and the rural North Downs.

Tell me more

The River Wey was the first river in Britain to be canalised for commercial traffic – an amazing 350 years ago! It's both a historic and scenic waterway, which is deservedly popular for paddling and everyone has their own favourite stretch. The one below is our top recommendation. It takes you through the centre of historic Guildford and then out into peaceful water meadows and Surrey countryside.

Start and Finish

Guildford, Woodbridge Meadows

GR SU992504   Post code GU1 1BA

There is small car park here next to the river, with easy launching and free at weekends. However it has a height restriction, and there are no toilets (nearest are at the NT centre at Dapdune Wharf). Note that this car park is now on a **new one way** stretch of the road (Walnut Tree Close) and can only be reached by car by travelling north from Guildford Centre - at first follow signs for the railway station then drive north on Walnut Tree Close.

Getting ready for a race on the River Wey at Guildford.   *Richard Cawthorn*

5 Wey at Guildford

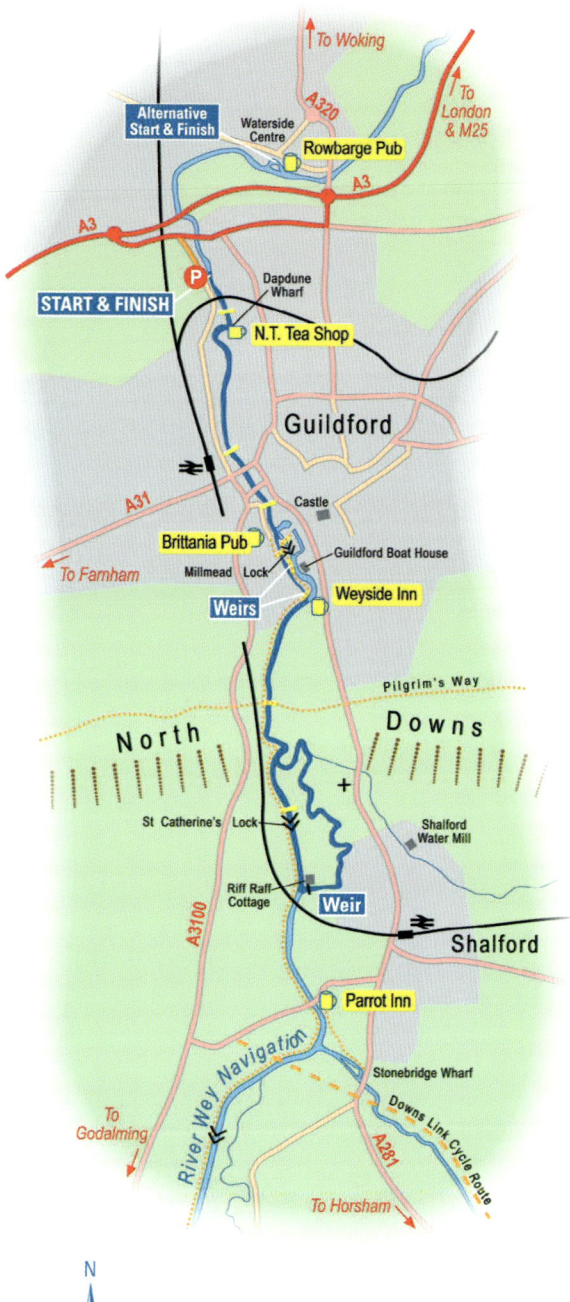

Pubs and tea shops

The **National Trust tea shop** at Dapdune Wharf is very close to the start point so makes a convenient place for a reviving cup of tea at the start or end of your trip – no admission charge if you just want to visit the tea shop. Tel: 01483 561389. In the centre of Guildford, the **Brittannia Inn** is a friendly, convenient pub and has a large sunny outside terrace overlooking a car park and the river. It has real beer and a good menu. Tel: 01483 572160. The **Weyside Inn** has a fantastic location on the riverside just upstream of Guildford, but fencing makes landing difficult.

Downstream, close to the alternative Start Point and with a riverside garden is the **Rowbarge** which was well recommended at the time of writing. Tel: 01483 570242.

Special thanks to Norm Teasdale

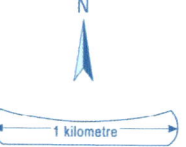

A summer trip on the River Wey. *Amelia Clarke*

Alternative start

An alternative start is to retrace your steps to the A3, go under the A3 bridge, straight over the round about and take the A320 towards Woking, over the River Wey, then turn left at the next round about into Stoughton Road. Take the immediate left and follow the road to where you can access the river near the Guildford Waterside Centre. GR SU996511, Post Code GU1 1LW. Parking and starting here will add approximately 1km to the trip.

Eels in the River Wey

Eels thrive along the River Wey and used to be part of the staple diet for those that could either catch them or afford to buy them. Trappers would set eel pots, funnel shaped baskets, along the river and snare their catch. Eels hatch thousands of miles away off the West Indies and swim for up to three years before reaching the Wey. Here they can stay for up to 30 years before returning to the sea to spawn. That is of course if they don't get caught first! www.weyriver.co.uk.

5 Wey at Guildford

One of many works of art along the Wey. *Norman Teasdale*

Other paddling trips nearby

There are lots of alternative trips on the river Wey. See www.canoedaysout.com for more details. Note that stretches of the old course of the river often make for interesting and quiet variants from the main navigation. The following can be especially recommended -

1. Guildford to Godalming This makes an interesting and scenic trip, 8km one way, provided you don't mind Guildford traffic and shuttling cars. Godalming is a good place to finish with a wide choice of pubs and convenient parking.

2. Upstream from the Anchor Pub at Pyrford Lock, near Wisley GR TQ053592. This is a pleasant evening paddle on a quiet stretch of the river – with a pint and a pie waiting at the end of it! Equally good for a family paddle at the weekend. The start and finish point is only 5 minutes drive from junction 10 of the M25 (follow the signs to the RHS gardens at Wisley and continue on the minor road past the entrance). There is a public car park just beyond the Anchor pub.

3. Burpham to Send. This is a scenic trip with the New Inn at Send as a fine destination. Easy parking at Bowers Mill – GR TQ010527.

The journey

The River Wey runs through the heart of Guildford and the riverside space forms a green lung for the city, with shoppers and office workers using the area for walking and picnics. From the car park, launch and then set off to your right, upstream. You go under a railway bridge and then immediately on your left is **Dapdune Wharf**, where there is a museum, interpretive visitor centre and an excellent interactive display about the River Wey Navigation which is free if you are a National Trust member. You can land just downstream of the quay to visit the visitor centre and the tea shop.

Continuing on your journey, further up there is the old Town Mill on the left and then just before the old road bridge is the Town Wharf - take a look here at the old treadmill crane – one of only three left in the country. Continue upstream and you will need to make a short portage across the island so that you are above **Millmead Lock**.

To your left is the theatre, behind you the shops and offices of the city: in front of you is a surprising green vista of open meadows and the wooded hill sides of the North Downs. On your left is the **Boathouse Cafe**, shortly followed by the **Weyside** Public House. A footbridge crosses the river and rounding the sharp bend, there is Guildford rowing club. On the right is a weir and the moving water in the weir pool below is a favourite spot for local paddlers to practice their skills. The towpath on your right is a favourite path for walkers and cyclists, so this is a friendly rather than a wilderness paddle. Ancient water meadows border the river, covered in wild flowers in the summer, and are actually lower than the river, giving

Kayak race through the centre of Guildford. *Richard Cawthorn*

Central Guildford. *Norman Teasdale*

lovely views of gnarly old willow trees and expensive houses nestling on the wooded valley sides. Look over your left shoulder and you will see the ruins of Guildford Castle.

Boat traffic is normally light, but do keep an eye out for any fast moving rowing sculls especially at weekends. On the left you can see an old sluice gate or penstock that allows the water meadows to be irrigated – in hard winters the meadows would be flooded and then the water froze to form a huge outdoor skating rink. Just before

Places of interest nearby

Shalford Water Mill is a well preserved working water mill. Tel: 01483 561389. www.nationaltrust.org.

Wisley R.H.S Gardens are ten minutes drive on the A3 towards London. www.rhs.org.

More information

O.S. Map 1:50,000 sheet 186

Tourist information
www.visitsurrey.com

River Wey information
www.weyriver.co.uk/theriver

River Wey Navigation, permits, etc.
www.nationaltrust.org.uk
Tel: 01483 561389.

Wey Kayak Club, Guildford
www.weykayak.co.uk

Hitching a ride through a lock on the Wey. *Amelia Clarke*

5 Wey at Guildford

the next footbridge look out for a Victorian grotto and some springs on the right hand side – these holy springs used to be famous for their medicinal properties. The footbridge is on the old pilgrim's way that follows the North Downs. The river skirts the edge of St Catherine's hill that bleeds its golden sands into the waters. It is said that this is the 'gold ford', which for thousands of years provided safe passage to travellers and gave its name to the town of Guildford. If you have kids with you then they will probably want to land and scale the sandy hill – the ruins of St Catherine's chapel are on the top.

Next, the river takes a couple of sharp bends - note the vertical roller on the towpath - this was used to control the tow rope when barges were pulled by horses. Soon after the bend the river branches – keep right here along the navigation, you will be returning along the left channel (alternatively, if you want to shorten the trip then we suggest that you just explore up the left channel). A few minute's gentle paddling brings you to **St Catherine's Lock** – portage here on the left. About 500m past the lock is the old lock keeper's cottage **'Riff Raff Cottage'** and a vertical weir and sluice to the old channel of the river. The weir is dangerous so land about 20m beyond it where there is a grassy stretch of bank and then carry across the corner of the meadow and put in on a little beach in the weir pool.

You are now in the course of the old river and have left the navi-

Locals are friendly! *Norman Teasdale*

St Catherine's Lock. *Norman Teasdale*

50

River Wey. *Roar Outdoor*

gation behind - all is wild and peaceful. The paddling seems adventurous but is easy, with fallen trees to avoid as the river winds. Ancient oak trees overhang from the banks and on this stretch we saw several herons and kingfishers. We came across a couple of cray fish pots along here – with several large American crayfish. A fleeting glimpse of Shalford Church through the trees is a rough half way marker for this loop – which always seems longer than it is! A gentle half hour of paddling brings you back to the main river and the paddle back towards Guildford.

When you reach Millmead Lock again it might be time for an ice cream or other refreshment before the last km of paddling back to your start point.

Extending the trip

We are not so keen on paddling downstream beyond our suggested start point as the A3 runs close to the river and traffic noise becomes intrusive. Going in the other direction, it is a pleasant paddle if you extend your trip upstream above Riff Raff Cottage – it's about 1.5km to the next upstream lock at Peabody.

Alternatively if you are feeling adventurous, then paddle upstream, but turn left a km after Riff Raff Cottage and explore the old **Wey and Arun Canal arm**. Some twenty or so interesting old boats are moored in the old arm of the Wey and Arun Canal, then, at the end of this, a right turn takes you to a wide arch under the main A281. This tributary of the Wey runs past some private gardens, and then continues as a beautiful small wild creek overhung with 300 year old oak trees - nature at its best and it can probably be paddled for about a km.

The Start and Finish point. *Norman Teasdale*

Basingstoke Canal 6

Canal

There and back

3 hours – 8km

Very Easy paddling

Parking	★★★
Launching	★★★
Portages?	None
Quiet?	Very few other boats

Why do this trip?

This is an ideal trip for families or beginners - yes it's a canal, but it's a really friendly one for paddlers - a scenic, quiet, winding one, with lots of things of interest.

Special points

Membership of Paddle UK or permit needed - available from Basingstoke Canal Centre or online.

Tell me more

The Basingstoke Canal winds through the heath land of Surrey with a profusion of mature trees and aquatic plants and is a Site of Special Scientific Interest besides being a wonderful recreational facility – with the accent very much on environmentally friendly sports like canoeing. The canal is effectively a dead end - so this section of the canal, above most of the locks, is quiet and peaceful and sees only a very few canal cruisers. The water is clean and clear and you can often see fish swimming under your canoe – the canal is a popular angling venue and it is a good idea to check with the website or with the canal centre to see if there are any angling matches.

Canoe Hire

Canoes, Sit on top kayaks, rowing boats, and pedalos are available for rent from **Basingstoke Canal Centre** 01252 370073 www.basingstoke-canal.co.uk .

Notes

Pub crawl on the Basingstoke Canal. *Brian Biffin*

6 Basingstoke Canal

Other paddling trips nearby

Another excellent family trip on the Basingstoke Canal is to **Odiham Castle** – see Trip no. 7.

If you are looking for a longer day trip then it is possible to start at Odiham and finish at Mytchett – about 28km with only the one portage at Ash Lock – peaceful and scenic, but a little long for many – our two suggested trips asset strip the best sections for more relaxed paddling! The rest of the canal through Woking has numerous locks, so is not ideal for paddling but is popular and can be recommended for walking and cycling.

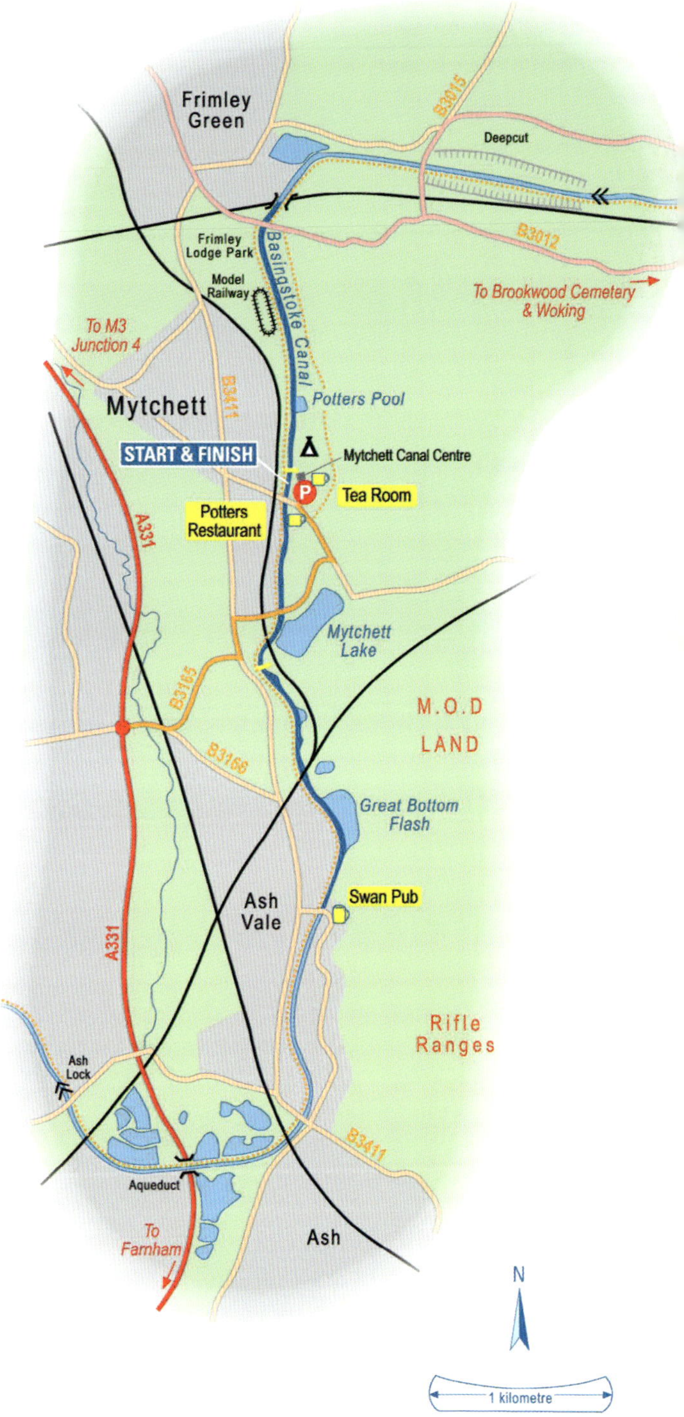

More information

O.S. Map 1:50,000 Sheet 186.

Angling Association –
calendar of matches
www.basingstokecanalaa.co.uk/matc

Tourist information
www.visitsurrey.com

Basingstoke Canal Authority
www.basingstoke-canal.co.uk
(Buy a permit online)

Basingstoke Canal Society
www.basingstoke-canal.org.uk/.

Basingstoke Canal Canoe Club
www.b3c.org

Frimley Lodge Minature Railway Society www.flmr.org

Special thanks to Dave & Sheryl Francis

Deep Cut lock.   www.canoedaysout.com

Start and Finish

Mytchett Canal Centre
GR SU893552   Post code GU16 6DD
Visitor Centre -01252 370073
www.basingstoke-canal.org.uk

Mytchett Canal Centre is an excellent facility and makes a perfect start for a paddling trip – a large free car park (clean tarmac), picnic tables, kiddies adventure play area, a free interpretative indoor exhibition, toilets, tearooms, and even camping! Launching is very convenient and easy from a slipway. On launching you may be asked to show your Paddle UK membership card – if you don't have one then you will have to buy a visiting pass.

To drive here, take junction 4 off the M3 and follow the signs for A331 towards Guildford. Take the second turn off the A331 and follow the signs to Mytchett and the Canal Centre.

Pubs and tea shops

The **Swan Inn** at Ash Vale is a large, friendly canal-side pub that can be recommended. It has a big lawn, lots of outside tables, and a children's play area. It serves real ale and normally does food all day - tel: 01252 325212. It has a large car park with access directly to the canal – there is a gate which is kept locked – but if you ring the pub, they will come and open the gate.

At the start or end of the trip there is a **tea room** at the Mytchett Visitor Centre for refreshments. It offers breakfasts, lunches, ice creams all day and even Thai food in the evenings – Wednesdays to Saturdays.

6 Basingstoke Canal

History of the Basingstoke Canal

The canal was opened from the River Wey to Basingstoke in 1794, however it was never busy and the last commercial traffic was in 1950. The Surrey and Hampshire Canal Society was formed and did a magnificent job over some twenty years to restore the canal and it was formally re-opened in 1991. The canal is now owned by Hampshire and Surrey County Councils.

Places of interest nearby

This area of Surrey has many military training bases and there are several museums in the locality -

• Air Science Museum, Farnborough. www.airsciences.org.uk

• Army Medical Services Museum, Mytchett www.army.mod.uk/medical/ams_museum/

• Aldershot Military Museum www.hants.gov.uk/museum/aldershot/

• Royal Logistical Corps Museum www.army.mod.uk/rlc/rlc_shop_museum/

Our top deviant recommendation is **Brookwood Cemetery** which is just five minutes drive away. This is a fascinating, huge Victorian cemetery built for the dead of London – this is wonderful for a spooky walk at twilight! It has its own railway station where special funeral trains used to arrive from London Waterloo. www.tbcs.org.uk

The journey

On summer weekends the visitor centre can be quite busy, so it's quite nice to launch and get away from the centre. We suggest that you turn left up the canal and set off south towards Ash Vale. You pass Potters Restaurant on the left. Huge mature deciduous trees – mainly oak and beech shade the canal on the tow path side, whilst on the other bank it is sandy heath land – pines, heather, rhododendrons and bracken. Mytchett Lake opens up after the next bridge - this is owned by the MOD at the moment and fenced off, but hopefully this will change. Another bridge brings you to Anglers Flash. Several more small flashes bring you to the railway bridge and then Great Bottom Flash – a haven for the great crested grebe. An old canal boat has been deliberately sunk here to provide an artificial island for the birds to nest in.

There is an army firing range on the left, note the flag mast – they hoist a red flag for danger, when firing is taking place (not usually at weekends). Soon after this is another road bridge complete with delicious cooking smells wafting through the arch – a welcome to the **Swan Pub** on the left bank which welcomes visiting canoeists.

We suggest that you perhaps make this your turning point and stop for a quick stretch and refreshment. Then on the return you may want to take your time and explore some of the flashes – try out your silent 'Indian Stroke', glide around the edge, and quietly observe the wildlife – if you are lucky you may see a water vole, but certainly all kinds of water birds – grebes, ducks, herons, etc.

Returning past the visitor centre, carry on for just under a km and on the left you overlook Frimley Lodge Park. If you are lucky you may hear a whistle and then see a cloud of steam as a **miniature steam train** comes out of the woods. It's worth landing here to visit the station and see the lines – on summer weekends (usually the first Sunday of the month) members of the Frimley Green Railway Club offer rides behind their small steam engines.

Continuing on a few hundred metres more and you come to a road bridge and then a rather bigger railway, the South West Main line

Minature railway at Frimley Lodge Park. *Flmr Society*

"The canal is clean, quiet and peaceful". *Brian Biffin*

crosses under the canal. If you take out on the right bank you can look through the fence down onto the tracks as an express rushes under the canal on one side, and then you can hear the roar as it comes out on the other side of the canal. This canal aqueduct is lined with lead to make sure no water leaks onto the railway line. This for many people probably makes a good turning point and then a return to the visitor centre, and an ice cream perhaps, and then a look around the interpretative displays which explain the history of the canal and will help make sense of all the things you have seen on your paddle.

Extending the trip

Paddling beyond the Swan Inn brings you past lots of back gardens in the village of Ash and then 2km from the pub you come to the impressive aqueduct which soars over the Blackwater Valley Expressway – where else in Britain can you canoe over a motorway? If you are still feeling energetic a further km brings you to Ash Lock, which makes a convenient point to turn round.

There is an alternative access point to the canal behind Ash Vale Station – where there is a free car park and launching platform.

Extending the trip the other way past Frimley Green brings you to the equally impressive Deepcut cutting – all the soil dug out of this cutting was used to make the embankment over the Blackwater valley - guess how many wheel barrow loads? (The answer is at the Canal Centre).

Great Bottom Flash. *Mal Grey*

Odiham Castle 7

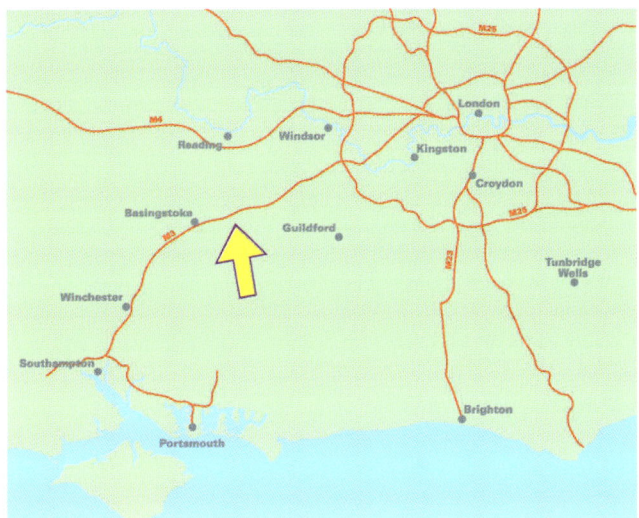

Canal
There and back
2 hours – 6km
Very Easy paddling

Parking	★★★
Launching	★★★
Portages?	None
Quiet?	Very few other boats

Why do this trip?

A short, easy paddle to explore a medieval castle - or if you prefer a more peaceful paddle through delectable countryside, then head in the opposite direction to a fine country pub.

Special points

Membership of Paddle UK or permit required - Permits available from Basingstoke Canal Centre or online.

Tell me more

This selected paddle takes us to Odiham castle which is near the end of the canal at the now closed Greywell Tunnel. There are very few boats and this is a peaceful dead end. The water is incredibly clear and pure as it comes from springs in the tunnel and there is a profusion of water plants and aquatic life so this section of the canal is a Site of Special Scientific Interest.

Canoe & SUP Hire

Sit on tops, canoes, kayaks, SUPs, Rowboats & Eboats are available for rent from Galleon Marine at Colts Hill Wharf www.galleonmarine.co.uk. Tel: 01256 703691.

Start and Finish

Colt Hill Wharf, Odiham
GR SU748517   Post code RG29 1AL

Colt Hill Wharf is only five minutes drive from the M3. Come off at junction 5 and follow the signs for the A287 towards Farnham, turn right at the second roundabout towards Odiham then take the first right in the village. There is a free public car park at the end of this road with a 2.1m height restriction.

Megan & Polly lead an expedition to Odiham Castle.   *Richard Ash*

7 Odiham Castle

The local Basingstoke and Deane Canoe Club meet here most Wednesday evenings in the summer. Note that there are **no toilets** and it is 50m carry to the canal tow path. If you have a skiff then it would be easier to launch at Galleon Marine opposite or at the public slipway at Winchfield 5km east down the canal.

Pubs and tea shops

The **Water Witch** at Colt Hill Wharf is a large comfortable pub, popular for its food and real beer and recommended by paddlers (Tel: 01256 702778). It has a massive garden and in the winter, after paddling, you can warm your backside up in front of a roaring log fire. The only down side is that understandably the pub gets busy on fine weekends in the summer.

There are a couple of other pubs in North Warnborough but neither is as convenient for the paddler. At Greywell, we can recommend the **Fox and Goose**, a fine 16th century traditional village pub near the entrance to the tunnel and 5 minute walk above the tunnel – Very reasonably priced Good Food.

If you fancy an ice cream after your paddle then Galleon Marine is the place. If you are looking for a tea shop then we recommend **Newlyns Farm Shop** which is five minutes drive away, just off the first roundabout from the motorway. This is famous for its award winning pies and free range meat and also has an excellent coffee shop - www.newlyns-farmshop.co.uk.

Going in the other direction, the **Barley Mow** at Winchfield is a well recommended pub that is popular with paddlers – tel: 01252 617490.

Greywell Tunnel

"Legging" through a tunnel.

The Greywell Tunnel is the second longest canal tunnel in southern England and was built using hand tools. It was lined throughout using local bricks using the traditional three-brick ring which was the standard specification for nearly all transport tunnels built during the canal era.

The tunnel had no towpath – the barge horses were walked over Greywell Hill while the barge was 'legged' through by the crew lying on their sides on the barge roof and pushing with their legs along the sides of the tunnel (n.b. if you want to try 'legging' a boat for yourself in the dark though a canal tunnel we recommend the Dudley Canal tunnel at the Black Country Museum.)

In 1932 a section of the tunnel roof collapsed however it was still passable in the early 1950s when two canoeists are reported to have passed through it. In 1985 it was discovered that a number of bats hibernated in the tunnel, and it was declared a Site of Special Scientific Interest (SSSI) to protect the colony of bats. A roof blockage protects the western end.

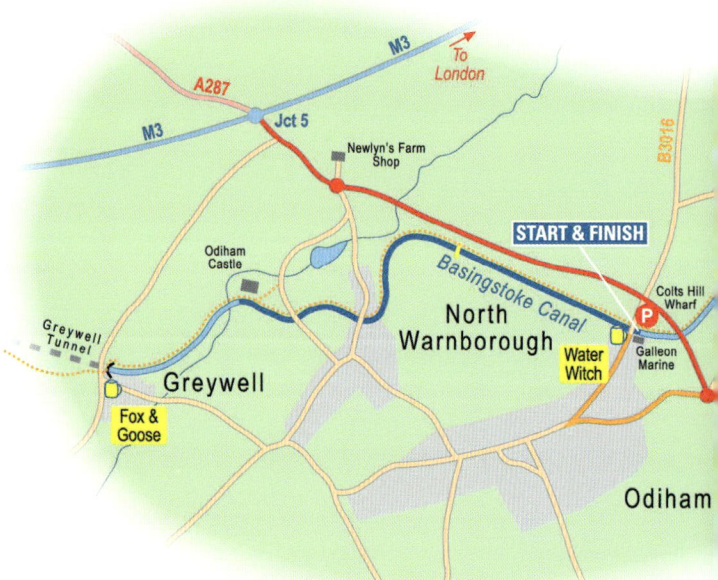

Limbo at the lifting bridge.   www.canoedaysout.com

Odiham Castle

Odiham Castle was built on a bend in the River Whitewater, on as site chosen because it was half way between Windsor and Winchester. It is said that King John stayed at Odiham Castle in 1215 and rode out from here to sign the Magna Carta at Runnymede. A year later the castle was captured by the French after a two-week siege during the First Barons' War in 1216. The castle was an important stronghold with a colourful history and was a base for plotting several rebellions. Later in the fourteenth century the Scottish King David II was imprisoned here for 11 years from 1346. By the 15th century Odiham was now used only as a hunting-lodge and by 1605 the former royal castle was described as a ruin. Access is usually available via the main gate on the East side of the castle.

Special thanks to Dave & Sheryl Francis

7 Odiham Castle

Shadowing a rare narrow boat. *Vitalijs Jasinskis*

Places of interest nearby

Basingstoke has a striking new museum inside a massive modern building called **Milestones** - imagine a network of streets with shops, a village green and even a pub - dating from Victorian times to the 1930s. www.milestones-museum.com.

Ten minutes drive away is one of Britain's top 50 gardens - West Green House N.T. www.westgreenhousegardens.co.uk.

More information

Angling Association – calendar of matches
www.basingstokecanalaa.co.uk/matc

Tourist information
www.visit-hampshire.co.uk

Basingstoke Canal Authority
www.basingstoke-canal.co.uk
(Buy a permit online)

Basingstoke Canal Society
www.basingstoke-canal.org.uk.

Basingstoke and Deane Canoe Club
www.badpaddlers.org

Odiham Castle www3.hants.gov.uk/hampshire-countryside/odiham-castle.

The journey

After launching turn right and paddle under the bridge. Ignore the temptations of the Water Witch opposite and set off down the a straight stretch of about a kilometer with pleasant views of open fields and hedgerows – a little spoilt by the noise from the nearby highway. The canal then bends away from the main road and winds alongside the back gardens of the village of **North Warnborough**. More gardens back down to the canal – this is great gnome spotting territory. A few more minutes paddle brings you to a lifting beam bridge which may require a limbo to get you under it.

The next stretch has crystal clear water and an abundance of plant and wildlife – glide along and see if you can spot any fish darting in amongst the water weed. Soon you come to **Odiham Castle** – often called King John's Castle, because it was from here that King John set out to meet the Barons of England and to sign the Magna Carta in June 1215. All stout hearted English Yeomen will want to land here to scout the ramparts and dream of distant battles and daring deeds! It's also fun to stand and play pooh sticks on the bridge where the canal goes over the river White Water – named for its white chalky bottom rather than any roaring rapids.

There is a turning point here for the narrow boats – called a 'winding hole' (supposedly so named because you put the bow of the boat into the bank and then let the wind push the boat round). The canal beyond here is protected as a nature reserve so you are not allowed to paddle any further, so if you want to carry on to **Greywell Tunnel** then you will have to leave your boats and do this on foot. It is only a fifteen minutes walk, and worth it to see the entrance to the second longest canal tunnel in Southern England. A flight of steps takes you down to the tunnel entrance and you can peer down the dark, dark tunnel and imagine what it must have been like in the old days to have to 'leg' your boat into this dark abyss! The tunnel is home to a huge colony of rare bats so an iron grill and gate has been built across the tunnel to protect their roost and discourage human visitors. More welcoming is the Fox and Goose, only a couple of

Odiham Castle. *Cathy Griffiths*

Natterer's bats. *Gerald le Claire Environmental Trust*

hundred metres away.

The return journey is much the same as coming, except of course all the views are different as you are doing it backwards. Returning to Colt Hill Wharf you have the difficult decision to take – refreshment at the Water Witch – or whether to extend the paddle and carry on to the Barley Mow another 4km or so.

Extending the trip

Continuing East towards Broad Oak the canal winds its ways through some delectably rural and peaceful countryside – mainly wooded and with lots of bird life. In many ways, if you are here just for a peaceful paddle, then this is a pleasanter alternative than paddling west to Odiham Castle. The obvious turning point is the **Barley Mow** pub, about 4.5km from Colts Hill Wharf – another canal-side pub which welcomes families and is popular with paddlers. There is a slipway and public parking 200m away, 2.1m height restriction so this can be recommended as an alternative start and finish point.

A further 7km past Barley Mow Bridge is the Fox and Hounds pub at Church Crookham GU51 5NP. This pub is right on the canal with a large carpark – and Good Reasonably priced food served every day.

Other paddling trips nearby

Another excellent trip on the Basingstoke Canal is at the **Mytchett Canal Centre** – see trip number 6. If you are looking for a longer day trip then it is possible to start at Odiham and finish at Mytchett – about 28km with only the one portage at Ash Lock – peaceful and scenic, but perhaps a little long for many people – our two suggested trips asset strip the best sections.

Marlow to Maidenhead 8

Wide River

One way trip

4 hours - 14km

Easy paddling

Parking	★
Launching	★★★
Portages?	2 locks
Quiet?	Some river traffic

Why do this trip?

This is one of the most picturesque trips on the Thames taking you past the famous Cliveden Country House.

Tell me more

Pretty riverside towns alternate with steeply wooded hills and open meadows. Victorian villas and their boat houses grow out of the banks and poke through the canopy of the trees. Coots and moorhens fight amongst the islands where the narrow boats moor up for summer gin and tonics. Much of this run is overlooked by one of England's great houses, Cliveden, an elegant memorial to when what was discussed by gentlemen in its dining rooms affected the rest of the world. The whole stretch, thanks in large part to the coming of Brunel's railway, is where London's wealthy Victorian day trippers came to relax and enjoy nature, and even today, the rural Thames manages to exist distinct from the bustle of London.

We recommend this as a one way trip. However, If you want to avoid a vehicle shuttle then we suggest you park at Boulters Lock, paddle upstream to Cliveden and return.

Special points

1. Beware of motor boats and weirs
2. Membership of Paddle UK or Thames permit required

Canoe and SUP Hire

www.moosecanoehire.com are based at Bisham Abbey near Marlow and offer canoes, kayaks and SUPs. Tel: 01628 566290.
Paddle Board UK are based at Bourne End. Tel: 07919228735.
Paddleboarding Maidenhead. Tel: 07505 147957

The painting opposite is 'Boulter's Lock, Sunday Afternoon', by Edward John Gregory, 1885-97 © National Museums Liverpool, Lady Lever Art Gallery.

8 Marlow to Maidenhead

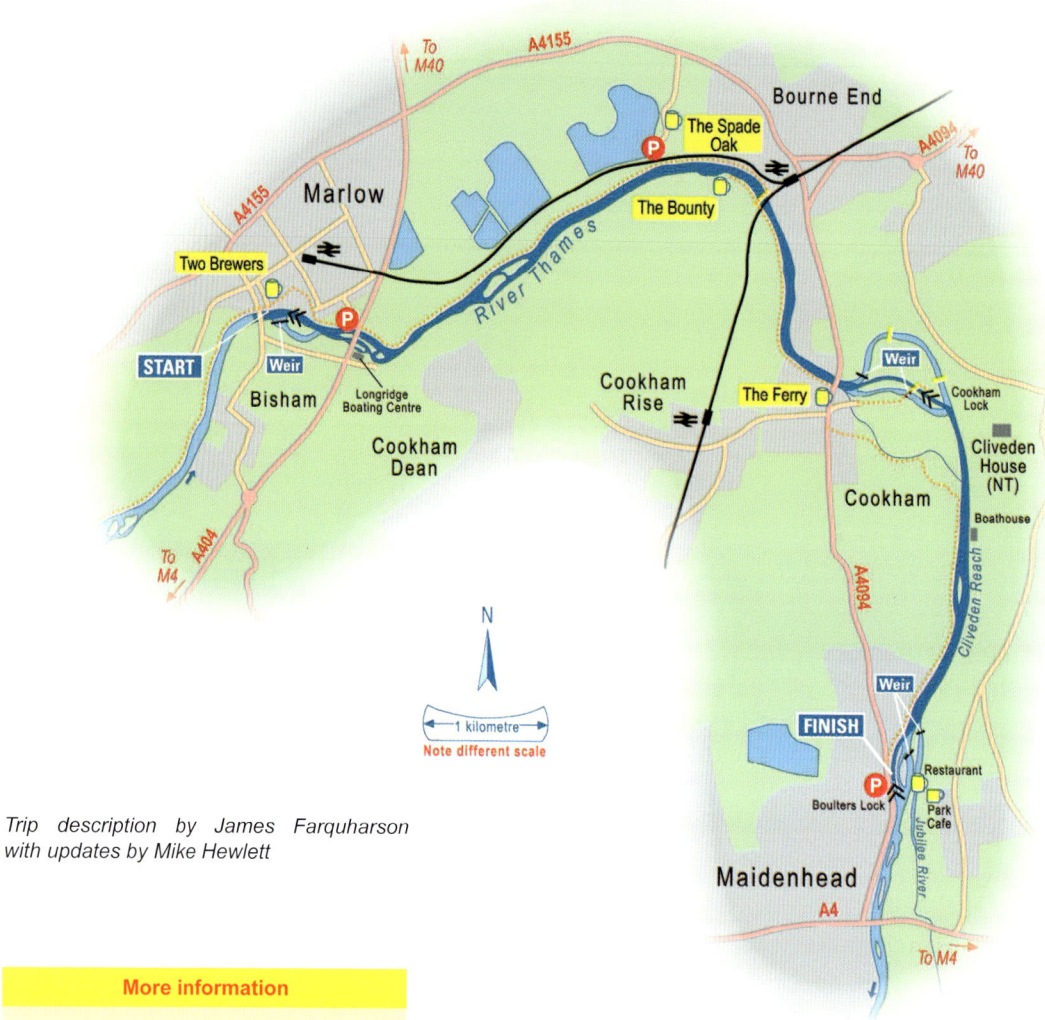

Trip description by James Farquharson with updates by Mike Hewlett

More information

River conditions
www.gov.uk/guidance/river-thames-current-river-conditions

Marlow visitor information
www.marlow-tc.gov.uk/visiting-marlow

Marlow Canoe Club
www.marlowcc.org.uk

Cliveden House
www.nationaltrust.org.uk

Longridge Boating Centre
www.longridge.org.uk

Start

Marlow
GR SU853862   Post code: SL7 1NQ

The most convenient place to start this trip is the public boat launching area and slipway at the end of Saint Peter's Street in Marlow near The **Two Brewers pub**. Car parking is very limited here so you will have to move the car after unloading to one of the public car parks in town. There is an alternative start point at Gossmore Recreation Grounds GR SU858861, under the A404 flyover. This has a large free car park, however the down side is a height restriction and launching is difficult, down a steep overgrown bank.

Cliveden House. *Robin Warwick*

Finish

Boulters Lock GR SU903826   Post code: SL6 8PE

From the M4, exit at junction 7. Turn west on the A4 and then after crossing Maidenhead Bridge, turn right and follow the river upstream to Boulters Lock. The car park is on the left about 200m beyond the lock and has a height restriction.

For the physically challenged we suggest you consider a finish at the slipway next to the Ferry Hotel in Cookham.

Shortening the trip

There is convenient access and car parking (height restriction) at **Spade Oak** GR SU884873 near the Spade Oak pub (SL8 5PS), sign posted road off the main Marlow to Bourne End road.

Alternatively, consider starting at **Boulters Lock** and do a return trip to **Cliveden House**.

Other trips nearby

Trip number 9, **Henley upon Thames**, could easily be combined with this one - perhaps as a weekend trip and camping overnight at Hurley Lock. Downstream, our next selected paddle is at Shepperton, trip number 3.

The **Jubilee River** is a flood relief channel that leaves the Thames at Boulters Lock and re-joins the river below Slough. Note that there is a dangerous weir near the start, so do not be tempted to try and paddle directly into the channel from the Thames. In normal summer conditions there's a very gentle flow interrupted by concrete weirs. No motorised boats are allowed so stretches between the weirs can be quiet and ideal for beginners - but uninspiring and noisy with traffic from the nearby M4. Check the internet - "Paddleboarding on the Jubilee River" for more information.

8 Marlow to Maidenhead

Pubs and tea shops

Marlow is one of the main attractions for food and entertainment in the area and the little town welcomes a great many day trippers attracted by its setting and array of fine shops, pubs, bars, cafes and

Ferry Hotel, Cookham. *Tim Hughes*

Upstream approach to Marlow Lock. *James Farquharson*

restaurants. The **Two Brewers** at the start is a very fine pub - tel: 01628 484140. The local ale is from Marlow's Rebellion brewery. Other local ales are brewed by Brakspear and Loddon breweries, which are also very good.

At Bourne End, on the riverside is the defiantly independent pub and restaurant, the **Bounty**, Tel: 01628 520056. This laid back but highly successful venture can only be accessed by river or on foot. As a result of this, it's a pub of character with a lack of pretensions - in the summer The Bounty is a sprawled out mass of adults, dogs and children all enjoying a drink and simple but well done pub food.

Under Cookham bridge on the right is the **Ferry**, a 'pub' enjoying a beautiful location and offering good food and beer, at a price. It's a lovely place to sip a cool beer in the summer. Tel: 01628 525123.

On the island at **Boulters Lock** there is the up-market **Boathouse at Boulters** and bar, Tel: 01628 621291. Also there is a friendly **café** in the public park.

Boulters Lock

In Victorian times, boating on the Thames was really popular and Boulters Lock was once the epicentre of river activity, with day trippers from London taking to the river in flotillas of small boats - It is said that on one Sunday in 1888 something like 800 boats and 70 steam launches passed through the lock. The painting by Edward John Gregory shows such a typical Sunday and the variety of boats using the lock – notice especially the 'new woman' energetically paddling her own canoe.

Boulters Lock is still a pretty and interesting spot, so we suggest you spend a little time here – watch the boats in the lock and then walk over to the island where there is really pleasant public park, café, toilets, and restaurant. The island makes a great view point to watch any freestyle paddlers who often train and play in the white water below the weir.

8 Marlow to Maidenhead

Extending the trip

If you carry on **downstream** below Boulters Lock the next convenient finish point is at Ferry Lane in **Bray**, about 3km more. Below Maidenhead Bridge is a railway bridge which is one of Brunel's many triumphs – when built it was the widest and flattest brick span in the world. As you approach the Church and houses of Bray on the right bank, you will see a small slipway next to a riverside restaurant – Michel Roux's fabulously expensive, Waterside Inn. This is our suggested finish point.

Starting your trip **upstream at Hurley** adds another very picturesque stretch of some 4km, however parking and launching are not ideal - it is a 200m walk to the river from the village car park (GR SU826841) which often fills up on summer weekends.

Freestyle competition at Boulters Island.
James Farquharson

The journey

Soon after your boat glides into the water at the slipway in St Peter's Street in Marlow, you'll be presented with a 360 degree view containing one of the classic picture postcard scenes of middle England. To your right is William Tierney Clark's suspension bridge. Across the water on the Berkshire bank is the justly famous Complete Angler Hotel and the graceful arc of Marlow Weir. Behind you is the beautiful All Saint's church (where this writer was married). Following the flow downstream to your left, after just a few hundred yards, is Marlow lock. The lock keeper is usually happy for you to enter the lock with the pleasure boats and pass through to the lower level, however if you need it there is an easy portage path.

Paddling out of the lock cut and onto the main river, you will see a large pink house high up on the hill (reputedly, once belonging to gap-toothed purveyor of piano fuelled pop, Elton John) and the bridge carrying the Marlow bypass – necessary as it is, this is the one jarring intrusion of modern life in the entire run. The channel passing through the right hand arch leads to **Longridge boating centre**. This has a claim to have launched more people into canoeing and kayaking than almost any other centre. It has a long history with the Scouting Association but has recently gone independent – long may they succeed.

After passing through Longridge and back out onto the main river to the right you will see some large houses set into Quarry Wood hill and by the riverside an odd castellated house, known locally as the cardboard castle. Soon after, Wootten's Boatyard will come into view and the opportunity to head right, leave the main river to skoot over clear water into a fast flowing backwater threading its way amongst a set of islands.

On emerging from the islands, ahead on either side lie wide flood meadows, often complete with wallowing cattle, and to the right the high grassland of Winter Hill. After a km or so you come to a picnic site and access point at **Spade Oak** on the left bank. The public car park is 300m on the other side of the level crossing. A short walk further is the former home of Enid Blyton – who people of a certain age will remember as writer of The Famous Five children's books.

Paddling on to **Bourne End** you'll first see the marina on the left. Directly opposite the marina is the distinctly unfussy **Bounty** public house and a little further on is the cast iron railway bridge, which provides foot access to the pub.

Continuing on past Bourne End, you float past what are to my eye, more extravagantly large houses leading up to Cookham. Underneath **Cookham bridge** and to the right is **The Ferry** pub. To the side of The Ferry is a public slipway where you might disembark to stretch your legs along Cookham's high street.

Beyond Cookham Bridge, make sure to take the channel marked as a navigation by the EA. The far left hand channel leads to a very **nasty weir** with no stopping above it. The far right hand channel leads to a duck pond, with a small but swift channel draining it that is too shallow for comfortable paddling. Of the two middle channels, the right ends in another even worse weir, the left runs on into the lock cut. As I said, it's altogether advisable to go down the marked channel!

If you have time to explore a bit then we suggest that on leaving Cookham lock, you turn left instead of right - you then paddle upstream underneath a wooden bridge into a sleepy, beautiful, backwater, with a wealth of flora and fauna and a giant riverside mansion house. This Hedsor Backwater has only recently been opened to public navigation. There is a long story and a short story as to why that is. The short story is that once upon a time this was the main route of the Thames. Then, a long time ago, the landowner put up a big sign that said, 'Private Navigation – No Entry'. Years went by and no one thought to question the sign. Then, in 2002, and after a long battle, the EA proved that the putting up of a sign does not a private navigation make. Another, narrower backwater to explore is the Lulle Brook, 300m on the right below Cookham Lock.

Below Cookham Lock is the famous **Cliveden Reach** one of the undoubted best vistas and wonders of the Thames – the high chalk cliffs have been planted with trees collected from all over the world. Above it all, is the house and golden tower of Cliveden House which is now is an exclusive country house hotel owned by the National Trust. This is not your usual NT property and they would prefer that you do not land here. At any time of year, but especially in May and Autumn, the view, the smell and the feel of this vista is enchanting.

About a km down from the lock is the Cliveden Boat House. Further downstream are some small islands that make nice picnic spots.

Another km or so and the high cliffs and forested valley sides gradually drop and meet the river as the weir at Boulters lock is approached. Keep to the right bank when you see the weir and paddle down the lock cut - our recommended **Finish** is 200m on the right where a section of the concrete bank is lowered to make landing easier. The public car park is just the other side of the main road – beware the traffic.

A winter paddle at Marlow. *James Farquharson*

Places of interest nearby

Cliveden House and Grounds are of course superb and well worth a visit and a stroll - it's great to look down from the House terrace onto the sweeping vista of the river that you have just paddled!

Windsor Castle and Eton are only 30 minutes drive from the finish. We suggest parking at Windsor riverside and strolling over the old bridge and along Eton High Street.

Windsor Great Park and the **Savill Gardens** are two other famous attractions that probably deserve a day to themselves.

Henley upon Thames 9

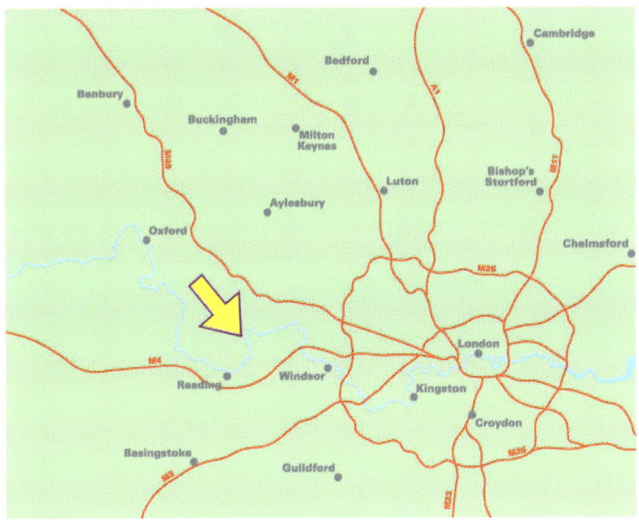

River Thames + backwaters

One way

5 hours - 18km

Easy paddling

Parking	★★★
Launching	★★★
Portages?	4 locks
Quiet?	Busy at weekends

Why do this trip?

A day trip on one of the most picturesque and famous stretches of the Thames including the delightful 'Wind in the Willows' Hennerton Backwater. See "Shortening the trip" for other options.

Special points

1. Check for rowing regattas. Henley is first week of July
2. Membership of Paddle UK or Thames permit required

Tell me more

You'll pass through everything from deserted rural backwaters to busy historic towns and ancient landmarks, plus a few famous folk's houses – you may see Uri Geller or Paul Daniels and we've even bumped into Rolf Harris down here too! There's also a great deal of British wildlife to spot – kingfishers are common on the northern bank, together with adders at the Thames Valley Nature, combined with common sightings of mink and even roe deer swimming the Thames on occasion. Ultimately though, this is a soulful paddle on the most picturesque section of the Thames – the numerous good pubs en route are just a convenient bonus!

Canoe & SUP Hire

Henley Canoe Hire have a base near the rowing museum and offer canoe, kayak and SUP hire. Tel: 0118 402 5820.

Family Picnic on the Thames. *Steve Weir*

9 Henley upon Thames

More information

O.S. Map 1:50,000 sheet 175

www.gov.uk/guidance/river-thames-current-river-conditions

Tourist information
www.henley-on-thames.org

River Thames
www.visitthames.co.uk

Henley Royal Regatta
www.hrr.co.uk

www.wokinghamwatersidecentre.com

www.wokinghamcanoeclub.co.uk

www.wargrave.boat-club.net

Henley Canoe & SUP groups
www.eyotcentre.co.uk

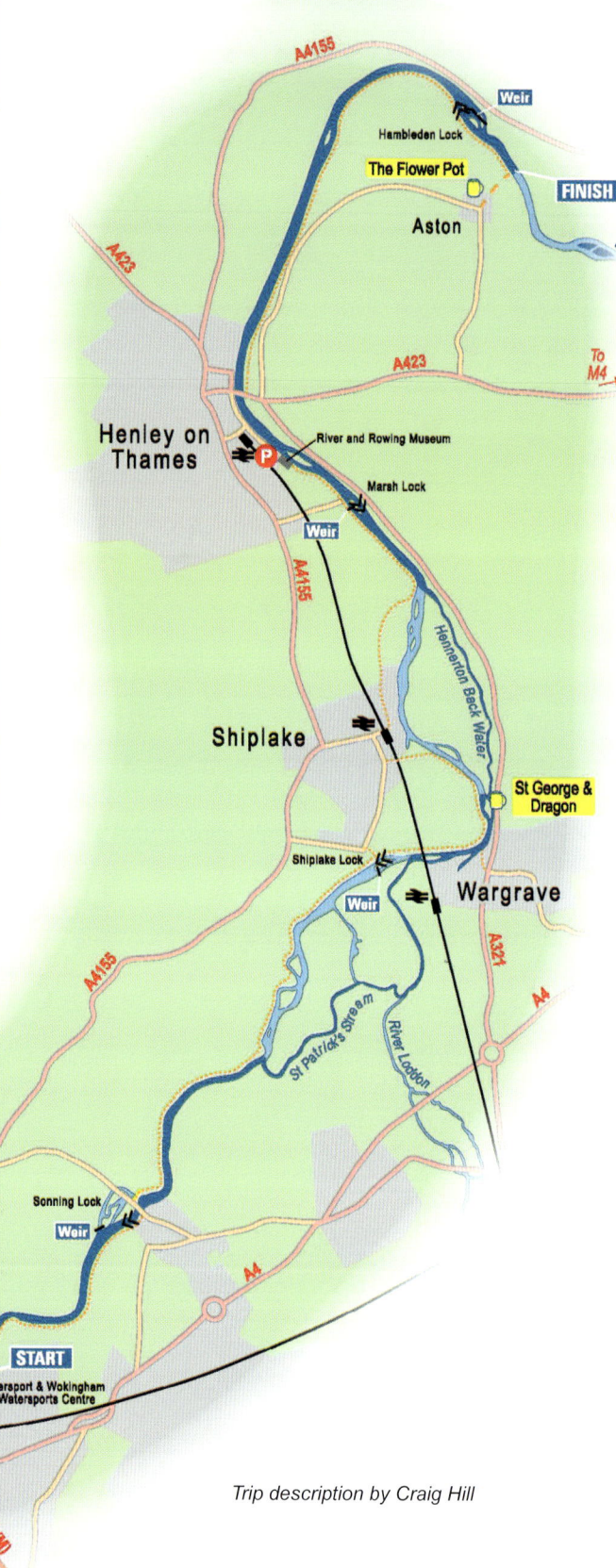

Trip description by Craig Hill

'I say, have you chaps got your BCU permit?' Oepkes.com

Start

Thames Valley Park, Reading
RG6 1PQ, GR SU737740
Public toilets available

From the M4 take the A329M towards Reading. Continue on this as it becomes the A3290 to the very end and a roundabout. Turn right and follow the road into the Thames Valley Business Park. Immediately on the left is Wokingham Waterside centre and home of Wokingham Canoe club with the River Thames just a quick walk across the meadows. Parking can usually be found along the Thames Valley Park Drive or on side roads. However if you have problems there is a large pay car park available just off the entrance roundabout.

Finish

Aston, Ferry Lane
GR SU787845   Post code: RG9 3DG

The best finish point is Ferry Lane, Aston. There is parking for a dozen or so cars here – but it does get busy on summer weekends, so it's best to leave the least number of vehicles here as possible. The best route for the shuttle is on the south side of the Thames through Wargrave. Whilst your drivers are doing the shuttle – the paddlers can occupy themselves in the Flower Pot – a very welcoming pub. We suggest you bring a lock for your boats whilst you are in the pub.

Pubs and tea shops

The Great House Hotel and Restaurant at Sonning, has an enviable location, with beautiful gardens. It looks up market but families and paddlers are welcome and it has a selection of real ales and menus to suit all budgets. Tel: 0118 969 2277. www.greathouseatsonning.co.uk

St George and Dragon at Wargrave, is a non-themed friendly pub, with a nice modern feel and restaurant. Sit out on the patio next to the river, or shelter from the sun inside the spacious bar.   Tel: 0118 9405021. www.stgeorgeanddragon.co.uk

The Angel on the Bridge is one of Henley's best landmarks and only inches from the river. It has a relatively up market restaurant and a patio. Tel: 01491 410678

The Flower Pot. This is at the take out at Aston and personally my favourite pub on the Thames, with good food and drink, and many footpaths to walk off that Sunday lunch! Tel: 01491 574721.

9 Henley upon Thames

The journey

As you paddle downstream you'll pass the business park on your right. As this ends, there is a small nature reserve on the right hand bank - this is one of the best spots in the UK to find adders in the wild – on hot days, keep an eye open – they are often spotted swimming the river! After another 10 minutes you'll pass a small island, followed by the Bluecoat School on your right hand side – Keep an eye out for their boats on Saturdays. Immediately beyond, you'll find the first of the four locks on the journey – **Sonning Lock**. There is a new SUP and canoe portage on the right or alternatively the Lock keeper may (at his discretion) be kind to you and let you go through the lock. There is a small tea room here, normally open in afternoons in the season.

Fiddler's Bridge, Hennerton Backwater. *Kathy Summers*

Below the lock the river winds round a couple of bends before coming to a very picturesque brick bridge built in 1775. Below this you'll find the gardens of **The Great House at Sonning** – a nice spot to moor up your SUPs or canoes and pop in for a swift pint or for an up market lunch, however a high sided landing.

From Sonning, the river continues north-east through the countryside. Just under 2km the river bends sharply to the left and on your right you will find the entrance to **St Patrick's Stream**, marked by two large white pillars and a sign. This is a fast flowing backwater that by passes Shiplake Lock, and we recommend this route if you are looking for a fun paddle and are suitably experienced – please see the full description Trip number 10.

Continue on the main river Thames and you will come to a number of small islands before passing Shiplake College on your left – (The main building, Skipworth House, dating back to 1890) before coming to Shiplake Lock. Below here is a far from aesthetic Railway bridge, built in steel and concrete in 1897, carrying the Henley Branch Line, and just before this bridge St Patrick's Stream re-joins the Thames.

The river banks get busier from here, with residential properties and boat houses, as you move into **Wargrave**. On your right you'll find Wargrave Boat Club – a friendly, family-orientated club for canoeists, rowers and punters. Below here is a great lunch stop – **The St George and Dragon Pub**. Many a trip has stopped here for lunch and not moved on: taxi's being called to collect the car from the finish point!

Continue on downstream keeping to the right bank, through the marina and you have the option, which we strongly recommend, of paddling under the tiny arched 'Fiddler's Bridge'. This side stream is called '**Hennerton Backwater**' and is a quite idyllic, peaceful stream –Toad of Wind in the Willows would have loved it - gently flowing through peoples' back gardens, woodland and meadows. Like St Patrick's Stream, it is navigable by SUPs, canoes and small boats but it is quite tranquil as it doesn't bypass any locks – Jerome K Jerome mentions a comic interlude on this very same backwater.

Henley Royal Regatta

A regatta was first held here in 1839 so it is one of the oldest rowing events in the world and a unique event in the English summer. It is held in the first week of July and is always colourful and entertaining with the men in brightly coloured blazers and the women in gorgeous summer dresses.

It's great fun to take a boat and there is no charge to paddle up to the regatta site and tie up to the booms that mark out the course. A large open canoe is ideal – preferably with a small table, crisply ironed cloth, and a well stocked picnic hamper. You need to research and plan your car parking - there are normally lots of extra car parks up and down stream as landowners cater for the thousands of extra visitors.

River Loddon near Wargrave. Tony Ward

Historically this stream was farmed by Hennerton House for eels in the 18th Century, though few remain these days.

Hennerton Backwater rejoins the main river after some 2km and then after a km you will come to **Marsh Lock** – marked by a wooden walkway crossing the weir to the lock. The portage here is a bit awkward (ask any Devizes to Westminster Race competitor) so if you have the option it is easier to go through the lock. On leaving the lock. In high water beware the flow from the weir. This is another point to shorten the journey, as on the left bank below the weir, next to the footbridge, there is a road to a public car park.

About 500m below the lock, keep left of the small island and there on the left bank is a large car park and a little way back from the riverside, the **River and Rowing Museum** – a really interesting modern museum devoted to rivers, rowing boats and canoes. The journey continues through a much more built up area as we move into the historic town of Henley – with the 5 span Henley Bridge

Attractions nearby

Henley on Thames is a delightful town and well worth looking round if you have the time –we especially recommend the **River and Rowing Museum** here. Tel: 01491 415600 - www.rrm.co.uk.

The Museum of English Rural Life is at the University of Reading. It teems with objects designed to draw out some comparisons between the village-based society of a century ago and our global, high-tech world of today. www.reading.ac.uk/merl.

Thames Valley Nature Park is near the start point.

9 Henley upon Thames

A modest boathouse. Richard Knight

Other trips nearby

You are almost spoilt for choice of trips in this area of the Thames Valley - knowledgeable local paddlers all have their favourite start and finish points and different trips on the main river, its backwaters and tributaries. We describe the St Patrick's Stream, the Hennerton Backwater, and the River Loddon in more detail in Trip number 10. The next section of the River Thames upstream of Reading is described in Trip number 11, the Goring Gap.

crossing the river here. There are lots of wonderful pubs and restaurants here, but it is a little harder to find somewhere nice to pull in to go exploring. If you want to stop here – the **Angel on the Bridge**, on the left hand bank of the bridge, is definitely worth a look and has mooring available.

Henley on Thames is the home of British rowing and the Leander Club on the right below the bridge is the famous club where many of our Olympic rowers train. This stretch downstream from the bridge is the famous Henley Straight – 3 km of dead straight riverbank, showing why it's the chosen spot for the rowers. This is notorious for headwinds so check the weather forecast before leaving if you want an easy paddle! It is heavily used by rowing clubs, and also hire boats, so keep an eye open for racing craft as they fly down this section of river. It's worth checking the calendar, as this reach gets incredibly busy during regatta season and it can be a little daunting trying to work your way through the many racing and support craft over a regatta weekend. In the summer months there is often an ice cream van parked half way down this stretch – a good morale booster for the last couple of km.

Towards the end of this straight you'll pass Fawley Court on your left – built by Sir Christopher Wren in 1663 for Colonel William Freeman – together with, ahead of you, the Temple on Temple island which was built to improve the view along the straight!

As you take a large sweeping right hand bend, you are nearing the end of the journey and returning to the countryside as you approach **Hambleden Lock**. Having portaged or passed through the lock, look back to the weir – in high water levels you can often see freestyle paddlers playing on the weir. A hydraulic ramp has been installed to allow paddlers to control the flow through the main gate to create a better surf wave – not for the faint hearted in an open

Sonning Bridge. *Craig Hill*

Hennerton Backwater. www.canoedaysout.com

canoe though! Paddling on downstream, after half a kilometre or so, you'll find a small wooden jetty on your right hand side, and a gravel slipway. This is our suggested **finish** and a few minutes walk, 300m, up the lane brings you to one of the nicest pubs on the Thames – The **Flower Pot Inn** at Aston. It's then up to you who gets the short straw of doing the shuttle run, and who gets to sample the delights of this fine pub.

Extending the trip

An excellent weekend trip can be made by combining this journey through Henley upon Thames with the next trip downstream, number 8, staying overnight at the lovely island campsite at Hurley Lock.

Shortening the trip

There are many options here – a good warm up is simply to paddle down to the Great House at **Sonning** for lunch, and then return. Sonning is only 3km downstream so this gives you an hour or two's paddling in total, giving you a good idea of your speed and lets you practise – an ideal short trip if you have hired your boat from Marsports.

If you have your own boats, then consider driving to the **River and Rowing Museum** in Henley on Thames and putting on here. We then recommend a paddle up river to **Wargrave** and then a return along the **Hennerton Backwater** – a delightful circuit that nearly made it into this book as a trip in it's own right.

Angel Hotel at Henley. Tony Ward

St Patrick's Stream 10

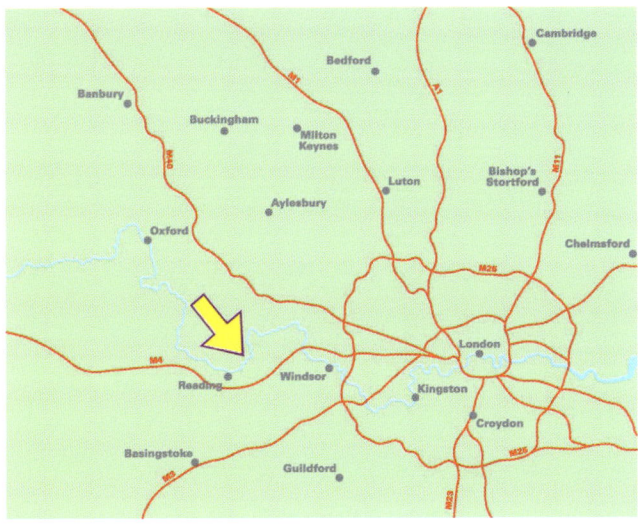

Small stream + River Thames

Circular trip

2 hours - 8km

Experience needed

Parking	★
Launching	★★
Portages?	One lock
Quiet?	St Patrick's Stream is quiet. Some river traffic on the Thames

Special points

1. Current, trees and possible blockages
2. Membership of Paddle UK or Thames permit required

Canoe & SUP Hire

Please check the internet.

Why do this trip?

St Patrick's Stream was a must for this book - a natural, navigable stretch of the Thames that by-passes a lock so it is a miniature free-flowing river. It makes a fascinating circular trip full of diverse interest in one of the most picturesque parts of the Thames valley.

Tell me more

Wargrave has a reputation as one of the prettiest villages in the Thames valley with some lovely old houses so it makes a lovely start and finish point. Our suggested journey takes you up a short and scenic stretch of the main river Thames and then returns down the St Patrick's Stream – the angling websites describe this as being like a 'miniature Hampshire Avon'. There is a gentle current – maybe 2mph, so you don't need to paddle hard, but you do need to be a proficient paddler so that the current doesn't carry you into any over-hanging trees. St Patrick's Stream (like other Thames backwaters) is a statutory navigation, but you are unlikely to meet any other boats and it seems a whole world away from the busy main river Thames. Look out for wildlife and especially herons, kingfishers, and crested grebes.

Young Luke on the River Loddon. *Peter Knowles*

10 St Patrick's Stream

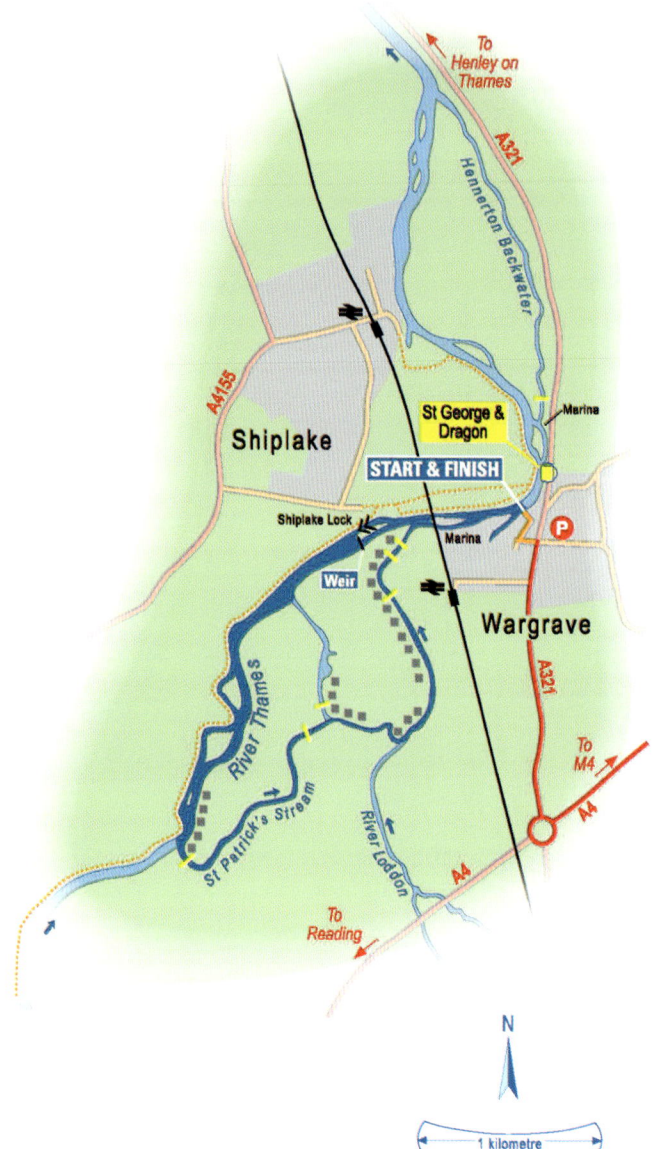

Start and finish

Wargrave
GR SU784787   Post code: RG10 8ET
Public toilets at the car park in village

Wargrave makes a great start and finish point and Ferry lane in the middle of this fine old village makes a quiet and easy launch point – but only for one car at a time. It is a narrow lane (see photo) with a tight corner that you will have to reverse round. Driving into Wargrave on the A321 from the south, turn left at the traffic lights and then after 50m turn right down Ferry Lane (a sign says 'no access to the river, except for small craft'). The lane takes a left turn after some 100m and then in 50m you are in the river. There is a public pay and display car park in School lane, 5 minutes walk away, on the other side of the traffic lights.

If this launch spot is busy then there is alternative launch spot on the main road to Henley some 100m downstream of the St George and Dragon – this should be o.k. for a minibus but beware the traffic.

Special note

St Patrick's Stream is one of the most noteworthy angling stretches of the Thames, so please be considerate:

1. We suggest that large groups should if they have a choice, try and schedule trips outside of the angling season
2. This stream is narrow and you need to be ready to give a friendly warning shout so that any angler has time to reel in their line.

Alternative start point for large groups

An alternative start is at Sonning at the north end of Sonning Bridge opposite the French Horn Hotel, where there is a grass bank for launching and free public parking for a few vehicles. Even at busy periods there is normally room here to unload a minibus and trailer (returning over the bridge there is usually parking space in Sonning Lane, B4446, some ten minutes walk back through the church yard). St Patrick's Stream is some 1.5km downstream so starting here will add another 3km to your trip.

Opposite - Ferry Lane start point.   *Paul Mackenzie*

10 St Patrick's Stream

The journey

After launching you might want to turn left and explore up the side creek that takes you up through some lovely back gardens and towards the church which was burnt down in 1914 by a suffragette – it is said that she objected to the words 'honor and obey' in the Anglican marriage ceremony. Happily the church has been beautifully restored. After being up the creek, cross the main river Thames and paddle upstream keeping near the north bank, under the railway bridge, to **Shiplake Lock**.

If it isn't too busy you may be able to go through the lock with other boats, otherwise paddle up the left hand side (river right) of the lock island to a landing stage clearly signed "Canoe portage". An easy 40m carry over the camp site brings you to the top of the lock. This campsite was originally bought by the Corporation of London in 1889 to provide clean air and relaxation for the poor people of the East End. Only men were allowed – women had to camp on a separate island!

Carrying on upstream, keep to the north bank and soon you will come to Shiplake College Rowing Club and then there are a couple of large islands – it is worth exploring the more peaceful side channels on this northern side of the river - these quiet meanders are a popular mooring spot for modern 'water gypsies'. Take time to look over your shoulder and you will see a fine old house up on the hill, and if you keep quiet and are lucky you might glimpse an ostrich in the distance in the large garden.

Paddle past some small islands and then ahead of you are some houses on the south side, the river bends right and this is the **entrance to St Patrick's Stream** – there are two white posts and a sign saying "Unsuitable for navigation by launches".

Now starts the adventurous bit! Overhanging trees and a bend in the stream means that you cannot see what you are letting yourself in for – the verdant green overhanging vegetation is reminiscent of the jungles of Ecuador – perhaps crocodiles and anacondas are lurking in the undergrowth? An appreciable current gives a gentle stir of adrenaline as you glide under a bridge (built by St Patrick in the 5th century AD, honest!). Then keep left between two white posts which mark a gentle chute – just keep the SUP or canoe straight, glide down with a gentle whoosh, and cruise on down the stream as it slowly twists and bends – the river is relatively deep with a mainly chalk bed. If it is the fishing season, keep an eye out for any anglers and give them a friendly warning shout if necessary. After a km you will float under another bridge and then another side stream of the Thames comes in on the left with a rather fine private house on the bank. You can paddle up this side stream for some 50m if you wish (but beware the dragons which you may see in the grounds of the house) and white water enthusiasts can play in the current jetting out from the bridge over this side stream.

More information

Wargrave Regatta is normally the first or second weekend in August.
www.wsregatta.co.uk

River conditions
www.gov.uk/guidance/river-thames-current-river-conditions

River Thames
www.thames.me.uk

Wargrave   www.wargrave.net

Wargrave Boat Club
www.wargrave.boat-club.net

River Loddon near Wargrave.   *Richard Knight*

St Patrick's Stream. *Paul Mackenzie*

Carrying on, the river twists and at each bend you will see a different riverside house. A wonderful diversity of attractive houses – one a superb olde world thatched cottage, the next surrealistic modern, the next a mere millionaire's shed. Drifting along it is all too easy to miss the river Loddon coming in from the right and then there is another km of paddling on what is now the river Loddon, and yet more highly desirable houses – some with their own private footbridge. This brings you back to the village of Wargrave and the main river Thames. You pass the Marina and then **Wargrave Boating Club** – a family orientated club, which has an active canoeing section. A few minutes of paddling and you are back to Ferry lane and the **St George and Dragon** pub beckons just 100m downstream.

Pubs and tea shops

The **St George and Dragon** is a famous riverside pub – featured in 'Three men in a boat'. It has a landing stage, grass banks, terraces, and lots of outside tables. It has a good selection of food with vegan options.

10 St Patrick's Stream

Other trips nearby

Trip no. 9 is a longer day trip from Wokingham to downstream of Henley on Thames and can include St Patrick's Stream. The **River Loddon** joins the St Patricks Stream and can be paddled from Aborfield but the section upstream of Winnersh is heavily fished so best paddled out of season. We recommend the section downstream of Winnersh for those looking for an alternative trip – see description below.

Extending the trip

Suitably revived after refreshment at the pub and game for more? Continue downstream keeping to the right bank, through the marina and dive under the tiny arched 'Fiddler's Bridge'. This side stream is called '**Hennerton Backwater**' and is a quite idyllic, peaceful stream –Toad of Wind in the Willows would have loved it - gently flowing through peoples' back gardens, woodland and meadows, before rejoining the main river after some 2km. Like St Patrick's Stream, it is navigable by canoes and small boats but it is more tranquil as it doesn't bypass any locks – Jerome K Jerome mentions a comic interlude on this very same backwater. Return up the main river Thames past the village of Shiplake on the north bank – admiring 'Millionaire's Mile' with its fabulous houses, most with lovely old boathouses that are probably worth a million in their own right. (beware, this mile left me salivating with a wicked lust for property!).

Top Tip - If it is a really windy day, before setting off, take an extra five minutes in the pub to think about whether this loop might be better in the reverse direction.

A welcome pub. *Chris Stephens*

River Loddon near Wargrave. www.canoedaysout.com

River Loddon from Winnersh

The River Loddon nearly made it for a main description however there were just too many other good trips in the local area. It's a surprisingly clean, swift flowing stream which makes a fine little adventurous expedition, ideal in summer at low water levels. Some experience is needed - there may be fallen trees to negotiate and you should dress for nettles and the occasional bramble.

We suggest a start at the **Winnersh Triangle Park and Ride**, just off the A329M, at GR SU767717. From here it is 7km to a possible finish at Twyford Mill, GR SU785760 - or continue another 3km to Wargrave. The George Pub is on the other side of the river at the put in - this is family friendly with decking overlooking the river.

At first the river is unpromising, however you will soon be into a beautiful stretch of swift flowing river populated by herons, big fish and enormous dragon flys. After one kilometre the river flows through **Dinton Pastures Country Park** where the Black Swan Sailing Club offers canoe hire on a sheltered lake. Just past here the river flows swiftly through Sandford Mill and under a double arch road bridge - approach carefully as it can be blocked by trees after heavy rain. Past the road bridge and under a rope foot bridge the river settles down and straightens out for a few kilometres. The next girder bridge carries a farm service road and marks the start of the most technical part as the river picks up pace and descends over several gravel beds. Just downstream from a white wooden house, watch out for the large willow directly after the bridge, depending on the amount of vegetation and water flow you may find yourself paddling through it! At the next island take the smaller left hand channel, the right is blocked by trees.

As you near the end of the trip you can make ridiculous owl noises through the Twyford railway bridge arches before reaching **Twyford Mill sluice**. This is great fun to run in almost any craft and at most water levels. Take the left channel down a simple chute and through a couple of waves. You can exit river left and carry over the footbridge to Silk Lane or continue out of the weir pool for 100m and exit left just after a small concrete bridge by the **Wagon and Horses**. If you plan to continue downstream it is a further pleasant 3km to Wargrave with the river running clear, shallow and fast flowing with gravel bars and small beaches.

Special thanks to Nick Mallabar

Goring Gap 11

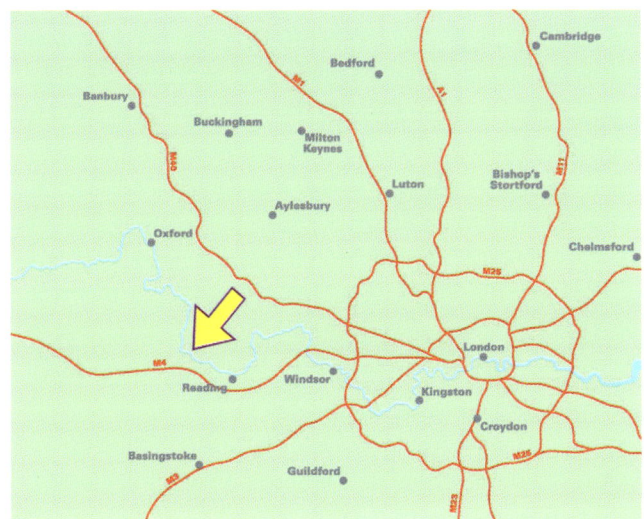

Wide river

There and back

4 hours - 14km

Easy paddling

Parking	★★
Launching	★★
Portages?	One lock to either portage or go through
Quiet?	Busy at weekends

Why do this trip?

This is perhaps the most beautiful stretch of the River Thames and it offers an easy paddle with plenty of interest.

Tell me more

This trip takes you through the 'Goring Gap' so called because this is where, at Goring, the Thames leaves behind the Oxfordshire clay flood plain as it is squeezed between the rolling chalk uplands of the Berkshire Downs and wooded Chiltern Hills, before emerging in the County town of Berkshire, Reading. Indeed, for most of the trip you will be paddling along the boundary between the two counties. As a result, it's a very pleasant trip, a gorgeous, classic stretch of the river Thames with wooded hills providing a picturesque backdrop. Along the way there are several attractive little islands to paddle between and several nice spots to get out for a picnic.

Goring is about 7km - an upstream paddle against the current, so this is probably best as a trip for summer water levels. One of the great things about a there and back trip is that you can turn around at any point, making it as long or as short as you want to. We would definitely recommend that you go at least as far as the railway bridge as this will allow you to appreciate the nature of the river and the surrounding countryside and note that there is a great picnic spot just upstream of the bridge!

Special points

1. Some river traffic
2. Membership of Paddle UK or Thames permit required

Canoe & SUP hire

The SUP Life are based at the Swan Hotel at Streatley. Tel: 01182 072482

Starting out at Goring Lock. *Chris Wheeler*

11 Goring Gap

Start and Finish

Pangbourne Meadow
GR 637768   Post code: RG8 7DA
Public toilets 200m

Pangbourne is a busy little town linked to Whitchurch by an attractive Victorian toll bridge. Just below the bridge, Pangbourne Meadows are a popular place to relax, especially on a summer's day. Just off the road to the bridge is a small pay and display car park next to the Adventure Dolphin activity centre. At the time of writing this is free on Sundays. Launch is through the gate and a short carry across the grass.

If this is full, there is alternative parking by the Recreation Ground at the end of Thames Avenue RG8 7BY, which has a slightly longer carry to the river. If you are physically challenged then check out the small slipway hidden away about 100m upstream of the bridge at the end of Ferry Lane.

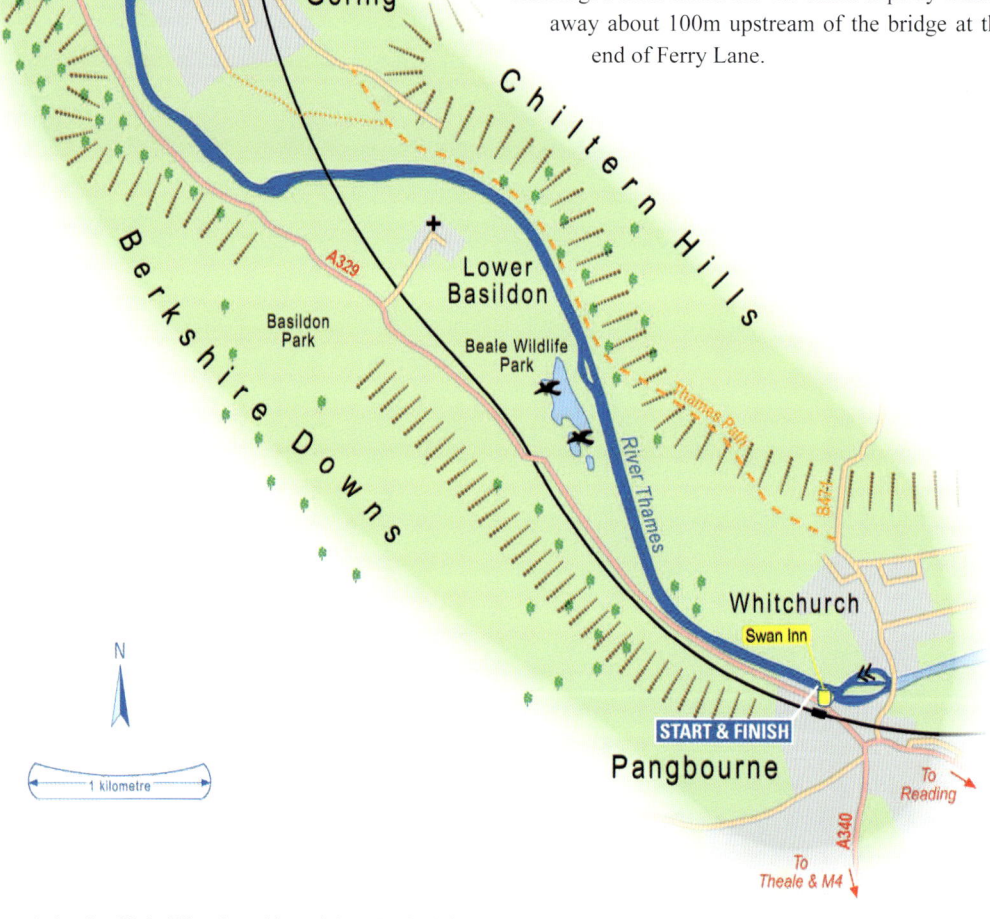

Trip description by Chris Wheeler with revisions by Mal Grey

Exploring downstream of Goring Weir. *Chris Wheeler*

Alternative One Way Trip

We used to recommend this as a one way trip however access at Goring has become more difficult since our first edition. The historic launch point is at the bottom of Ferry Lane (GR 596805) but some locals now object to this use of public land. We suggest that you park in the village car park which is quite close and then check the launching spot before dropping boats off. It is also possible to launch near the lock - but you cannot drive close. If you're OK with a 400m portage or trolley push then there is a launch spot from a meadow near Lower Basildon GR 611795, park at GR 611792.

Pubs, tea shops, etc

In **Goring**, the **Catherine Wheel** and the **John Barleycorn** are two modest, attractive, old Brakspear's pubs, tucked away south of Goring High Street, en route to the car park – both have gardens and welcome children. There is also sometimes a kiosk selling ice creams and hot drinks at **Goring Lock** during the summer. Just upstream of the lock on the Streatley side of the river and overlooking the weirs is the **Swan at Streatley** which offers a smart riverside dining experience. SUP Life are based here.

At Pangbourne, the **Swan pub** is just upstream and overlooks the Weir – this offers a very convenient egress and riverside drinking spot. Tel: 0118 984 4494

11 Goring Gap

More information

O.S. Map 1:50,000
sheets 174 and 175

River conditions
https://www.gov.uk/guidance/river-thames-current-river-conditions

River Thames
www.thames.me.uk

Reading Canoe Club
www.reading-canoe.org.uk

Adventure Dolphin Centre Pangbourne
www.adventuredolphin.co.uk

The journey

Leaving **Pangbourne Meadows** head under the interesting iron Victorian toll bridge and take the obvious channel up to Whitchurch lock. The other channel takes you to the weir, which is quite attractive but should be treated with care. If there is a lock keeper on duty, they are almost always happy to work the lock for you. If not you may be able to tag along with boats, though be cautious of inexperienced crews. Alternatively, portage the lock, which does involve a few steps.

Above the weir you will see the 17thC Swan Inn, though its probably best to leave a visit until your return later. It is here, at Pangbourne, that Jerome K Jerome's 'Three Men in a Boat' journey ended and here that Kenneth Grahame, author of 'Wind in the Willows', lived in his later years. On river right, in between the main road and river, is a row of splendidly ornate and individualistic Edwardian villas, and Pangbourne College's boat house (2 km away at the College, is the new Falklands memorial chapel, a legacy of the College's naval tradition). A long straight takes you away from Pangbourne before turning and taking you towards distant wooded slopes and some small islands.

The Swan Pub at Pangbourne. *Chris Wheeler*

Goring Gap. *Mal Grey*

A narrow flood plain is on the river right side of the river, your left as you head upstream, and here, on the site of flooded old gravel pits, is the very pleasant and intimately sized **Beale Park** Wildlife Park. Cruisers moor up here to visit - so why not do so too? Soon you come to those tree-clad hillsides. This is Hartslock Wood, a beautiful nature reserve where the beech woodlands of the Chilterns drop steeply to the river. At the northern edge of the woodland, grassy hillsides are a haven for wildflowers including rare hybrid orchids. You're now around the halfway point, and both banks offer the occasional place to stop or get out, though the easiest spot is a little further on.

After another kilometre you reach an obvious large brick railway bridge, Gatehampton Viaduct. This is actually two bridges parallel to each other, with the western spans designed and built by Isambard Kingdom Brunel as part of his original Great Western line, and completed in 1840. The eastern spans were added half a century later. Just upstream of the bridge, a sandy beach appears on the northern banks, often with cattle wading in the river. This makes for an excellent stopping point, and is the easiest place to land on the journey.

Places of interest nearby

Beale Park Wildlife Park
www.bealepark.co.uk

Basildon House and Park
www.nationaltrust.org.uk/places/basildonpark

Mapledurham House and watermill
www.mapledurham.co.uk

11 Goring Gap

Heron seeking guidance on where to feed. *Chris Wheeler*

Less than 2km later, after swinging in a more northerly direction, paddling between tree-lined banks, you reach the twin villages of **Streatley and Goring**, on the west and east banks respectively. both very attractive, and there are various inlets and channels to explore downstream of the lock, where islands are interspersed with weirs. At Goring, it is possible to get out and stretch your legs, most easily just below the lock. Make sure you don't get in the way of lock operations though. This is an old historic Roman and pre-Roman crossing point and one of the places where the Icknield Way would have forded the river, long before there was a bridge. Today, it is where two long distance paths cross each other- the Ridgeway and Thames Path, and also where two modern day 'Areas of Outstanding Natural Beauty' meet- the Chilterns and North Wessex Downs AONB. As a result, whilst the Bristol to London main line railway, an 'A' road and the Thames are all squeezed together through the Gap, down at water level, it is a surprisingly rural and quiet paddle.

The return leg will usually be a little easier, as even in summer there will be a bit of flow. On the way back, we recommend going behind the various long, wooded islands, most of which hug the river right bank. These make for interesting little diversions, though please do so quietly as both wildlife and humans live close to the river here. Eventually you'll find yourself back at Whitchurch lock, and hopefully there will still be a lock keeper on duty to allow for a nice, relaxed passage at the end of a lovely day on the river.

Other trips nearby

There are several other good trips on the River Thames close by – please see the relevant descriptions. The **Kennet** also offers an interesting urban paddle as it flows through central Reading just before the confluence with the Thames. However, the flow can be fast, so you can only paddle upstream when the river is at low, summer levels. The confluence with the Thames is downstream of Reading Bridge.

Cattle wonder how to respond to a navigation buoy. *Chris Wheeler*

Sunset paddle on the Thames. *SUP life*

A terrible drowning

Goring Bridge was built in 1873 and before this a large ferry boat used to carry people and wagons across the river below the weir.

It is recorded that in 1674 there was "sad and deplorable news from Oxfordshire and Berkshire". Sixty people had been drowned in the weir pool by the watermen imprudently rowing too near to the weir and the boat capsizing. Reading between the lines the ferryboat must have been over-crowded and of course most of the passengers probably couldn't swim. However, here is a warning not to venture too close to the weir!

Extending the trip

If you have the energy and time, and are willing to go through or portage Goring lock twice, the next short section upstream to Cleeve Lock is equally pleasant.

Alternatively, at the Pangbourne end it would be very easy to paddle downstream for a while before returning to the start.

Wolvercote Circuit 12

River Thames + canal
Circular trip
3 hours - 10km
Easy paddling

Parking	★★★
Launching	★★★
Portages?	4 (or 1 - see note)
Quiet?	Canal is quiet but the Thames can be busy

Why do this trip?

This is a diverse and interesting paddle through Thames meadows and gardens, on the outskirts of Oxford.

Special points

1. Wolvercote car park may be busy on summer weekends
2. Membership of Paddle UK or permits needed

Tell me more

This trip offers a unique opportunity to take in both the River Thames and the historic Oxford Canal in the one afternoon and to paddle alongside Port Meadow, an ancient, large expanse of common land, where horses and cattle graze and come down to the riverbank to drink. It was here, on a boat trip in 1862, that Charles Dodgson (Lewis Carroll) is said to have first told the story of 'Alice in Wonderland'. This stretch of the Oxford Canal gives you a delightful tour of a plethora of people's back gardens.

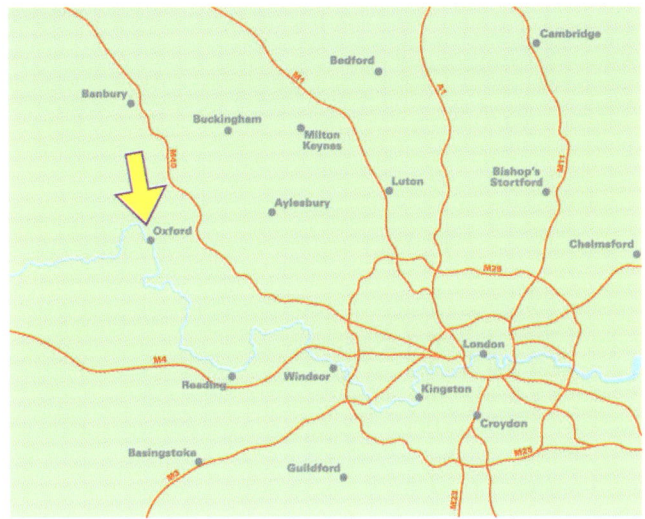

Starting out from Wolvercote. *Peter Knowles*   Opposite - Isis Lock on the Oxford Canal. *Chris Wheeler*

12 Wolvercote Circuit

Start and finish

Wolvercote Car Park
GR SU487094
Post code: OX2 8PN
Public toilets

Wolvercote village is located within the boundaries of Oxford, on the north western edge of the City, just inside the Ring Road. There is a large public car park with toilets, situated on the western edge of the village, next to water meadows and a backwater of the River Thames.

If you are driving: head for the **Peartree Roundabout** on the Ring Road north of Oxford, where the A34 meets the A44. From here, head southwards, following the sign for Oxford City Centre. At the next roundabout take the fourth exit following the signs for **Wolvercote**; drive through the village until you see the public car park on the left. This car park is free at the time of writing but has a **height restriction**. It is popular and can get very busy on summer weekends. The nearest alternative is to park on the roads near to the Plough pub – see below.

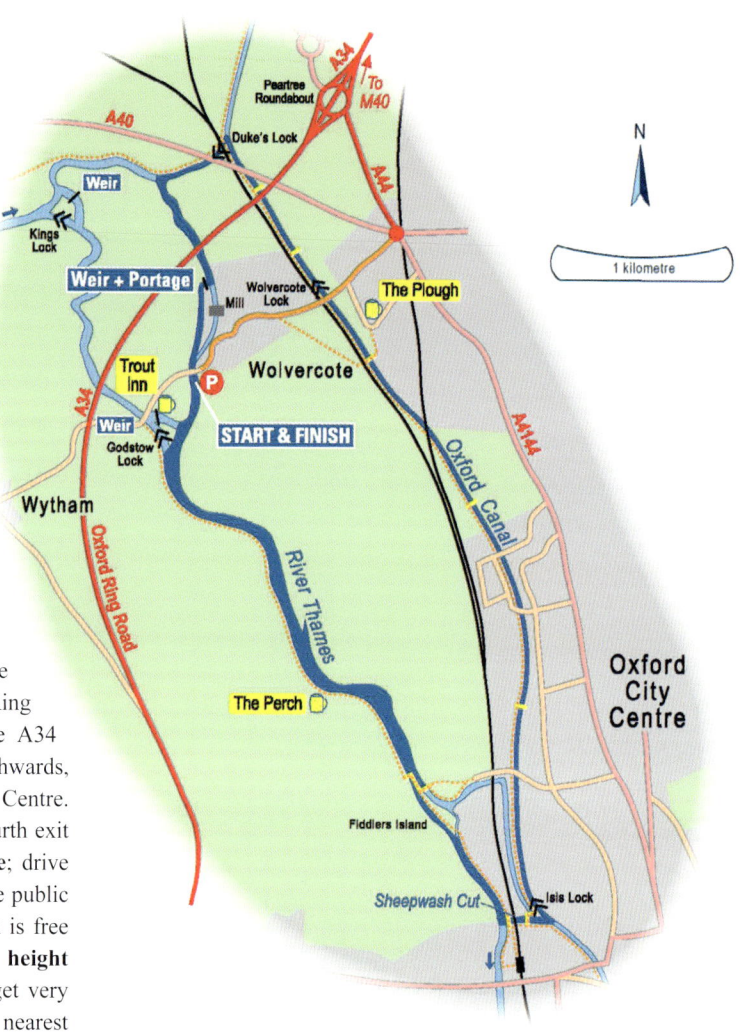

Trip description by Chris Wheeler and updated by Dave Surman

Shorter trip and only one portage

Instead of completing the full circuit, you can cut out the northern most part of the loop to create a U shaped trip, by finishing at the **Plough pub** (GR SU497097). This reduces the number of portages from 4 to 1 however it involves a short walk, just over a km, through Wolvercote village to pick up the car. On street parking is available here near the Plough and so if the car park at Wolvercote is full, one can simply run the shuttle first, parking the car here. It also provides an alternative launch point for the full circuit if the car park is full.

Family recreation on the Thames. *Chris Wheeler*

Pubs and tea shops

The Trout at Wolvercote offers a pleasant riverside terrace and garden and is very convenient for refreshment before or after the trip Tel: 01865 510930.

The Perch is a long established thatched pub amongst fields, 200m from the river, dating back to the seventeenth century. Tel: 01865 728891.

The Plough is our recommended pub and we suggest this as a finish point if you want to shorten the paddle. It is a very pleasant pub set back a mere 50m from the Canal, alongside open fields and receives good reviews from paddlers. Post Code OX2 8BD. Tel: 01865 556969.

More information

O.S. Map 1:50,000   sheet 164

River conditions
https://www.gov.uk/guidance/river-thames-current-river-conditions

River Thames
www.thames.me.uk

Oxford Visitor Info
www.visitoxford.org

Oxford Canal
www.canalrivertrust.org.uk

Chris Wheeler

12 Wolvercote Circuit

Other trips nearby

Please see trip number 13, the Oxford Cherwell.

Other possibilities for circular paddles in the local area are the Oxford backwaters – the **Seacourt and Hinksey streams** – best paddled early in the spring before weed and vegetation become too much of a problem. See www.canoedaysout. for more details.

Attractions nearby

Oxford is of course a world famous historic city and is a must for a visit.

Woodstock and Blenheim Palace is just a few km north of Wolvercote along the A44. www.blenheimpalace.com

The Oxford Canal

The Oxford Canal was designed by the famous engineer James Brindley and completed in 1790. It is one of the most historic canals in the country and it was planned and built to bring coal from the mines near Coventry south to London. It was designed as a narrow, 7ft wide, 'contour' canal, winding round the rolling hills of North Oxfordshire. This saved money for the builders, but then a 14ft broad canal, the Grand Union, was built in the 1820's also connecting the coal fields of Warwickshire to London. This was bigger and faster so most barge traffic switched to this so that the southern end of the Oxford Canal was bypassed by most traffic, and so it remains today hardly changed in two centuries. The stretch that we paddle sees relatively little boat traffic (most boats use the Dukes Cut) but it is popular for recreation and it is well maintained.

The journey

From the launch spot head left and downstream and within 100 yards you can detour to the right (upstream) to visit the **Trout pub**, a long established and locally famous pub which some of you may recognize from watching Inspector Morse. The riverside setting is very pleasant but can tend to get very busy during the summer months. Beware of and stay away from the adjacent weir.

Paddling downstream, you pass Godstow Lock on your right, behind which are the ruins of Godstow Nunnery which was dismantled by Parliamentary forces during the Civil War. To your left, for the next couple of miles, is Port Meadow. The people of Oxford enjoy legal right over the entire 440 acres, with common rights to graze cattle, horses and geese and have done for hundreds of years ('Port' derives from an Anglo Saxon trading place). Every few years the entire area floods just leaving the towpath on the western side of the river above water.

This stretch of the river Thames is a popular training stretch for rowing eights and other rakish and backward craft, so keep a watchful eye open both behind as well as ahead of you. After another mile or so, look out for a landing stage and sign on the right advertising the Perch pub - it's easy to miss because the pub is set back 100m from the river. After this, stay alert to avoid crashing into sailing dinghies as you approach the local sailing club, beyond which there is a small boatyard and marina.

Short Cut - Fork to the left here, paddling between the two rows of boats and under a small footbridge, to take a small backwater, which provides a link to the Oxford Canal. Watch out for two low railway bridges, particularly in flood, although most of the time they are easily passable by means of an easy boat 'limbo'. From here the Stream turns rightwards/southwards to run parallel with the Canal. Pick your spot and portage over the left hand bank and turn left up the Canal.

Or **A bit longer** – Keep right after the marina and when some houses come in sight on the left, after a km, take a left turn under an arched foot bridge. This is called the 'Sheepwash Cut': it is quite narrow and must be quite exciting in a narrow boat. Paddle under the railway bridges and then land on the left to portage **Isis lock** the first on the Oxford Canal.

From here, heading north up the Canal, the scene is urban but remarkably quiet and peaceful. You pass, to your left, endless houseboats - canal barges that people do actually live in, complete with cats and dogs, bikes, wood burning stoves and some splendid decorative art work (and dubious smoke). To your right, are the back gardens of attractive, expensive Jericho cottages, an old concentration of terraced workers' cottages houses that have been 'gentrified' and are now eye wateringly expensive! It is fascinating to dawdle and admire the huge diversity of back gardens that could

Houseboats on the Oxford Canal. *Chris Wheeler*

be straight out of a 'Homes and Gardens' magazine – indeed, you could almost produce a coffee table book of garden designs from all the ones laid out here for your delight!

Over the next two kilometres you will paddle under several bridges and then under a railway bridge. Then there is a footbridge number 236, and just beyond and through the trees on the right, is the **Plough Pub** – our suggested option if you wish to shorten the trip.

Just past the next road bridge is **Wolvercote Lock** which will need a short portage. Another km brings you to the Ring Road and the roar of traffic intrudes. Just beyond is a canal junction, **Duke's Lock** and Lock House. You need to turn left here, portage the lock and take the 'Duke's Cut' that links the canal and Thames. 500m will bring you to a T junction, where the cutting meets the Wolvercote Mill Stream. The shortest way back is to turn left, downstream, signed 'Mill stream'. This Mill stream is only navigable by canoe so may change due to falling trees etc.

You paddle under the ring road and then after 100m land on the right to portage the weir. Indicated by a boom across the stream. This can be a little bit slippery – seal launches are the order of the day. From here it is just 600m to Wolvercote Bridge where there is a bit of a shoot of water under the arches to add a final little bit of excitement as a climax to the trip.

(If you want to avoid the portage at the weir, an alternative route, 2km longer, is to head right, upstream to join the main channel just upstream of King's Weir and Lock - you have to portage, or pass through this lock and then also Godstow Lock).

Extending the trip

If you want a longer trip we suggest that you continue **downstream** down the Thames through the Oxford city centre to the **Isis Tavern** and then return - about 8km return from Sheepwash Channel. You will need to portage or pass through Osney Lock and you then paddle past Christ Church Meadows and then the college boat houses. This stretch can be busy with fast rowing eights.

The river Thames **upstream** of Kings Lock is pleasant, but not as interesting as the circuit described here.

Strange encounters on the canal. *Chris Wheeler*

101

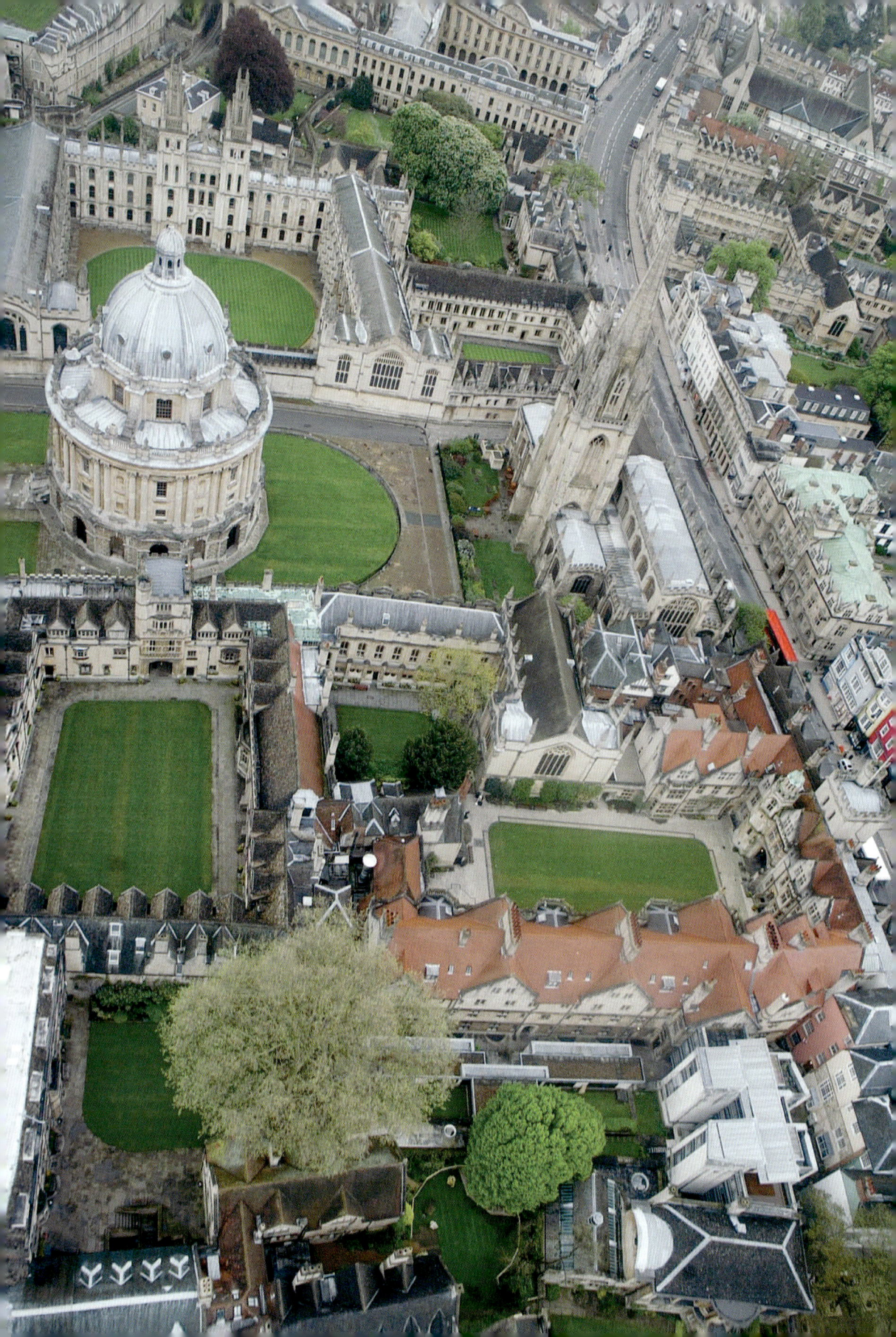

Oxford Cherwell 13

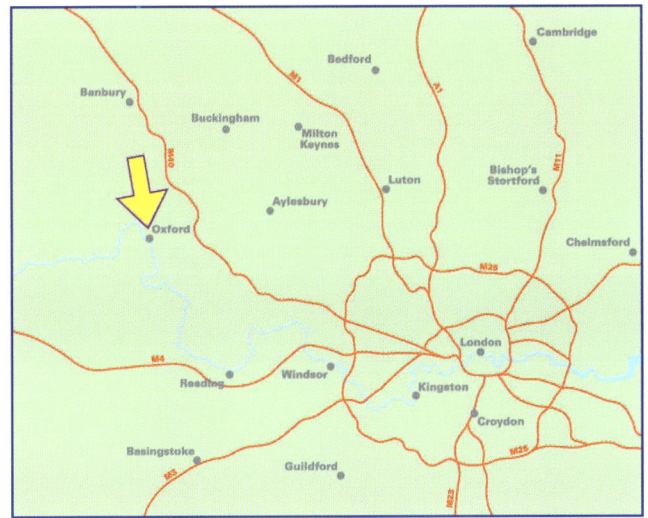

There and back
Small river
4-5 hours - 13km
Easy paddling

Parking	★
Launching	★★★
Portages?	1 - but rollers to help!
Quiet?	No motorboats, but busy at weekends

Why do this trip?

This is a classic trip that takes you to the heart of Oxford – with idyllic views of dreaming spires, sunlit meadows, students punting, and a welcoming traditional pub at your destination.

Tell me more

The Cherwell is a tributary of the Thames which passes through beautiful meadows with over-hanging trees, past many famous historic colleges and the University Parks to a lovely river side pub. If you prefer, there are also many lovely spots ideal for picnics. There are no motor boats and it has always been popular for punting - on fine summer days it is likely to be busy and entertaining with people who have hired punts trying to learn the skills of handling them!

Our suggested starting point is on the River Thames and takes you along the main rowing stretch past the famous college boat houses. This is a really interesting section of the Thames (or 'Isis', as it is known in Oxford) but you may have problems on this short stretch if you have chosen a day when there is a **rowing regatta** or the exciting 'Oxford bumps' – we suggest you check on the web for details:
www.oxfordrowingclub.org.uk/events (City events)
www.ourcs.co.uk (University events)

Special points

1. Fast Rowing boats-see notes
2. Membership of Paddle UK or Thames licence is in theory required

Canoe & SUP Hire

The Cherwell Boat House mainly hires punts, however it also has some quality 'Old Town' canoes for hire.
Tel: 01865 515978
www.cherwellboathouse.co.uk

Radcliffe Camera and All Souls from the air.
Kingpin Media Ltd

13 Oxford Cherwell

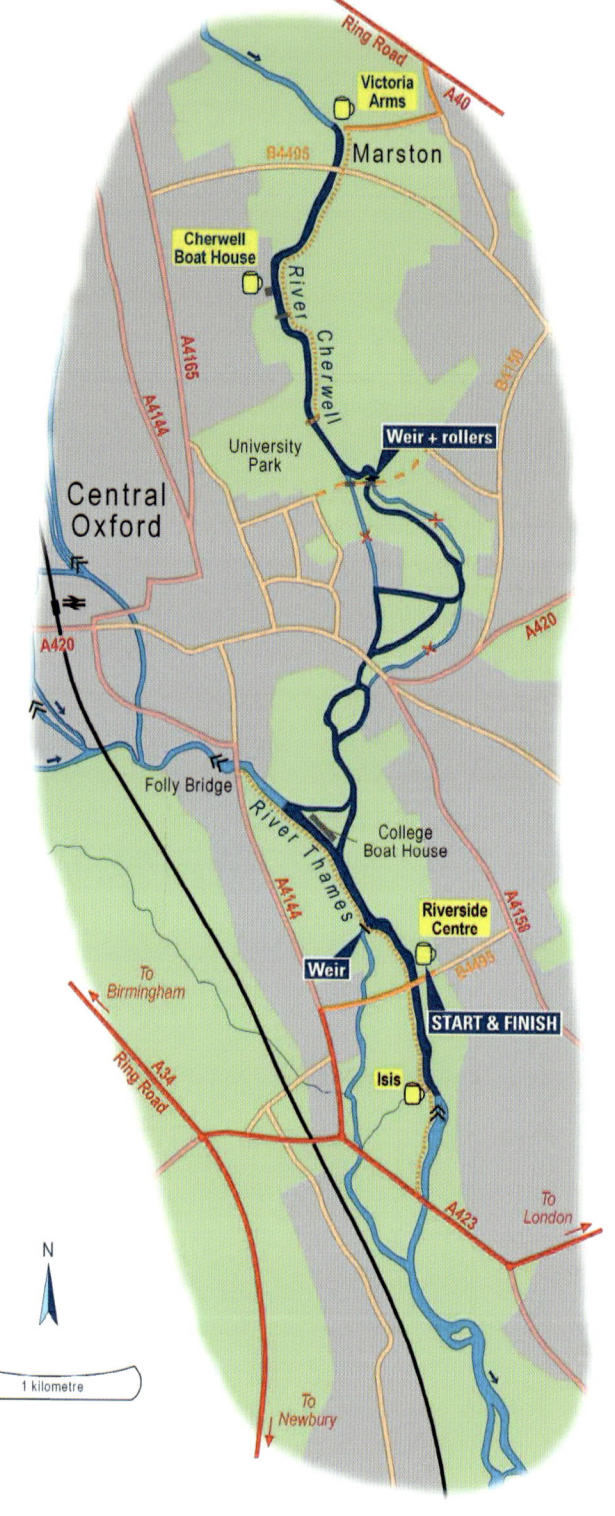

Start and finish

Slipway next to Donnington Bridge GR 525045   Post code: OX4 4BJ

Oxford City centre is closed to private traffic, so from the North, East or West follow the Oxford Ring Road to the South of the city and then follow the signs to Redbridge Park & Ride. You may want to use the toilets here but otherwise stay in the centre lane of the A4074 and continue towards the City Centre. At the next traffic lights, just past Tesco, turn right - this will take you over the river Thames at Donnington Bridge. Take the first left after the bridge, Meadow Lane, and then immediately turn left down to a large concrete slipway with a grassy area to unload boats and gear. Having dropped off your boats the driver will probably need to take your vehicle back to Redbridge Park and Ride which is the nearest car park - it has good facilities and no height restrictions but is a 15 minute walk.

Alternative Start

If this section of the Thames is busy due to a rowing regatta then it is probably best to start from the Victoria Arms, Old Marston OX3 0PZ and do the trip in reverse. (They have a large car park, but please phone the pub first as a courtesy - 01865 241 382)

Trip description by Peter Hennessy

Magdalen Tower and Botanic Gardens. *Glynn Carter*

Pubs and tea shops

The **Victoria Arms** is at the far end of the trip at Old Marston. It is a well-known, traditional, riverside pub that we can recommend and it has been around for centuries as it used to be site of a ferry linking Marston with north Oxford. It has a landing stage with a large lawn, terrace and outside tables. The food is usually good depending on how busy the pub is - however the beer is always excellent! The pub has a big car park and so could be used as the start and finish point of the trip, but do please give them a ring to ask permission first. Tel: 01865 241382.

The **Cherwell Boat House** has a restaurant with a reputation for fine food. However it also has a "Tea Hut" hatch that serves drinks and snacks, so this makes a convenient refreshment stop for punters and paddlers. Tel 01865 552746.

If you want to extend the paddling trip down the Thames, then the **Isis Tavern** is less than a km downstream from Donnington Bridge. This is another classic Oxford riverside pub with a big garden and great location - no road access, the only way to it is by the towpath or by river. It is rightly popular in the summer months.

More information

Oxford Visitor Information
www.oxfordcityguide.com

River Thames
www.thames.me.uk

Falcon Rowing and Canoeing Club
www.falconboatclub.org.uk

Isis Canoe Club
www.isiscanoecluboxford.co.uk

13 Oxford Cherwell

The journey

Oxford is a city that is dominated by the rivers and the University. Many of the University colleges take rowing seriously and this stretch of the river Thames (known locally as 'The Isis') is a popular training ground. Racing craft are fast, have sharp bows, and the rowers are of course a backward crew – so after setting off keep looking behind you to make sure you are not about to be cut in half. After launching turn right and keep to the right hand side heading upstream along side a tree lined meadow. On the left you will see two foot bridges marked 'Danger' as the towpath goes over two channels in the Thames, it is not unknown to see whitewater play boaters heading this way - strangely there seem to be fewer coming back!

After less than a kilometre on the Thames you will come to the River Cherwell joining the River Thames from the right. Provided it is not too busy we suggest you continue along the Thames and paddle past the **University Boat Houses**.

If the river is really busy with racing boats, then we suggest you take the first branch of the Cherwell and miss out the boat houses.

The College Boathouses are a distinctive part of the riverside landscape and at weekends in term time and especially at regattas they can be hives of activity as crews get in and out of boats. Immediately after the last boat house turn right under an arched bridge, and up the second, smaller branch of the Cherwell. It is worth going along this route for the views across **Christ Church Meadow** to Christ Church, Corpus Christi and Merton colleges (from left to right). If you haven't seen the Oxford colleges before then it is worth getting out, to have a proper look as the path around the meadow is open to the public during daylight hours. After about 600m this pleasant, winding backwater, bright with daffodils in the spring time, joins the main River Cherwell.

Continue up the main River Cherwell with 'the views of dreaming spires' ahead of you. When the river splits again, continue along the left fork keeping the meadow path on your left. By now, on a nice day in spring or summer, you will be passing punts. Originally used for goods transport along shallow rivers they are now a feature of both Oxford and Cambridge (although the punters of Cambridge traditionally stand on the wrong end).

The open meadow on the left gives way to the large glasshouses of the Oxford Botanic Gardens which are the third oldest scientific gardens in the world. Keep left and then ahead of you is the attractive Magdalen Bridge and behind it is **Magdalen Tower**, the bell tower for Magdalen College.

Jake reckoned that the rollers were the best bit of the trip.
Marcus Draper

Other trips nearby

See Trip no. 13, the Wolvercote Circuit for another pleasant nearby trip.

The valley of the River Cherwell is followed by the Oxford Canal in its upper stretches (also by the M40 motorway) and if you are looking for a longer paddle then you can do a **Cherwell circuit** from Oxford up the canal to Thrupp and then return down the river Cherwell back to Oxford. Other possibilities for circular paddles in the local area are the Oxford backwaters – the **Seacourt and Hinksey streams** – best paddled early in the spring before weed and vegetation become too much of a problem. See www.canoedaysout for details of these trips and expect an adventure.

Magdalen Mill. *Glynn Carter*

Look out for punts. Oxford's central punt hire place is immediately after the bridge (on the left) and the river is narrow and easily blocked by a handful of novice punters. It's generally best to sit back, watch the chaos and laugh along with everyone else!

After the bridge continue straight ahead (or slightly right) along the main river, ignoring the small channel to the left (your return route). The bridge is soon left behind and the crowd of punters rapidly thins out. If you are ready for a break then the meadow on the right (Angel Meadow) is a pleasant picnic spot. The gardens on the left may look more attractive but they are private to Magdalen College. From April to June the banks along this stretch of the river are covered with daffodils and other spring flowers.

About half a kilometre from the stone bridge a footbridge crosses over and you come to a T-junction where the main river, which you should follow, turns right and soon after, turns left again. Just over 100m later the river forks again, around a long narrow island. Keep to the right and you should be able to catch glimpses through the trees of Oxford's newest and strangest spires - the minaret and dome of the Centre for Islamic Studies.

This building has been beautifully constructed and is an inspired addition to Oxford's famous skyline. At the end of the island is an old sluice weir beside Mill House, the weir is generally only open at times of high flows in the river and there is little cause for worry about the current.

"The Cherwell - winding, secretive, alluring, willow-girt, whispering of men and maidens, and of the dream days of ambitious youth"
E.W. Hazelhurst.

Magdalen College

Magdalen College was founded in 1448 (the name is pronounced "maudlin"). Since Medieval times, at dawn on the first day of May every year the college choir assemble on the top of the tower and sing for a large crowd - typically 8000 or so - who come to listen from the bridge. Many of the people are students who have stayed up all night at their college spring balls so there is a festival atmosphere.

13 Oxford Cherwell

Parsons Pleasure

This grassy area beside the rollers and weir is known as 'Parsons Pleasure' and was an area for male-only nude bathing that was only closed in 1991. This was before the cycle path was built so it would have been a quiet corner of the river and decency was maintained with hedges and a wall of bathing huts. One anecdote goes that a number of University dons were skinny-sunbathing here when a group of students floated by in a punt. All but one of the startled dons covered their modesty — the other placed a flannel over his head instead. When asked why he had done that, he replied haughtily, "Oh, well my students recognise me by my face." There was of course equality for the sexes - an adjourning swimming area was reserved for female bathers and known as 'Dame's Delight'.

After this point the river is split in two; you stay on the lower channel while a higher channel (with very low bridges) runs just the other side of the path on your right. The lower route passes another sluice weir about 300m later *Warning - normally all sluice gates are shut, but if any are open be wary here as there are strong feeder eddies that will pull you towards the weir.* This is followed by a smaller weir with a pretty wooden bridge over it 300m later again. By now the channel is getting noticeably smaller with trees on both sides and the current will be stronger here if there is any flow in the river - but it's not for long. At dusk this is a great place for watching bats flying around!

The river goes under a wooden footbridge and after the next corner it suddenly opens out in a pool with a landing area on your left and a final weir on the right. Ahead of you are **'rollers'** that can be used to portage the 10m or so up to the next stretch of river.

After portaging up the rollers continue on, and soon after, the river bends right. At this point there is a fairly significant and very straight channel downstream to the left, this comes to a dead end after about 10 minutes at Magdalen Mill - it's worth noting the direction you have come from for your return trip. For the next half kilometre, the land on your left is owned by the University Parks and is probably the most attractive place to have a **picnic**, unless you value seclusion over landscaped gardens, in which case later fields will suit you more. The approaching end of the park is indicated by the 'Rainbow Bridge' after which the fields on your right can make good landing places as they are open to public access all the way to the end of the trip. These old meadows are carefully grazed in a traditional way to maintain an abundance and diversity of wildlife – especially scenic with wild flowers in May and June.

You may have noticed the number of punts increasing again, this is because you are approaching the **'Cherwell Boat House'** which has punt and canoe hire, besides a restaurant and tea hut. Immediately after the boathouse is Wolfson College, a graduate college only founded in 1965 that has beautiful setting with a punting harbour connected to the river by a couple of small channels.

After the college and its bridge, a few twists of the river brings you in sight of the road bridge and your final destination. The **Victoria Arms** was the site of a small ferry across the River Cherwell that was available until the modern road bridge was built in 1967. Visitors have been arriving here by boat for many centuries and it seems only appropriate to maintain traditions and partake of a refreshing pint of ale! On a warm summer afternoon many of its customers still arrive by punt and moor along the foot of the large south-west facing lawn.

Medieval Oxford from a different angle. *Glynn Carter*

Cherwell Boat House stretch. *Jon Stay*

After a suitable period of maintaining traditions, return the way you came - although there isn't usually much current in the river, the journey back always seems quite a bit quicker.

Take note not to take the dead end turn off to Magdalen Mill, however we suggest that about a km after the rollers, and where you turned right and left on your way up, you turn right and then continue straight ahead to explore the narrow and shallow channel that takes you to where the mill stream comes out, and so back to Magdalen Bridge by a different route. The other deviation you can take is soon after Magdalen Bridge - stay left of the island and also likewise stay left at the second island and take the main channel of the Cherwell to join the river Thames and so back to your **start point**.

Extending the trip

Suitably revived after refreshment at Victoria Arms and game for more before heading back? – Then continue **upstream** - the river gets progressively narrower, with more trees to negotiate, and feels very remote. The small village of Islip is about 6km away and the Red Lion pub there is just back from the river.

If you want to extend the paddling trip down the Thames, then the **Isis Farmhouse** is just half a km down from Donnington Bridge.

Grand Union at Tring 14

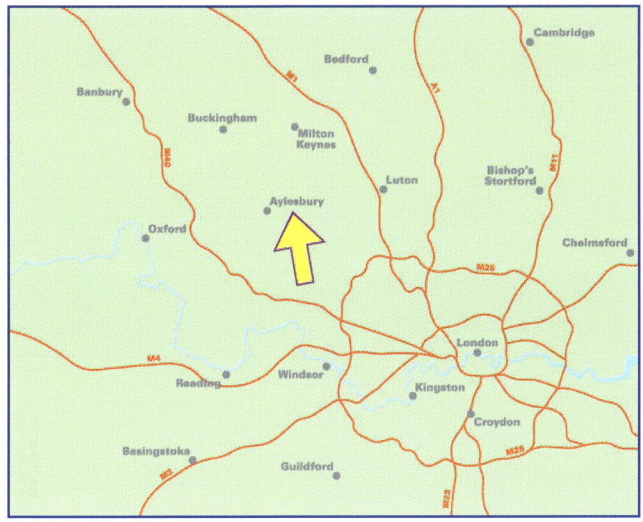

Canal

One way trip

2 hours - 7km

Very easy paddling

Parking	★★
Launching	★★
Portages?	None!
Quiet?	A few canal boats

Why do this trip?

This is one of the most interesting sections of the Grand Union Canal as it cuts through the Chiltern Downs and we also recommend an exploration of the renovated and sinuous Wendover Arm.

Special points

Membership of Paddle UK or a Canal & River Trust licence is required.

Tell me more

The Grand Union Canal used to be one of the most important canals in Britain linking Birmingham to London. It was opened in stages between 1793 and 1805 and this canal was part of the industrial revolution which transformed Britain. This is the Summit stretch of the canal - some 57 locks lift the canal 400ft up from the River Thames. This stretch of the canal was cunningly chosen by friend Bill Lockton because, being the summit stretch, it has no locks or portages and it has interesting scenery as it cuts through the Chiltern Hills. Then the second part of the trip explores the Wendover Arm which over the last twenty years has been renovated by a huge army of volunteers. We recommend this trip as a one way paddle - a cycle shuttle along the tow path is an easy option and won't take long. Those needing easier parking and launching should consider starting from the Grand Junction Arms at Bulbourne.

Bulbourne Junction lock. *Chris Wheeler*

14 Grand Union at Tring

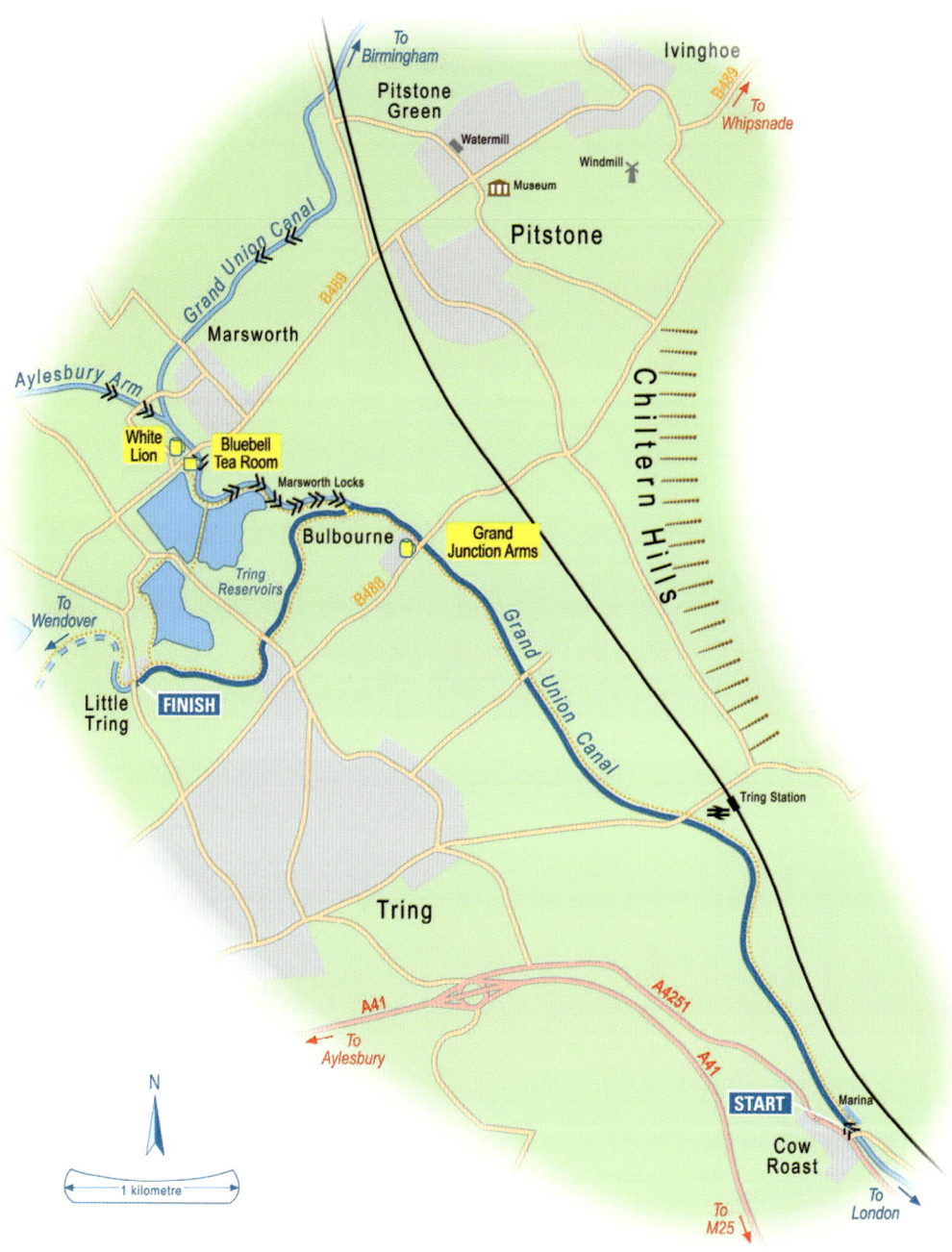

Tranquil paddling.   *Chris Wheeler*

Start

Cow Roast Lock
GR SP957103   Post code: HP23 5RE

Take the A41 north from the M25 and then come off at the first Tring junction. Head back south on the A4251 for some 3km to the Cow Roast. Turn left here, go over the canal bridge and then park in the small lay-by just past the entrance to the marina. Launch just beyond the lock – a carry of about 100m. If this is full, there is alternative parking just off the main road at Cow Roast.

Finish

Little Tring
GR SP916129   Post code: HP23 4NR

If you are arranging a shuttle and need to leave a car at the take out, then take the second Tring exit off the A41 and head north east on the B488. This is the old roman road, the Icknield Way. Turn left after 2km, signed 'Little Tring' and after 1km park on the left before the canal bridge. It is about a 100m walk up from the canal to the road.

More information

O.S. Map 1:50,000 sheet 165.

Wendover Arm Canal Trust
www.wendovercanal.org.uk

Canal licence
www.canalrivertrust.org.uk

Tourist information
www.visitbuckinghamshire.org.uk

Tring Reservoirs
www.hertswildlifetrust.org.uk

Chiltern Canoe Club
www.chilterncanoeclub.org.uk

14 Grand Union at Tring

Start point. *Chris Wheeler*

The Cow Roast

"What an intriguing name!" I thought when I first read this - so I did a little bit more research. The route that you are paddling is an obvious main gap and route through the Chiltern Hills and so there has been an ancient trackway and drove road here from time immemorial. Then a Roman settlement and road, the Akeman Street, followed many centuries later by a turnpike coach road, then the canal, the main railway line to the North West, and more recently the modern A41 highway. So over the centuries, this quiet spot has seen millions and millions of people travelling the same route as yourself and the Cow Roast is a very ancient settlement – and the name you ask? Prosaically it is merely a corruption of "cow rest" - a place where the drovers rested their cattle as they drove them to market in London.

Pubs and tea shops

We recommend the **Grand Junction Arms** at Bulbourne which is a traditional canal side pub with a big garden, car park, real beer and good food. This is also an ideal place to park as it's only a short walk down to the canal. The Chiltern Canoe Club has a base here just west of the Pub along the canal with adjacent access steps. Tel: 01442 890677.

Near the start point, the old Cow Roast Inn has been renovated and is now the **Artisan Bar and Grill**. It has a large garden and appears to be popular. Tel: 0333 366000.

Places of interest nearby

Pitstone Wind Mill is believed to be the oldest post mill in the British Isles. It was given to the National Trust in 1937 and is now fully restored. It is fascinating to see it working and it is open to the public on Sunday and Bank Holiday afternoons during the summer months. Tel:01442 851227. www.nationaltrust.org.uk.

Just a few minutes walk down the hill from Pitstone Wind Mill is **Ford End Water Mill**, Ivinghoe. Built in the early 1700s, it has been restored to recreate the atmosphere of a small corn mill in the 1800s. It is one of few watermills that are still working. Stoneground wholemeal flour for sale on open days. Tel: 01442 825421. www.fordendwatermill.co.uk.

Pitstone Green Museum is mainly a Rural Life Museum, with many exhibits relating to farming, country life, trades, and professions from the area. Tel:01582 605464.

Whipsnade Wildlife Park is about 9km North East of Tring. This is home to over 2,500 wild animals: lions, tigers, rhinos and giraffes can be seen in almost natural conditions. Tel: 01582 872171. www.zsl.org.

If you feel that your kids prefer to swing around in the trees by themselves, then maybe you should take them to the high ropes course run by **GoApe** near Wendover. www.goape.co.uk

The journey

Setting off from the Cow Roast, put in above lock 46 (numbered from the north) and set off past the small marina. The canal is pleasantly rural with views north to the Chiltern Hills. Over in the beech woods is Stokes Golf and Country Club, one of the playgirl clubs from the permissive 60's. My friend Bill used to train on this section of the canal in the evening time and talks about seeing bats, badgers, voles, and water snakes: We only saw a kingfisher.

After two bridges and a couple of km the banks get higher and you paddle into the **Tring Cutting** – a peaceful, green, leafy tunnel, cut off from the rest of the world. This was all dug out by pick and

Tring Cutting. *Chris Wheeler*

shovel by the navies who built the canal - how many wheelbarrow loads it must have taken! This cutting has always been at risk of landslips and best avoided at times of volcanic activity – see www.earthquakes.bgs.org.uk.

The next bridge marks the end of the cutting and the old BWB workshops at **Bulbourne**, where the wooden lock gates used to be made and repaired for much of the waterways of Southern England. Each took around ten days to make and were crafted from huge baulks of unseasoned oak. Nowadays the old boat yard has been converted into private residences. Over on the left is a very welcome sight – the old Victorian pub called the **Grand Junction Arms** – where the bargees would have stopped for refreshment – a fine tradition that you might like to continue...

Shortly after Bulbourne you come to the junction with the **Wendover Arm** of the canal. The main canal continues to the right - if you took this then you would have 7 locks to descend in less than a km. A lot of portaging! So we recommend a left turn and a paddle down the Wendover Arm of the Canal. Note the Toll keeper's house on the junction with a bay window so he could have a good view

Other trips nearby

Much of the Grand Union Canal has locks at frequent intervals; however there are stretches at Milton Keynes and Leighton Buzzard that offer trips with only one or two locks. At Leighton Buzzard there is the possibility of paddling the **River Ouzel** when water levels are sufficient, and then returning along the Grand Union canal. At Rickmansworth there is the possibility of a circular paddle using the **River Gade** – see www.canoetrips.org. The river **Great Ouse** offers several attractive stretches for paddling – again see www.canoetrips.org.

14 Grand Union at Tring

of approaching boats. This branch originally connected the town of Wendover to the Grand Union Canal but fell into disuse and is now being restored by the Wendover Arm Trust.

This branch of the canal is a narrow canal, with locks that are 7ft wide – unlike the Grand Union which was built with locks that are 14ft wide so it could take a wide barge or two narrow boats side by side. The Wendover Arm is also different in character in that it is what is called a 'contour canal' because it winds around the hillside. Winding round the hillside like this, different views open up ahead of you – one moment you are picking blackberries, the next you are looking into someone's bedroom window! After a km you come to Tring Wharf and Heygates Flour Mill - this is where the flour in your local shop is packed.

The Wendover Arm is also very peaceful because it is a dead end. At the time of writing the navigation finishes at Little Tring – just 2km from Bulbourne and this is our suggested finish. If you want to end your trip here, then take out next to the bridge and walk up to the road. However, looking to the future, as restoration continues apace it should be possible to explore further another 6km to Wendover - see "Extending the trip".

Bulbourne Junction. *Chris Wheeler*

Tring Reservoirs

57 locks lift the Grand Union Canal up from the River Thames to this summit stretch at Tring and every time a boat passes up or down through this summit level it takes nearly 200,000 gallons of water! So these Tring reservoirs were built in the early 19th Century to supply water when the canal was really busy with hundreds of barges passing up and down and there was a shortage of water. The reservoirs are now designated a Site of Special Scientific Interest on account of their wealth of birdlife and are a popular visitor attraction with waymarked trails which explore the woods, fields, locks and towpaths surrounding the reservoirs.

Adrift at the finish. *Chris Wheeler*

Wendover Arm Junction. *Davepaddles.co.uk*

Extending the trip

If you have the time then we suggest that you consider exploring up the **Wendover Arm** and then returning to Little Tring. Note that this stretch may have problems with weed. About 2km beyond Little Tring the new A41 highway bridge swoops over the canal and then after 400m is the old bridge at Buckland Wharf. A further 600m brings you to Wellonhead Bridge where there is an alternative car park about 100m up the hill on the east side of the road at GR 888114, Post code HP22 5NE. Continuing on from here after about another 3km the canal takes you into the heart of Wendover -, but at the time of writing there were no obvious park and launch spots.

We don't recommend that you extend your trip on the Grand Union Canal - as in either direction you will have to portage a lot of locks.

Stort 15

Canalised river
One way trip
2 hours - 7km
Very easy paddling

Parking	★★
Launching	★★
Portages?	4 locks
Quiet?	A few canal boats

Why do this trip?
A pleasant paddle close to North East London. Despite its proximity to Greater London, this is a surprisingly rural trip winding through ancient parkland and quiet water meadows. The trip can be easily shortened or extended and is close to the railway with convenient stations.

Special points
Paddle UK membership or Canal & River Trust permit required

Tell me more
The river Stort was canalized in 1769 and today it is a quiet and peaceful cul-de-sac, with a total of 15 locks and passes through a corridor of nature reserves. Our recommended paddle selects the most convenient and pleasant stretch of the river. There are four locks to portage but all have landing stages designed for canoes so this is relatively easy. The journalist Paul Heiney summed up the Stort as "that most friendly of rivers" – we hope you agree!

Start
Sawbridgeworth Maltings
GR TL489150   Post code: CM21 9JX
Sawbridgeworth Maltings are a converted old Malthouse and a good place to start. From the M11, come off at junction 7 and follow the A414 to Harlow and then the A1184 north to Sawbridgeworth. Turn right in the village down the hill to the river, over the bridge turn

Family paddling on the Stort. *Jim Sollars*

15 Stort

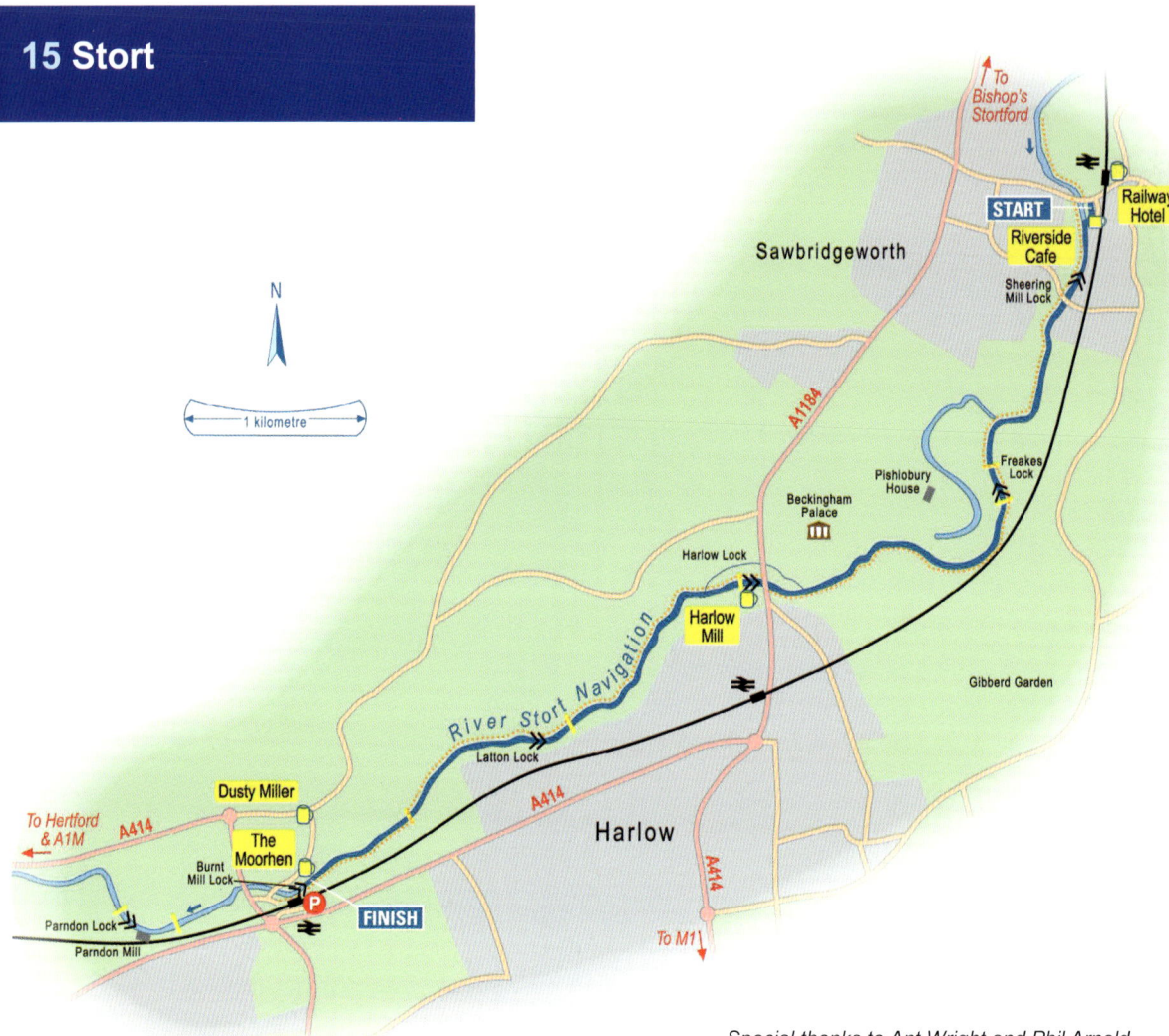

Special thanks to Ant Wright and Phil Arnold.

More information

O.S. Map 1:50,000 sheet 167.

Canal & River Trust
www.canalrivertrust.org.uk

Harlow visitor information
www.visitessex.com

Bishops Stortford Canoe Club
www.stortfordcanoe.org.uk/

Whoosh Explore Canoe Club
www.whooshexplore.co.uk

right and then the Maltings are the quay alongside the river. We recommend this as a convenient place for launching. You can park your car at the pay & display parking at the railway station which is only 2 minutes walk away (where there are toilets) or perhaps a better idea is to shuttle first and park your car at the take out.

Finish

Harlow Town Station
GR TL446113   Post code: CM20 2QS

We suggest taking out at Burnt Mill Lock which is just upstream of where the A414 crosses the river and very near Harlow Town Station. If driving south on the A414 take the first turning on the left immediately after crossing the river, this is Burnt Mill Lane, then continue straight on into Burnt Mill Close which leads you to a small riverside car park. The Moorhen pub is on the opposite bank

Collecting invasive Floating Pennywort. *Whoosh Explore Canoe Club*

and Harlow Town Station is just behind you. However there is no entrance this side.

There is a frequent train service, usually every 7 minutes, so we suggest that the driver returns by train to fetch the car: alternatively the tow path is in good condition and makes a pleasant cycle or run.

Pubs and tea shops

The **Shed** coffee house is near the start in the Maltings. Tel: 01279 723853.

The **Harlow Mill** is a beefeater pub and restaurant alongside the river at Harlow Lock, tel: 01279 217535.

The **Moorhen** is on the riverside at the end of the trip and has a large car park, garden and children's play areas so is popular with Essex families, tel: 01279 423066. Local paddlers recommend the **Dusty Miller** which is a smaller and quieter alternative just 300m up the road. This is a more traditional pub which welcomes well behaved families and has real beer and good food, tel: 01279 424180.

15 Stort

Other trips nearby

The **Chelmer**, trip no 18, the **Cam**, trip no. 17, and **Constable's Stour**, trip no. 19 are all less than an hour's drive - please see the relevant descriptions.

The **Lea Navigation** is busier than the Stort and we feel it is less attractive with long, straight, featureless stretches and steel piled concrete banks

Lee Valley White Water Centre

This was built for the London 2012 Olympics, is 15km from the River Stort and close to the M25. It looks like a short stretch of some powerful Alpine river landscaped by rolling green hills - so if you have the time do check it out. Admission to the centre is normally free (unless it is hosting a slalom or World Cup event) and it is exciting just to watch the white water action! Obviously it is even more exhilarating to have a go, and the centre offers white water rafting, kayaking, hot dogging and hydrospeeding. With two White Water courses the "Legacy" and the "Olympic" it caters to all skill levels, though an assessment is required to go on the water. The centre also offers lessons, equipment hire, a well stocked shop, and hosts the friendly Lee Valley Paddlesports Club.

Mike Shaw

Places of interest nearby

Mountfitchet Castle is 4km north of Bishops Stortford and is a recreation of a Medieval Castle and village which will delight most kids.

The **Gibberd Garden** at Marsh Lane, Harlow, is a more adult attraction - a fascinating and very different garden featuring over 80 sculptures and pieces of architectural salvage. "There are few gardens in England where the eye and mind are so consistently stimulated and amused".

Biggles fans will want to head to the **North Weald Airfield Museum** which recreates the days of the Battle of Britain and is 2km East of junction 7 of the M1.

The **Forge Museum** at Much Hadham 8km NW of Sawbridgeworth is a working forge.

Rye House Gatehouse is near the junction of the Rivers Lee & Stort at GR TL386099. Started in 1443, it is a fine example of early brickwork. The gatehouse has a lively display about the infamous 'Newmarket Plot' to murder King Charles II on his way back from the races at Newmarket in 1683.

The journey

Setting out from **Sawbridgeworth**, only a few minutes paddle will bring you to Sheering Mill Lock - the first lock to portage. The river twists and turns, with weeping willows, ancient meadows and shady woodland on both banks. There is the occasional swan, lots of ducks and other water fowl and the river seems incredibly peaceful – just the sound of the occasional train on the main line to Cambridge to disturb you. Just before the next footbridge you can see a sluice that goes off right to the old course of the river which runs past the old Thomas Richards Orchard that used to supply nursery trees and seeds to all the great Victorian Houses of England.

Freakes Lock, which comes up next feels like it is in the heart of the countryside and makes a pleasant place for a refreshment break. As you paddle round the next big bend you will see old Pishiobury House on the right, whilst on the left and out of sight is the fascinating Gibberd Garden. Perhaps more famous is Rowneybury House that comes into view on the right bank ahead – this used to be a school for disabled children but is now known by the locals as "**Beckingham Palace**" – This used to be home of the Beckham's and was sold in 2017 for £11.35 million.

Harlow lock, bridge and Mill all come up next and will need another short portage. The Harlow Mill is now a pub and restaurant and

Winter paddling on the River Stort. *Whoosh Explore Canoe Club*

can provide refreshment if you need something to keep you going on this arduous paddle. The river seems to widen after Harlow bridge but stills twists and turns through fine wooded scenery. The only clue to the New Town of Harlow is the number of people walking and cycling the towpath and who usually give you a friendly wave. Hidden away somewhere to your left is the site of a Roman Temple and it seems probable that the Romans transported the stones for building it up the old river Stort – a lot harder before it was canalized. Latton Lock comes up after a few more twists in the river and you may well meet other paddlers here from the Essex Outdoors. Then another kilometer brings you to our suggested **finish point** opposite the Moorhen Pub and just before Burnt Mill Lock

Extending the trip

There is convenient parking and easy launching at Twyford Lock in Pig Lane near Bishop's Stortford CM22 7PA. This would add 5km to the start of the trip. The other option, although perhaps not as interesting, would be to continue on another 5km to Roydon Railway Station which again is close to the river.

A short and interesting extension is to continue another km to Parndon Mill which is now a community of artists studios with some excellent artwork to be seen.

River Stort Navigation Tonnage Rates

For Wheat, Rye, Beans or Peas... 0s 6d per Quarter.
For Malt or Oats. 0s 4d ditto.
For Barley, or any other Sort of Grain not before enumerated. 0s 5d ditto.
For Meal or Flour (Five Bushels to a Sack). 0s 4d per Sack.
For Coal, Culm or Cinders.. 2s 6d per Chaldron.
For Lime 2s 6d ditto.
For Oil-cakes, Malt-dust, Pigeon Dung or Manure of any kind 1s 6d per Ton.
For Goods, Wares or Merchandize not before enumerated.. 2s 6d ditto. And so in proportion for any less Quantity.

Cam 16

Small river

There and back

6km - 2 hours

Easy paddling

Parking	★★★
Launching	★★★
Portages?	None (1 with rollers if you extend the trip)
Quiet?	No motor boats but busy with punts?

Why do this trip?

This is a gentle, quintessentially English river trip that can be split into two excellent but contrasting paddles -

1. A rural paddle upstream though quiet pastoral scenery and meadows to the old village of Grantchester,

2. An urban paddle downstream along the famous and touristy 'Backs' of the historic Cambridge colleges.

Each trip is about 6km long and will take a leisurely two hours. Combine the two and you have a very pleasant and diverse day.

Special points

Busy with punts on sunny afternoons along the 'Backs'.

Trip no 2 needs membership of Paddle UK or Cam licence.

Canoe Hire

Granta Boat and Punt Company hire quality 'Old Town' canoes, Tel: 01223 301845. 01223 301845
www.puntingincambridge.com

Tell me more

The River Cam rises in Hertfordshire and then gently meanders through farmland to Cambridge where it flows along the famous 'Backs' – the green riverside lawns of the backs of the colleges. At Cambridge it becomes a navigation and flows north to join the Great Ouse and then onto the Wash. It can be paddled in winter from Barrington and all year from Byron's Pool at Grantchester. Seeing Cambridge is a tourist must - seeing it for free from the comfort of your own SUP or canoe makes it all that more enjoyable! Note that the trips we recommend here are free of motor boats

Kings College Cambridge. *Hiroshi Shimura*

16 Cam

Trip description by David Savage

Setting off from Newnham. *Colin Southward*

Grantchester meadows. *Hiroshi Shimura*

Start and finish

Newnham
GR TL448574   Post code: CB2

From the M11 follow the A 603 towards Cambridge until the road takes a sharp left at some traffic lights – you want to take the narrow road that goes straight ahead, but you are not allowed to, so follow the main road round to the left, and carry on next to the meadowland alongside the river -called 'Lammas Land'. At the next roundabout turn round and return to the traffic lights and so turn left down the small lane, Driftway - there is a tall hedge on your left and speed bumps. There is a pay and display car park at the bottom of this lane, however note that there is a **2m locked height barrier** at the entrance. If your vehicle is over this height then probably the best alternative is to start your trip at Chesterton – see 'Extending the trip' below. There is also pay & display parking on Newnham Rd next to Lammas land. There are **toilets** here at Newnham near the paddling pool.

> **More information**
>
> O.S. Map 1:50,000 sheet 154
>
> Cambridge Tourist information
> www.visitcambridge.org
>
> River Cam information
> www.camconservators.co.uk
>
> Cambridge Canoe Club
> www.cambridgecanoeclub.org.uk
>
> The 'Secret Rivers' dvd features the River Cam.

Pubs, tea shops, etc

The **Orchard Tea Gardens** at Grantchester are a historic and delightful place with green deckchairs and wonderful cakes. It has a licence and also does pub style lunches. Tel: 01223 845 788. www.orchard-grantchester.com.

The **Granta**, the **Mill**, the **Anchor**, and the **Fort St George** are all popular riverside pubs which can be recommended at the time of writing.

16 Cam

Journey 1

Upstream to Grantchester (6km round trip)

Launch into the Mill Stream which runs next to the car park – it is easier launching from the far bank which is concrete so we suggest you cross the footbridge and put in there. Head upstream and after 50m or so you meet the main river. Now turn right (upstream) towards Grantchester. The river winds with only a very gentle current. After a few hundred metres under the trees the vista opens out onto Granchester meadows – on warm summer evenings this is a popular spot with local people and you will pass lovers and Labradors, punts and picnickers. You will also pass the fine lawn and hedges of the Newnham Riverbank Club – one of the last of the river swimming clubs in England. The famous artist Augustus John once lived here in a caravan with two wives and ten children. You can stop and picnic almost anywhere on the right hand bank, but we suggest you carry on until you see a stone cottage and Granchester church can be glimpsed through the trees – on your right you will see a small landing stage. (GR TL436553).

Depending on your timing and inclination, we suggest you pull your canoe up on the grass to enjoy afternoon tea at **the Orchard** - in true Cambridge style, this is not signposted - walk up the field and climb the style at the top left hand corner and there you are in a

The Grantchester Group

From 1909, when Rupert Brooke moved into Orchard House, to 1914, when the First World War began, the Orchard, with its wooden Tea Pavilion, provided a backdrop to a very remarkable group of friends - Rupert Brooke (a poet), Russell and Wittgenstein (philosophers), Forster and Virginia Woolf (novelists), Keynes (an economist), and Augustus John (an artist).

It was an idyllic period in an age of relaxed elegance - energetic and optimistic. Rupert Brooke formed the centre of this group and whilst at Orchard House he would spend his days studying, running, swimming in the river, living off fruit and honey, and commuting to Cambridge by canoe.

Thanks to the Orchard Tea Gardens.

*Would I were
In Grantchester, In Grantchester!
.....Oh, is the water sweet and cool,
Gentle and brown, above the pool?
And laughs the immortal river still
Under the mill, under the mill?
Say, is there Beauty yet to find?
And Certainty? And Quiet kind?
Deep meadows yet, for to forget
The lies, and truths, and pain? oh! Yet
Stands the Church clock at ten to three?
And is there honey still for tea?
By Rupert Brooke.*

The Orchard Tea Gardens. *Hiroshi Shimura*

Sprint C1 training on the Cam. *Hiroshi Shimura*

quintessentially English tea garden. This was founded in 1897 and associated with Rupert Brooke and his circle of friends including Virginia Wolfe.

Fully refreshed, invigorated and educated you can continue to paddle upsteam: a little further ahead is a large garden running almost to the river - this is Geoffrey Archer's house and is adjacent to the Orchard. The river branches (sometimes hidden by over hanging trees) and if you take the right hand fork, after 200m you will come to the picturesque Granchester Mill with a large weir pool and some dark spooky mill tunnels. Note the beautiful sculpture of a horse that guards the weir pool.

The left hand branch is also narrow and winding. After 800m it brings you up to **Byrons Pool**, a well known bathing spot in times past, where Rupert Brooke and Virginia Woolf skinny dipped in those innocent days at the beginning of the 20th century. Nowadays, an ugly concrete weir and sluice structure rather detracts from any romantic atmosphere.

On the return you will be helped by the gentle current and soon be back at Newnham footbridge. If you are short of time you can of course finish the trip here, and come back another day for this next section – one of the most famous tourist river trips in Britain.

Other paddling trips nearby

Trip no. 19 'Constable's Stour' is the nearest convenient quality paddle in this guidebook. The Bedfordshire Ouse, Little Ouse, and Wissey are worth considering – see www.canoedaysout.com and www.canoetrips.org. Further north is the pretty Waveney – see www.discoversuffolk.org.uk

Places of interest nearby

Cambridge is a fascinating, famous old city with lots of things to do and see – too many to list here! See www.visitcambridge.org.

16 Cam

The 'Backs'. *Simon Whitney*

The 'Colleges along the Backs'

The Cambridge colleges along the 'Backs' are located in the following order going downstream -
Darwin (ugly new buildings on the right of the Mill Pool)
Queens' College – on both sides connected by the 'Mathematical Bridge'.
St Catharine's College, to the right, set back and before the next bridge which belongs to King's College.
Kings with the chapel to the right.
Clare College, connected by a bridge identified by a series of spheres on the parapets.
Trinity Hall to the right immediately before 'Garret Hostel' bridge, a graceful parabola which is the only public bridge in the area.
Trinity College with a stone bridge (with dated flood marks) immediately before the Wren Library on the right.
St John's College New Court (1831) appears before its two bridges – the first with flood marks, the second is the stone built, enclosed, 'Bridge of Sighs'
Magdalene (pronounced "Maudlin") College on the left immediately after the Magdalene Road Bridge.

Journey 2

Downstream along the 'College Backs' (5km round trip)

This section can be very busy with large chauffeured punts so is perhaps best avoided on fine summer weekend days. Please don't be in a rush and allow plenty of time to enjoy the aquatic dodgems!

Continue on the main river past your launch spot and under a footbridge. Pass Cambridge Canoe Club on your left (on Sheep's Green) under The Fen Causeway highway bridge and then, opposite the Garden House hotel, stop before the sluice. Portage next to the punt rollers and launch into the Mill Pool. It would of course be thoroughly irresponsible to think of seal launching down these rollers! (Take care if the sluice is open; unless of course you like rough water!)

Bear left at the back of the Mill Pool and turn left into the old mill stream – some 200m will bring you to the **Granta**, a busy student pub with some landing steps and next door **The Millwork** with some public landing steps next to it. Granta Punt Hire is based here and hires punts and canoes - how about hiring a punt and having a go yourself? If, at the Mill pool you instead go right, you can take out on the right bank onto Laundress Green and stroll 50m to the **Mill**, with a good range of real ales - sit on the grass and enjoy a sup. A little downstream is an alternative pub, the **Anchor** which also sells a fine pint of real beer.

Suitably refreshed, you are now ready to tackle the tourist invasion. Continue under Silver St Bridge (keep left and look out for monster double or triple chauffeured punts who take no prisoners) and the colleges come into view. Now you are on the famous 'Backs'. Enjoy a leisurely paddle on past the colleges – note that unfortunately

Putting on again below the rollers. *Colin Southward*

Bridge of Sighs. *Colin Southward*

you can't land (there is a public landing place on the right below Magdalene bridge at Quayside, but it is monopolised by Punt Hire). Be amused by the antics of those who have hired punts; your good deed of the day may be to return a lost pole to an inept punter.

Soon you'll see Jesus Green on the right and a boom protecting the weir. Land at the steps on the right before **Jesus lock** and consider rewarding yourself with an ice cream from the kiosk before turning round and returning to Newnham.   This is just as interesting as a return trip because you'll see everything from a different angle on the way back.

Extending the trip

You can make a longer trip by starting (or finishing) at the riverside car park in Water St, **Chesterton** (GR TL470670). Paddle upstream and keep to the right bank to avoid being mown down by rowing eights. The **Green Dragon** is just by the footbridge to Stourbridge Common, has a small public slipway and is welcoming, with good beer and good food! You'll pass some very desirable houses on the right and then all the University and town club boathouses are along the right hand bank. The **Fort St George** is a pleasant riverside pub (left bank) with reasonable food, then you soon arrive at **Jesus Lock** and can now join the main paddle along the 'Backs' described above. From Chesterton to Jesus Lock is about 2.5km.

There is quiet exploring on the River Cam for a few kilometers upstream of Grantchester. The river downstream of Cambridge is wider and flows through flat but pleasant countryside as far as Ely.

Extending the trip below Jesus Lock. *Colin Southward*

Houghton Mill 17

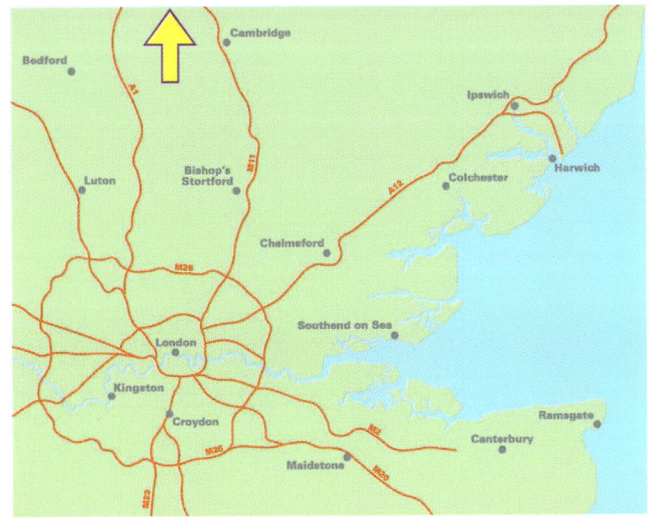

River and backwaters

Circular trip

6km - 2-3 hours

Easy paddling

Parking	★★
Launching	★★
Portages?	4 short portages (but an easier option)
Quiet?	Mainly backwaters

Why do this trip?
A short and varied paddle through quintessentially English countryside. Starting and ending at a splendid old water mill.

Tell me more
The Great Ouse is one of England's longest rivers and our suggested paddle is the best short trip on the most beautiful stretch of this fine river! Most of this trip is on quiet backwaters with willow trees fringing sylvan water meadows, connecting picturesque villages and to top it all some wonderful pubs!

The Great Ouse is a historic river navigation however these days it is surprisingly quiet when compared with say the River Thames or the Norfolk Broads. Our suggested paddle is a short circular route and is mainly on quiet backwaters - there are also many options for extending or changing the route.

Houghton Mill is an old water mill, now restored and owned by the National Trust, with a car park, tea shop and camp site - this makes it an iconic and very pleasant place to start and end a paddling trip.

On our research trips we saw lots of bird life - herons, kingfishers and red kites; also voles, water snakes and looking at us over a hedge, some llamas! Other paddlers have seen otters, mink, and at first we didn't believe it - seals!

Houghton Mill pool. *Peter Knowles*

Special points
1. Houghton Mill NT car park may be busy on summer weekends.
2. Paddle UK membership or E.A. licence required
3. Six Sluices Stream is dangerous at times of high flow

Canoe and SUP Hire
Houghton Boats is a well-established company, next door to Houghton Mill, with canoes, rowing boats and punts for hire. Tel:07759 316260

Go-paddle is at Hartford Marina 2km upstream and rents paddle boards and canoes. Tel: 07856 940113.

Millside Canoe Hire offers canoes and kayaks for rental at Godmanchester. Tel: 07952 642956.

17 Houghton Mill

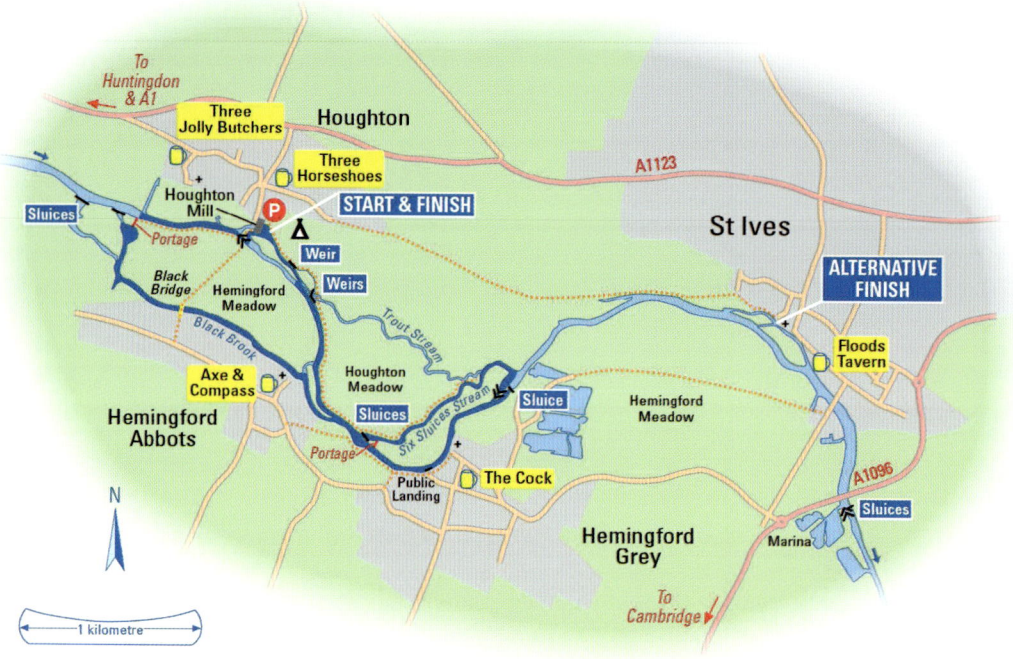

Start and finish

Houghton Mill - *pronounced "Ho" as in "Ho, ho, ho"*
GR TL281719   Post code: PE28 2AZ

The village of Houghton is 20km northwest of Cambridge and close to the A1 and A14. Houghton Mill is well sign posted off the A141 which bypasses Huntingdon on the north side. The National Trust car park is free to members and is a pleasant grassy area. Next to it is a small tea room with toilets around the back. There is easy and convenient launching about 30m away into the mill pool off a low concrete bank. Note that this car park gets busy and can fill up on popular days in the summer, so do please take this into account in your planning. If parking is an issue then an alternative option is to do the extended trip in reverse by starting at St Ives. There is good launching here from the slipway in Church St, next to the Parish Church of All Saints, PE29 1XP.

Hemingford Grey Church. *Paul Mackenzie*

The journey

The mill pool is a popular spot for both local families and visitors. So apart from being a bit busy at times, launching into the mill pool is fairly straightforward off the concrete bank. Take note of the mill sluice - the outflow current can be deceptively powerful, and capsize those who aren't expecting it.

When you are ready, set off by turning left and paddling through a green, tunnel like, oasis of trees and bushes that makes a great introduction to the trip. After a 100m you can spot a small weir and foot bridge that leads to a backwater called the Trout Stream. This used to be recommended as a canoe route but over the years it has become heavily overgrown (if interested we suggest you take a walk to scout it out beforehand). Continue along this quiet, pleasant oasis for another 200m and then you pop out onto the main river - look out and beware of pleasure boats! Remember the navigation rule to "Keep Right".

More information

O.S. Map 1:50,000 sheet 164

River Ouse information and permits
www.visitanglianwaterways.org

River conditions   For Strong Stream Advice phone the EA 24 hour SSA hotline: 0345 988 1188. Choose option 1 followed by the quick dial code for the Great Ouse - Bedford to St Ives. 033211.

Pubs and tea shops

This trip offers a plethora of choice -

At Houghton Mill there is the **National Trust tearoom** with its yummy homemade cakes. Only a few minutes' walk away in the village is the family run, **Houghton Tea Room**. There are also two village pubs which get good reviews - the "**Jolly Butchers**" tel; 01480 463228 and the "**Three Horseshoes**" tel: 01480462410

In Hemingford Grey we especially recommend "**The Cock**" tel: 01480 463609, which is only 50m from the public landing and has twice won the award of "Britain's Best Pub". A mile away in Hemingford Abbots is its rival, the thatch roofed "**Axe and Compass**" tel: 01480 463605.

A couple of miles downstream at St Ives and backing on to the river is the "**Floods Tavern**" Tel: 01480 700676, an ancient hostelry that has always extended a warm welcome to those arriving by water - Dutch bargees, English sea dogs, and modern paddle boarders.

Portage at Four Gate Pit. *Peter Knowles*

Houghton Mill 17

Passing Houghton Mill.

Attractions Nearby

St Ives is a small, pleasant market town well worth exploring on foot. Check out the recently renovated Norris Museum and its old fenland ice skates.

If you, or your children are into snakes and crocodiles then we recommend **Johnsons of Old Hurst**, which is a wildlife zoo, farm shop and steak house, just a few miles north of St Ives

Canoe Pass at Houghton Lock.   *Peter Knowles*

Coming up next on the right hand side you will see a sign and a channel that is a shortcut to Hemingford Abbots with it's church steeple poking up above the trees. This also marks the start of Battcocks Island that continues for half a km.

Soon after the island you will see a long line of huge green buoys on your left. We thought "How nice of the EA river team to put these here to protect paddlers" - It turns out that they are not here to safeguard paddlers but rather to protect the sluices - to prevent big trees and other debris getting washed down the side stream in times of flood. Keep a safe distance from the buoys and just 10m past them you will see a large tree, a short stretch of cleared bank, and an obvious metal stake. Land here to inspect the "**Six Sluices Stream**" - do not attempt this if there is a high river flow and/or a powerful current.

If you are happy to continue then carry or slide your craft a few meters down the bank and put in again in the weir pool - take care and keep well clear of the four sluices (you guessed it right - there used to be six). Now the fun starts as you enter a green jungle that reminded us of expeditions in Ecuador - a sinuous channel that makes you wonder what is around the corner - thankfully there are no boa constrictors! However, you will have to maneuver around several overhanging trees and bushes that have grown out into the channel - local paddlers normally prune these back but if you are here early season then you may find a folding pruning saw useful. The channel becomes easier the further you go and in about a

17 Houghton Mill

Seals 50 miles inland?

Yes, it's true - landlocked Cambridgeshire has a small resident population of common seals that in recent years have regularly been seen on the river Great Ouse. They were thought to have come from the North Sea and the Wash and have followed pleasure boats up through the locks into the heart of Cambridgeshire and beyond. Digital photography and tagging in the last few years has confirmed that some individuals are now resident in the river and are not just lost or roaming individuals as was once thought. One pair are well established and at home in the St Ives. There are other clusters of resident seals on inland rivers in the Fens, all be it in small numbers, and they now appear to be breeding - with a number of reports of pups and at least one photo of a mother suckling a pup!

So do keep your eyes open, and if you see a seal, enjoy the experience, but please keep a respectful distance.

Seals now at home on the Great Ouse! *Houghton Boats*

kilometer the Trout Stream joins from the left. Shortly after you come out on the main river with two channels to your right separated by a small island.

If refreshments are your focus, then now comes a difficult decision - Turn left for the Flood Tavern at St Ives or turn right for the Cock at Hemingford Grey? The Cock is nearer, so we recommend that you turn right and take the first channel which in 100m leads to **Hemingford Lock**. (the second channel leads to a large sluice and a private house). Take out at the landing stage which is on the right as you face the lock. A short portage brings you to the top of the lock, which is a pleasant spot to perhaps take a rest and watch pleasure craft working their way through the lock.

When you set off again you will now be paddling upstream on a wide river with panoramic views. You will see the houses of **Hemingford Grey** to the left and the parish church of St James which lost its steeple in 1790, leaving it with an unusual hexagonal tower. More lovely "chocolate box" cottages and houses line the river bank along with private moorings. Then after about 200m you will see a sign for the public landing stage. We recommend you land here and take a stroll 100m up the high street to the idyllic "**Cock Inn**". Purely for a photograph of course!

Setting out again you have a fine straight stretch of river on which the village hold an annual regatta. On the left is a green bank, public footpath and the gardens of 11th century Hemingford Manor. On the other bank you will see the line of green buoys at the entrance to the Six Sluices Stream. The end of Battcock Island comes up in 200m and you need to keep left here, leaving the main channel, and most of the pleasure craft behind.

This quiet stretch of river takes you past the village of **Hemingford Abbots**, with glimpses of expensive houses and gardens dropping to the river. The village has another fine church, this time with a spire. In less than a km you come to Black Bridge where it is possible to land and walk back to explore the village and its pub, the **Axe and Compass**. From the bridge, looking to the north over Houghton Meadow you can see the steeple of Houghton Church, close to your start point and only 15 minutes' walk away.

Continuing on, the channel bends to the right and then forks - take the right hand channel and this brings you to a pool called Four Gate Pit. Land on the right well before the dangerous sluice. It is an easy 30m portage here over the wild flower meadow, back to the main river. Look to your right downstream and you will see the building of Houghton Mill in the distance, so turn right, keep right and head straight for the lock which is on the right of the mill building. Just to the left hand side of the lock there is a small canoe-sized slipway and SUP and canoe pass, however sadly it no longer has its rollers. It still makes for a quick portage and you soon find yourself in a hidden backwater just off the mill pool, very close to where you first set off. The tea shop and ice creams beckon?

Six Sluices Stream or a jungle river of Ecuador. *Peter Knowles*

Easier trip with no portages

For a shorter trip we suggest paddling directly to Hemingford Grey and return. This misses out the Six Sluice Stream, locks and portages, so makes a simpler trip of about 4km. But it's less fun!

Extending the trip

1. If you have the time then we recommend continuing downstream to St Ives, about 2km further (making a total trip distance of 10km), turning round after the wonderful 15th century stone bridge, with an old chapel in the middle, and next to the old Dutch quayside. The Floods Tavern has a back garden dropping to the river and makes a convenient rest stop.

2. Alternatively, you could extend your trip upstream to Godmanchester and Huntingdon, both historic old towns, but this stretch of the river has more marinas and associated boat traffic so maybe consider the option of taking the Cook's Stream backwater for part of the route - however there may be problems with weed later in the summer.

3. Many paddlers prefer to do this scenic and historic stretch, from Brampton Mill or Godmanchester to St Ives as a **one way journey**. There is a convenient start point at Brampton Mill next to the riverside pub or in the middle of Godmanchester. We suggest finishing at the slipway next to the Parish Church of St Ives.

Other paddling trips nearby

Trip 16 the Cam is only half an hour's drive away. It offers two very different paddling trips and can be highly recommended.

There are many other paddling trips on the Great Ouse. If you continue downstream from St Ives the river and scenery become less interesting as you enter the flat fenlands, however there are one or two fine riverside pubs! Further upstream check out the area around St Neots and the "Danish Camp" downstream of Bedford.

The River Nene has a fine quiet, scenic stretch of river around Oundle, upstream of Peterborough.

The Little Ouse offers an adventurous trip from Thetford to Brandonsome with good opportunity for wildlife sightings.

For more information on these rivers please see www.gopaddling.info/rivers or www.canoedaysout.com

Chelmer 18

Canalised river

One way trip

2 hours - 8km

Very easy paddling

Parking	★★
Launching	★★★
Portages?	4 locks
Quiet?	A few canal boats

Special points

Chelmer permit required. (Membership of Paddle UK does NOT cover you)

Canoe Hire

Essex Waterways has open canoes & sit on tops for hire. Tel: 01245 226245.

Why do this trip?

Escape to rural Essex with a pleasant trip on this peaceful and historical waterway.

Tell me more

The Chelmer and Blackwater Navigation is some 20km long and was built in 1798 to connect the city of Chelmsford to the sea at Heybridge. It stands on its own, separated from other inland waterways, so there is little traffic, and it retains an old fashioned rural charm. It is now owned by a charity, the Chelmer Canal Trust.

Purists would say "Why not paddle the whole river from Chelmsford to the sea?" However the reality is that Chelmsford is now a modern city – a concrete jungle of industrial estates and retail parks. Then sadly there is the A12 – a noisy, noxious, six lane super highway which is close to the river for the first few km after Chelmsford. So all in all, we suggest that you ignore the upper river and step back in time by heading for the Paper Mill Canal Centre.

We think that this paddle is best done as a one way trip, but if a shuttle is a problem, or you are hiring canoes at the Paper Mill Canal Centre, then it is easily done as a 'there and back' trip with Hoe Mill as a convenient turning point. The tow path is well maintained so a cycle shuttle is worth thinking about as a pleasant alternative.

Shooting the weir at Rushes Lock. *David Crosson*

18 Chelmer

Pubs, tea shops, etc

There is not a single pub on this trip – "Heresy, sham, swindle!" - I hear you cry. There are though, lots of lovely, quiet, peaceful, grassy picnic spots – several of the locks are miles from any roads or houses. Also at the start of the trip is the **Paper Mill café** which is renowned for its home made cakes – a popular place to take Auntie May for afternoon tea on a sunny afternoon.

For those heroes who have paddled the extra miles to **Heybridge Basin**, you can reward yourself with a pint of real beer at the **Jolly Sailor** (tel:01621 854210) or the **Old Ship Inn** (tel: 01621 854150) whilst looking out to sea over the Blackwater estuary. Also overlooking the waterfront with fine views is the **Lock Café** which is run by Tiptree jams - www.trooms.com.

More information

O.S. Maps 1:50,000 – this trip overlaps sheets 167 & 168.

Permits, canoe hire, etc.
www.essexwaterways.com

Chelmer Canal Trust
www.chelmercanaltrust.co.uk

Tourist information
www.visitmaldon.co.uk.

Local canoe clubs
www.chelmsfordcanoeclub.co.uk
www.southendcanoe.org.uk

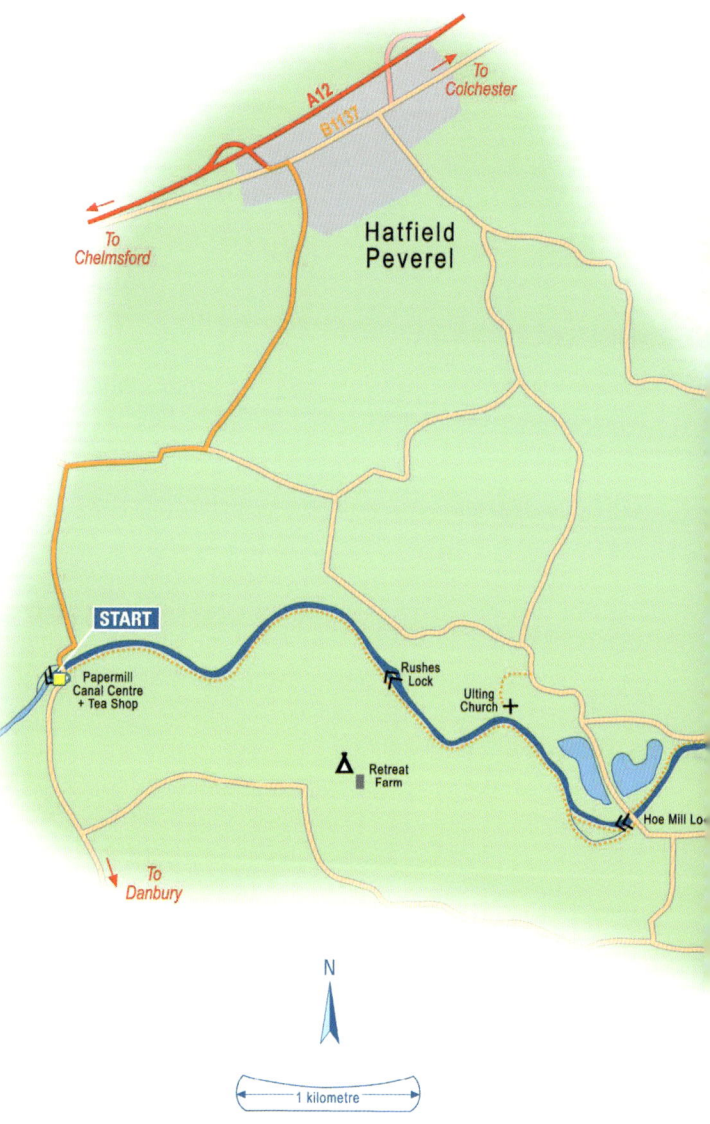

Start

Paper Mill Canal Centre   GR 777090
Post code CM3 4BS

From the A12, come off at Hatfield Peverel and follow the signs towards Little Baddow. Cross the canal and turn into the car park on the right. This car park offers secure parking at a fee (£5 a day in 2023) and is open in the summer at weekends and busy times. Next door is a much smaller car park which is reserved for customers of the Paper Mill café - short term only.

Pop into the Navigation Office next to the café to buy your daily licence - £5 a boat in 2023 - or save time by buying it online. There are toilets behind the café and easy launching from a landing stage just 5m from the car park.

Ulting church. *Richard Grieve*

Alternative Start

If parking is a problem then check out parking and a start from Church Road at Little Beddow, a further 1.5 km upstream.

Finish

Beeleigh Falls
GR TL839085
Post code: CM9 6LL

Drive towards Maldon on the B1019: on entering Langford, look out for the sign to Maldon Golf Club and take this right turn which is just after the Museum of Steam engines. Follow this small road until you reach the river and park before the bridge.

18 Chelmer

Other paddling trips nearby

Constable's Stour is only a half hours drive away and a classic paddling trip – see trip number 19.

Local experts recommend a tidal trip on the **Blackwater Estuary** for the more adventurous and experienced paddler - a circular paddle using the tides, setting off from Heybridge Basin, out into the Blackwater estuary, **around Northey Island**, then upstream through Maldon to arrive at Beeleigh Falls for high tide, and so back along the canal to your starting point.

The upper Chelmer and the river Blackwater have been paddled but for most of the year have insufficient water – for more information see: www.ukriversguidebook.co.uk.

Places of interest nearby

The Museum of Power, at Langford is set in seven acres of grounds of the steam pumping station and has many working examples of power sources of all types. www.museumofpower.org.uk

Maldon and the seaside

After your paddling trip we suggest that it's a great idea to load up the car and head for the seaside which is only some ten minutes drive away. Drive towards Maldon and follow the signs to Promenade Park. Hythe Quay is next to the park and is home port to a large fleet of fully rigged sailing barges. On any week day, up to ten of these vessels can be seen alongside at the Quay. There are also lots of other interesting things and activities for children and bigger kids, including; Maldon oysters, candy floss, fish and chips, ice cream, swings and round-a-bouts and being sick in the car on the way home.

Willow for Cricket Bats

Essex is famous amongst cricketers for the manufacture of some of the best cricket bats in the world and some of these are still made today from willow trees which have been grown alongside the canal. Trees are felled when they are around 15 years old and about 5ft in circumference and if you look closely you will see where new trees have been planted to replace the old ones.

Paper Mill Café. *Mark Baigent Photography*

Pudding Stones

If you look at the west wall of Ulting church you can see that it is built with a lot of brown boulders surrounded by flint and mortar. These pudding stones are found in river beds and are in fact one of the few naturally occurring rocks found in Essex so in former days they were much prized by our ancestors as a building material.

Paper Mill Canal Centre. *David Crosson*

Rushes Lock. *Phil Arnold*

The Journey

The **Paper Mill Canal Centre** can be quite busy on sunny afternoons, but if quiet, we suggest you take a few minutes to explore the lock and the old buildings. The Paper Mill used to make high quality paper from recycled rags and is said to be the oldest paper mill in Essex.

There is easy launching on the stage downstream of the lock and setting off from here you are soon away from people, roads and houses – just you and a pleasant river winding its way through old-fashioned fields and woods. There are a few walkers and the occasional angler who normally give you a friendly greeting. The Chelmer is popular with SUPs but on a sunny summer's day in August we only passed three power boats – the latter considerably slowed down to a snail's pace.

The banks of the canal are lined with a diversity of ancient trees and vegetation – this would be a wonderful paddle when autumn colours are at their best – we just had to make do with picking some blackberries for jam, and some sloes for Sloe gin. For much of its way the canal is has fine views over fields and woods, low hills and the occasional distant view of a farm. Much of the local farmland appears to be well tended in an old fashioned way – Retreat Farm over to the right is an idyllic certified farm campsite reserved for members of the Camping Club. Further along the canal we were

Fluffy at the Start point. *Peter Knowles*

18 Chelmer

returning at sunset and spotted a badger crossing the towpath as bats swooped overhead.

About 2km from the start brings you to **Rushes Lock**. If you take out on the left at the top lock gate, then a little path through the bushes allows you to slide your boat an easy 10m or so down into the weir pool. The weir is gently sloping and could perhaps be shot in the centre by the adventurous. The weir pool offers a very gentle introduction to white water and can be a fun place for kayak play.

After another kilometre of quiet, rural paddling – only the sound of doves and wood peckers to compete with splash of your paddle - and the small beautiful ancient church of Ulting comes into view. This is a wonderfully peaceful spot to land, explore, and perhaps have a quiet picnic. **Ulting Church** dates back to the 13th century - in the 14th century it was a famous holy place and the third most

History of the Chelmer and Blackwater Navigation

Chelmsford used to be just a small Essex market town and most of its bulk imports were carried by pack mule and heavy cumbersome wagons from Maldon which was then an important coastal port. As early as 1677 some people suggested the possibility of making the small river Chelmer into a navigable waterway so that goods could be transported more cheaply. However, it was not until 1793 before work started on the canal and it was then soon completed and opened in 1797. The navigation was designed to accommodate lighters 60 feet long by 16 feet wide, and despite only having a draught of two feet, each lighter could carry twenty five tons of cargo. Trade now boomed with all kinds of goods and materials being carried to the fast growing town of Chelmsford.

The railway line from London to Colchester was constructed in 1843, and once built this then captured a lot of the barge traffic and the navigation declined with the last commercial barge traffic in 1972. Thankfully, in 1992 the local branch of the Inland Waterways Association spearheaded the restoration of Heybridge basin and in 1997 the navigation was formally re-opened to Chelmsford with a large rally of pleasure boats.

Papermill Lock. *Mark Baigent Photography*

Little Baddow Lock. *David Crosson*

important place of pilgrimage in England. The site was obviously well chosen, although only a few feet above the level of the river it has never been flooded.

About 500m after Ulting there is a vertical weir (not shootable) on the right into the old river channel. Keep left and follow the lock cut with its line of moored picturesque barges and pleasure cruisers – this leads up to the lock and canal work depot at Hoe mill. Note the massive timbers from old lock gates piled on the bank. There are picnic tables and benches here, so it's a pleasant place to stop for refreshments and to sit, relax, and watch boaters working hard to hand work the lock – no flashy electrically operated gates on this waterway!

To portage the lock, land on the right next to the top gate and slide your boat some 10m down into the weir pool on the right. Just beyond Hoe Mill was Britain's first Sugar factory, established in 1833. After the lock a minor road comes close for a short distance, but this is again a peaceful paddle with few signs of houses or civilization. Another solitary lock, Ricketts, comes up after 2km with an easy portage and then it is just 1.5km to Beeleigh Falls.

At **Beeleigh Falls** there is an old mill and lovely old house hidden away in the trees to the right of the lock – the latter again easily portaged. The river Blackwater comes in from the left after the lock and opposite is a long weir with a footbridge running along the top. Below this weir the river is tidal with a lot of mud banks. Our suggested Finish is on the left, just before the footbridge. If you still have lots of energy then you can continue on for another 4km along the 'canal cut' past Tescos, factories, shops and industrial estates to the sea at Heybridge Basin – see below.

Extending the trip

There are several possibilities for further paddling –

1. Do the whole trip as a there and back trip, however this could maybe be a bit boring on the return.

2. Extend the paddle another 4km to Heybridge Basin and the sea lock – a dramatic and natural finishing point with the wide open estuary and North Sea ahead. The downside is that this last 4km of canal is straight, featureless and industrialised. Persevere though and there are two popular pubs to welcome you and there is also a large car park at Heybridge Basin.

3. Paddle upstream of the Paper Mill – pleasant, rural scenery but after 2km spoilt by traffic noise from the busy A12.

What better way to see wildlife? *Phil Arnold*

147

Constable's Stour 19

Small river

There and back

13km 4 hours

Very easy paddling

Parking	★★★
Launching	★★★
Portages?	1 lock
Quiet?	Quiet but rental row boats at Flatford

Why do this trip?

Put yourself in the picture on a river that epitomises idyllic English countryside.

Tell me more

This is "Constable Country" – **John Constable** was one of England's most famous landscape artists and he lived here in the Dedham Vale and we are fortunate that the landscape he recorded in the early 1800s has changed little along the course of the River Stour. The location of a number of his famous paintings will be evident along the route and the meadowland forming much of the river bank provides plenty of options for picnics. The Vale of Dedham and this delightful river is so beautiful that it is protected as an Area of Outstanding Natural Beauty.

Our selected paddle takes you from Cattawade as a there and back trip - the Stour is such a delightful river that it is nice to set out without any definite plans in mind - if it's a warm day pop a book in your dry bag and see where you get to. If you want a short trip then Cattawade to Flatford Mill is just 8km return – beautiful and quiet!

Special points

Membership of Paddle UK or EA permit required

In 1821 the local Constable (John) recorded an obstruction of the waterway by a hay cart driven by a man called Wayne. Fortunately recurrences have been few.

Canoe & SUP hire

Constable Park is 300m upstream from the start point and hires canoes, kayaks & SUPs. Tel: 01206 984100.

Flatford Mill by John Constable. *The Tate Gallery, London*

19 Constable's Stour

The Stour

This, the Suffolk Stour, is a navigation from Brundon Mill, just upstream of Sudbury, down to the tidal estuary below our start point at Cattawade, a total distance of around 40km. Stour means "mighty river" however this is a misnomer – the impression at the start of a small, placid, SUP and canoe-sized river is true for most of the navigable, non tidal, length.

Start and Finish

Cattawade Picnic Site
GR TM101332
Post Code: CO11 1QW

From the A12 take the B1070 eastwards through East Bergholt. Continue on the B1070 towards Brantham and just before the roundabout junction with the A137 there is a turn off to Cattawade Picnic Site on the right. There is a small car park here (no ice cream vans or toilets) and a short flat path (wheelchair friendly) leads to a low launching platform on the river bank. This branch of the river is now non tidal with an embankment downstream of the two bridges.

Trip description by Julian and Cathie Taylor

Paddling through Constable Country. *Environment Agency*

Pubs, tea shops, etc

Close to the Start point, the **Crown** at Cattawade is a friendly local pub just on the other side of the main A137 with tables outside and views across the Stour valley. Tel. 01206 392800

Constable Park is 250m upstream from the Start Point and has a welcoming café and ice cream kiosk. Tel: 01206 984100.

At **Flatford Mill** the National Trust has a Tea room and ice cream shop.

At **Dedham**, the **Boat Yard Restaurant** is alongside the river. 01206 323153.

19 Constable's Stour

More information

O.S. Map 1:50,000 sheet 168

Constable Country (see his paintings online)
www.eastbergholt-bells.org.uk

Tourist information
www.constablecountry.co.uk

River Stour Trust
www.riverstourtrust.org

Flatford Mill   www.nationaltrust.org.uk

Dedham Vale AONB
www.dedhamvalestourvalley.org

The 'Secret Rivers' dvd features the River Stour.

Dedham lock. *River Stour Boating*

Other trips on the Stour

Upstream of Stratford, most of the locks are disused and the river has reverted to a more natural state, shallower and with more current. This makes for a very scenic and interesting river with physical and ecological diversity, however there are frequent portages around the old locks and weirs - this means that you need to be physically fit and we suggest that trips are best done as one way journeys downstream with the current. A detailed map & guide can be purchased online from the River Stour Trust website under "Paddling the River Stour".

Sudbury to Bures is a particularly fine trip of around 10km with good parking at both ends. The put in at Sudbury Quay is adjacent to the Stour Trust premises which include a tea room, and the take out is at Bures recreation ground car park. There is a recommended riverside pub at Henny Street, The Swan, at around the 3 km mark.

Paddling the whole navigation from **Sudbury to Cattawade** makes a memorable and enjoyable **weekend trip** covering one of the best stretches of water in East Anglia. There is a small riverside campsite, **Rushbanks**, at around the halfway point at Wissington and another small campsite, **Constable Park** near Cattawade.

Other trips nearby

The Cam is about an hour's drive and offers another classic but very different paddle – see trip number 17.

Further north is the pretty river **Waveney** and there are also several tidal paddles on the estuaries of the Deben, Butley Creek and River Alde – see www.canoedaysout.com.

The Journey

Setting off upstream, the small Constable Park campsite is on the right after 250m and welcomes paddlers to its café and ice cream kiosk. The river winds peacefully with meadows on the left and a few gardens on the right. All is quiet and peaceful - on this stretch you probably won't see more than one or two other canoes or SUPs on the water, and perhaps an occasional fisherman. After a km you will come to the remains of **Brantham lock**. This used to be the tidal limit – now this branch of the river is dammed up so the lock is no longer needed and the gates have been removed.

The river continues, winding through the meadows, with rushes and water weed on the bends and pleasant pastoral views. Looking over to your left you will see another branch of the river, running parallel to our route – this branch is tidal up to the weir where you will

Flatford Mill. *River Stour Boating*

encounter after another 2km, a spot known as Judas Gap, where the two waterways join. Take care here and hug the right bank to keep clear of the **sluice gates**.

The next stretch up to Flatford Mill, (4km from the start point) is quite enchanting. The banks are wooded and the mix of habitats passed through in this short distance usually displays a wide diversity of wildlife. Around this point in addition to the usual kingfishers, heron and ducks, you may come across a few Egyptian geese, an exotic feral breeder around these parts.

The landing point for the portage of the **Flatford lock** is the platform on the left of the lock. However, before doing this, you will get a better view of the mill if you complete a lap of the pool downstream of the lock. Willy Lott's cottage, the subject of one of Constable's best known paintings, is tucked away up the overgrown mill stream and best seen from the lane behind the National Trust tearooms. Flatford is quite a tourist hot spot and together with Dedham the focus of much of the Tourist Boards "Constable Country" branding of

Places of interest nearby

East Bergholt Church has a unique bell cage that dates back to 1525. This was built to house the church bells because they couldn't afford a church tower and the bells have been here and are in regular use ever since.

East Bergholt Place is a garden and arboretum that covers some 20 acres and has many rare trees. www.placeforplants.co.uk.

19 Constable's Stour

the area. From the water it's none the worse for that and despite the lovely riverside walks between those two places few people venture far away from their vehicles.

Portage around the left side of the lock and put in again. Is it time for a rest and explore? – or are you going to leave this to the return journey? There are public toilets up in the car park up the lane. Next door to the tearoom is **Bridge Cottage**, also National Trust owned, which houses a display of Constable related exhibits. Many of Constable's paintings record a mass of barges and lighters on this river and one of his paintings depicts a lighter under construction in this dry dock which has recently been rediscovered and renovated.

Continuing upstream, the landscape has changed little from Constable's scenes of the 19th Century with grazing meadows and fine views of the villages of Dedham to the left and East Bergholt up on the hills to your right - don't expectantly elevate your gaze too much and miss it, we are talking Suffolk hills here! You meander through these meadows and after about a km come to Fen Bridge. This stretch is used by hire rowing boats from both Dedham and Flatford and particularly on sunny summer Sundays the river is busy with them lurching along the river like aquatic drunks, bouncing off each bank as they go. Try not to look too smug at their amazement as to how anyone can proceed swiftly in their desired direction by using only one paddle!

Paddling near Cattawade. *Constable Park*

Flatford to Cattawade. *River Stour Boating*

A further km and a half brings you to **Dedham Mill** (6.5km from the start point). Downstream of the bridge is the **Boat Yard Restaurant** and ice cream shop or alternatively If you are using Dedham as the turnaround point there is a good picnic spot on the right hand side of the mill pool just beyond the bridge – pull your boats up on the shelving beach, and relax on the riverside meadow. This is also the portage point to the river beyond. The village of **Dedham** is just a short walk over the bridge and in the church the Constable painting "the Ascension" is on permanent display. On the bank opposite (river right) and upstream of the bridge is a small car park.

Returning downstream is every bit as pleasant and of course, a little bit faster. If you have time to spare at the finish then we recommend carrying on past the take out, under the new road bridge, and under the old bridge at **Cattawade**. It quite interesting to land briefly here on the embankment, built in the 1970's to dam the tidal river, and look out at the tidal estuary – imagine some Stour lighters being 'poled' down river towards Mistley and the sea.

Extending the trip

Upstream from Dedham the river very much maintains its interest and the paddle up to Stratford Lock, another 2km, is well worthwhile. The portage around the lock is on the left, getting out at the platform up a few steps and back in, and one possible incentive for this further portage is the **Swan Pub** around 100m further upstream.

Medway 20

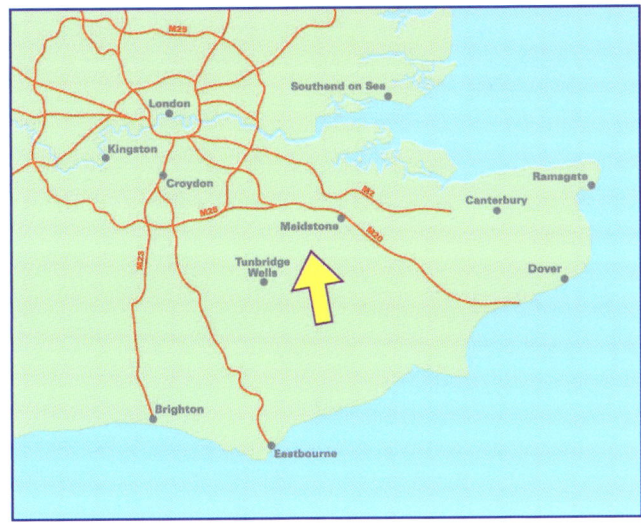

Medium canalized river

There and back

12km 3 hours

Easy paddling

Parking	★★
Launching	★★★
Portages?	1 (None if you shorten the trip)
Quiet?	A few motor boats

Special points

Membership of Paddle UK or EA licence required

Canoe & SUP hire

Elveys Canoe is a well-established company based at Yalding that rents canoes and kayaks. Tel: 07704 357025

River Medway Canoes are based at Wateringbury and rent canoes, kayaks and SUPs. Tel: 01622 816723

Paddle Cabin is based at East Peckham and specialises in SUP rental.
01892 249089

Epic Life is based at Tonbridge and rents SUPs.
Tel: 07494712144

Why do this trip?

Paddle through the 'Garden of England' with close-up views of oast houses, orchards, fields and woods on this, the most interesting and popular section on the historic River Medway.

Tell me more

This is the heart of the 'Garden of England' and it is naturally a popular place on fine weekends in the summer - paddlers come to play and practise their white water skills in the weir pool, powerboat owners come to the marinas, families come to picnic on the Lees meadow, a few come to walk along the river; however only a privileged few come to make the journey along the river by paddle board, canoe or kayak. It is a popular spot, but don't be put off by this – it can generally cope with a lot of people and you will soon paddle away from them with just fields, woods and beautiful tranquility as your companions.

David and Jacob shooting the canoe pass at Sluice Weir. *John Lengthorn*

20 Medway

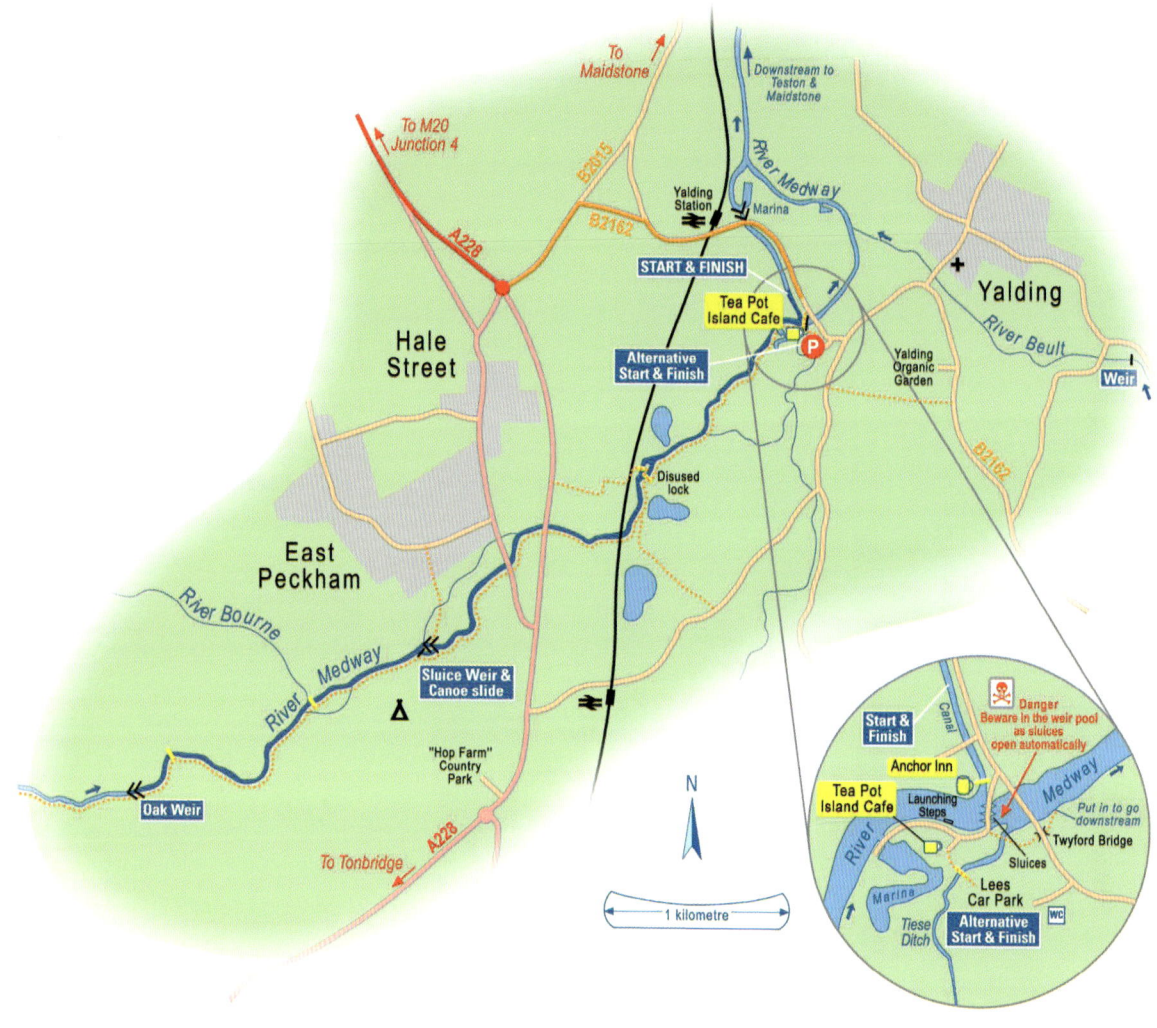

Trip description by Matt Oseman

Start and Finish

Twyford Bridge, Yalding
GR TQ690497   Post code ME18 6HG

From the M20, exit at junction 4 and head south on the A228. South of Mereworth, turn left at a roundabout and take the B2105 signed 'Nettlestead and Yalding', then take the next right on the B2162 towards Yalding. Follow the road until you cross the level crossing over the railway. Immediately after this you cross the canal and then drive alongside it. Just before you reach the first building on your right, you will see some wooden fencing at the river side. Just here is a purpose built put-in and parking here is free alongside the road.

Autumn day on the Medway. *Matt Oseman*

Alternatively, carry on with the Boathouse pub on your right, then cross over Twyford Bridge and you will find The **Lees car park** on your right. For a fee (£4.00 in 2023) you can stay here all day. There are toilets and a huge grass field in which to park and picnic - for some folks this is a better and safer parking spot. The weir pool is accessible by a convenient slipway, but sadly you need to access the river **above the weir**, and unfortunately a muddy ditch, the River Tiese, is in your way.

So launch into the Weir pool, paddle a couple of metres across the Tiese and drag your boats up the other side onto Teapot Island. *N.B. Beware the automatic sluice that can open at any time without warning and wash you down to pin on the chain hung between the bridge piers!*

Start platform near Twyford Bridge. *Phil Munslow*

20 Medway

Pubs, tea shops, etc

The Boathouse is a popular pub on the riverside at Yalding with many outdoor tables and a landing stage. It was formerly 'The Anchor' Tel: 01622 814359

Hop Pickers Rest is a cafe on the other side of the roads close to the main put in at Yalding. Tel: 07526148947

Teapot Island is a riverside café at Yalding and is a popular place to watch comings and goings on the river. It now has its own small landing stage. Tel: 01622 814541

The Waterside Café is on the riverside near East Peckham next to the Paddle Cabin rental company. Tel: 01622391521

Other trips on the Medway

The River Medway can be paddled from Tonbridge to the sea, and there are few parts with nothing to recommend them. For family paddling, the non-tidal sections are best – the Environment Agency have done a lot to encourage paddling and have built a lot of new facilities for paddlers. See internet links for up to date information. A free 'Medway Canoe Trail' leaflet, published by the EA team, covers the 29km from Tonbridge to Allington.

Tonbridge to Yalding is an excellent one way trip and takes in the very best of the river and it can easily be paddled in reverse in summer flows. If you head downstream from Yalding the next convenient access point is the picnic site at **Teston**, or you can continue beyond to East Farleigh and Maidstone where you are greeted with views of the beautiful Arch Bishops Palace and the Millennium Bridge. The **Maidstone** river side is a good spot to land, where you may be sure of an ice cream and a well earned rest.

Allington is an excellent launching spot - the EA have recently built a special facility here for paddlers, with toilets, showers, slipway, launch point and parking for cars, minibuses and trailers.

Note that there are a couple of riverside **campsites** and also some limited wild camping so the Medway makles a great weekend trip!

Deer upstream of Hop Farm campsite. *Ed Bassett*

Other paddling trips nearby

The River **Rother to Bodiam Castle** is less than an hour's drive away and offers a quieter alternative to the Medway – see trip number 22. The **River Beult** is a pretty river and has been paddled from near Headcorn in spring water conditions - see www.ukriversguidebook.co.uk/beult.htm..

Places of interest nearby

Teapot Island has a working potter and an exhibition of over 3500 teapots.

Yalding Organic Garden is only a km from the Lees Car Park, has many different gardens and an excellent whole food café. www.gardenorganic.org.uk

Oast house on the banks of the Medway. *Kent Canoes*

The Journey

From the Tea Pot Island Café set off and paddle upstream. The Anchor pub is on your right. Pass the entrance to Twyford marina on your left, then public moorings. A few houses line the bank to your right – an oast house among them, whose pretty architecture sits in stark contrast to the WWII bunker in its garden. It's hard to imagine but in 1941 the Medway was a possible front line in the defense against an invasion that was viewed as a near certainty, and these defenses exist all the way along the river. Paddle on, and in moments you leave behind the day-trippers and playboats. The roar of the weir descends to nothing and you quickly find yourself in a tranquil landscape. Huge willows lean over on your right, offering some shade on a hot day.

A kilometer or so beyond the houses is a small opening on the right to entice the explorer into a secret Amazonian world. Paddle quietly and observe nature.

More information

O.S. Map 1:50,000 - this trip is covered on sheet 188.

Kent tourist information
www.visitkent.co.uk

Paddling information
www.therivermedway.co.uk/medway-canoe-trail

River levels, etc.
www.check-for-flooding-service.gov.uk/station/9124

Tonbridge Canoe Club
www.tonbridgecanoeclub.org.uk

White Water Action Medway Canoe Club.
www.whitewateraction.co.uk

20 Medway

Second World War pill box. *Matt Oseman*

Extending the trip

See 'Other trips on the Medway' for extending your trip up or downstream.

However, if you have a little time on your hands and are feeling adventurous, our suggestion is a short foray up the **River Beult**. Land at Tea Pot Island, carry your boat across to the Lees Car Park and then under a small archway to put in safely downstream of Twyford bridge. Paddle downstream for 500m and then turn right up the river Beult. This is a beautiful small river that flows through Yalding village and passes under its marvelous medieval bridge. Look out for a glimpse of the unusual minaret of Yalding church. The River Beult is not a statutory navigation but is regularly paddled at all times of year as far as Mill Lane Bridge about a kilometer upstream of the village (a pretty weir lies just beyond this bridge). For the return journey, if you want a change, and depending where you are parked, you can paddle down the Medway for 700m and then return up the Hampstead canal, portage the lock, and so back to your start point.

Also keep your eyes open as you paddle on the main river - kingfishers are a common sight and it is a rare trip that does not see one. Watch the river ahead for the next 100m - they will shoot low over the water, heading away from you and into the trees. Herons are sometimes seen, and the occasional water vole, though the latter are getting harder to spot; the reason? Mink have been seen around Sluice Lock, and are a fierce predator of water voles.

After a couple of hundred metres or so you reach a big meander in the river, where it turns left and widens out into a broad glassy surface. The sun gleams off the water, and this is a good spot to stop and take a look about. Just around the next bend are the broken piers of Stoneham Old Lock (or Broken Lock as it is sometimes called) which is now disused and can be another pleasant spot for a break. You may follow the navigation signs through the old lock, or paddle around the side, but watch out for fishing lines as this is a popular spot for anglers.

Presently you will pass under the railway bridge whose huge iron construction seems almost artful amidst the beautifully wooded riverbanks. Then after 200 metres or so you are at **Branbridges**, passing first under the A26.

You then pass under the older road bridge, and watch the colony of pigeons depart as you pass through. They will congregate on one of the roofs of the small industrial units on your right, and wait for you to be gone. A hat is recommended when passing under the bridge!

You quickly leave the noise of Branbridges behind. A few more twists and turns in the river and you reach **Sluice Lock**. On your right as you approach is the lock and a landing stage, the right hand side of which is built especially low for SUPs, canoes and small craft. There are usually fishermen here, so watch their lines again as you land. To the left lies the eponymous sluice along with its overflow weir and SUP and canoe pass. If the journey here has taxed you enough then this is a natural place to land and stretch your legs before heading home. Otherwise a short portage will take you around the lock.

The next section upstream from Sluice Lock to Oak Weir is a pleasant and quiet paddle – it tends to be even quieter than the first section, is more heavily wooded, and has a couple of features of interest. Some 500m above the lock you will see a channel open up to your left with a footbridge across it - this is the entrance to a small backwater around an island which we suggest you explore on your way back downstream, ignore it on the way up, and stay on the main river. After 100m an iron footbridge crosses the river, you will see the River Bourne entering the Medway on your right and this small stream can be explored for some distance. Tree lined banks con-

Summer day on the Medway. *Matt Oseman*

tinue on the Medway for a one km or so and then you will see the old blasted oak which identifies **Oak Weir**. Green Woodpeckers inhabit this stretch in surprising numbers - listen out for their distinctive high-pitched calls. The river here is alive with fish and very healthy. In rare low water conditions, fresh water mussels can be seen on the surprisingly rocky riverbed.

Oak Weir has its own canoe pass, easily runnable by most SUPs, canoes and kayaks. The lock island has a nice large picnic table and "wild camping" is permitted here.

On your return, if conditions are right and you are feeling adventurous, then think about shooting the **canoe pass** which is on the extreme river right as you head downstream at Sluice Lock. Be warned it is a swift descent, a little hard on the fabric of your boat, and a little wet on reaching the bottom. Open canoes may be better taken down solo - tandem boats will get very wet! Canoe shoots like this are common in France (see the 'White Water Massif Central' guidebook) but rare in Britain. In high water the sluice can create a very fast and powerful flow, making approach difficult and dangerous.

Setting off from Oak Weir. *Matt Oseman*

Canterbury Stour 21

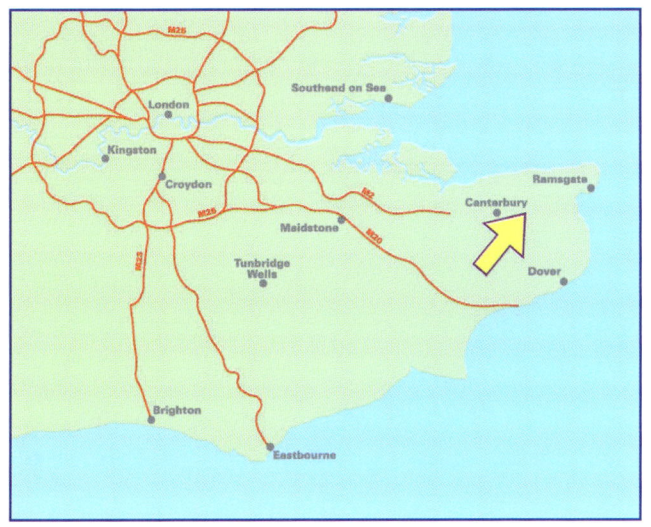

Small tidal river

There and back

16km return 4 hours

Easy paddling

Parking	★★★
Launching	★★
Portages?	None
Quiet?	A few other boats

Why do this trip?

A pleasant rural paddle to the 'smallest town in England'. "It's a beautiful river" a local paddler told us – "don't tell anyone!"

Special points

Tidal planning advised.

No permit needed.

Tell me more

The river Great Stour has been a public navigation from the sea to Canterbury since time immemorial – the stone for Canterbury Cathedral was shipped up this river through Fordwich. Our suggested paddle is on the top part of the tidal river close to Canterbury and the prettiest stretch of the river. However let us stress that this is in no way like your usual muddy tidal river - it is more like some inland trout stream as the river flows through the Stodmarsh National Nature Reserve with clear water, wooded banks, and Kingfishers darting through the trees.

We suggest that this trip is best planned as a return journey - use the tide to help carry you upstream from Grove Ferry to the old town of Fordwich at the tidal limit. Rest here for refreshments and to explore whilst the tide turns - then return on the ebb. If the time of the tides isn't convenient then you could equally well make this a very relaxing one way journey.

Canoe & SUP Hire

Canoe Wild rent canoes, kayaks and paddle boards. They have bases at Fordwich and Grove Ferry. They also operate a regular shuttle service if you want to do a one way paddle.
Tel 07947 835688

River Stour at Canterbury. *David Illiff*

21 Canterbury Stour

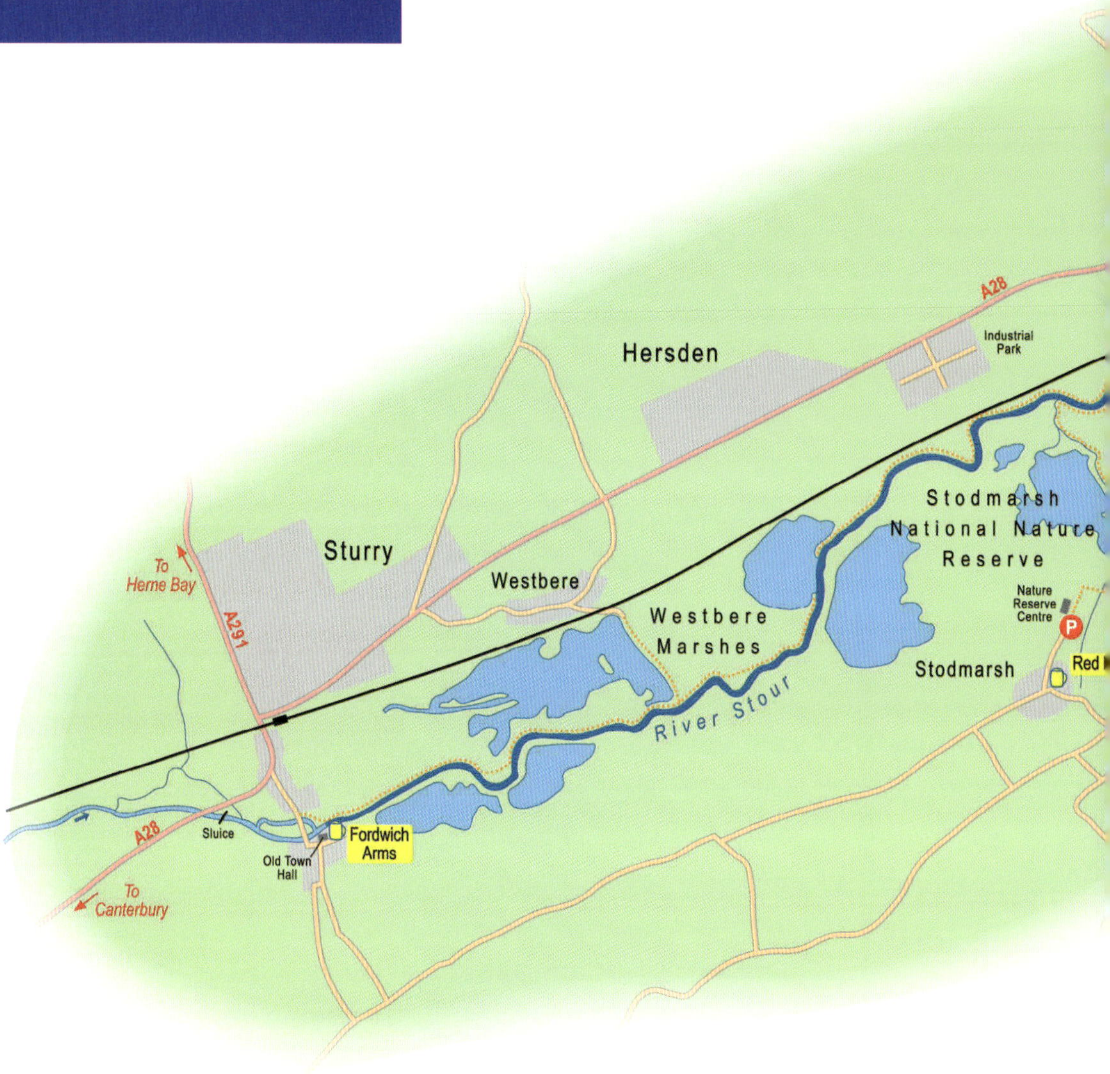

Special thanks to Chris Taylor

Fordwich Old Town Hall - note stocks for mutinous crew. *Peter Knowles*

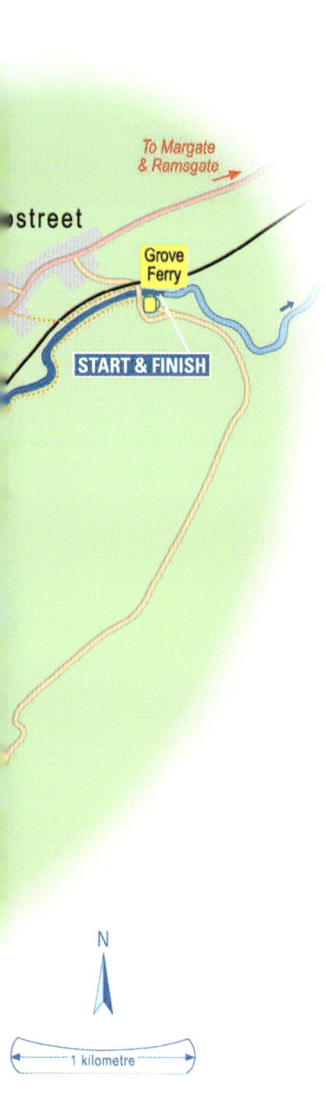

Winter day on the Stour. *Matt Oseman*

Start and Finish

Start and Finish Point   Grove Ferry
GR TR235632   Post code: CT3 4BP

If coming from London, it is better to bypass Canterbury by taking the M2 and the A299 towards Ramsgate and then turning right when you meet the A28. About 6km from this junction look out for a sign left to Grove Ferry. Turn left after crossing the river and park in the picnic site near the public toilets. The river is just 15m away over the grass with easy launching. This has always been a historic ferry crossing point and there used to be ferry operating here until 1960. The Grove Ferry Hotel is next door to the picnic site. Lavender was once grown here and there used to be a distillery where they would distil the oil from the lavender.

Pubs, tea shops, etc

The **Fordwich Arms** is next to the river and a Michelin starred restaurant. Tel: 01227 710444.

Also at Fordwich, close to the bridge is the recommended **George and Dragon**. Tel: 01227 710661.

The **Grove Ferry Inn** has been offering sustenance to old river dogs for centuries. Tel: 01227 860302.

21 Canterbury Stour

Beavers have big teeth! *Chris Taylor*

Tidal planning

Tidal planning is not essential but will make your journey easier!

High tide at Grove Ferry is the same time as London Bridge (or 3 hours and 15mins after Dover). The tide is said to flood for 3 hours and ebb for 9. The tide will take about an hour to flow up to Fordwich so we suggest that you plan to launch and set off from Grove Ferry about an hour or more before high tide. That having been said, the tidal effect this far upstream is not as much as we imagined – the tide in effect dams the river flow so there may be only a little current to help you upstream – however more to help you downstream. Reasonably fast paddlers can reckon on an hour and a half to paddle up to Fordwich and an hour to return. Note that at really low Neap tides, the tidal influence may not reach Fordwich and you may be struggling to make the last few km.

Places to visit nearby

Stodmarsh National Nature Reserve covers 241 hectares of diverse landscape comprising reed beds, grazing marsh and lagoons. There are several bird hides located on the reserve and these are great places for identifying the abundance of bird life.

Canterbury is of course a famous historic cathedral city and well worth a visit.

If you have driven out from London, then why not finish your trip with a visit to the seaside? – **Herne Bay** and **Whitstable** are only a few minutes drive.

Beavers in the Stour

Beavers have been reported here since at least 2008 but it is not known how they arrived. They are mainly seen in the Stodmarsh National Nature Reserve to the south of the river and the Westbere Marsh to the north - paddlers are asked to respect and stay out of these wildlife reserves. They offer a peaceful habitat ideal for the beavers and by 2023 there were around 50 beavers living in this area!

Whilst you are unlikely to see a beaver on this trip, you can often find signs of their presence - the main signs to look out for are chewed bark and gnawed trunks. Another common sign are slide marks on the bank where the beavers slide into the river. These can sometimes show beaver foot prints but the tracks are often wiped out by the beaver dragging its tail. These slides are easier to see in the winter months as in the summer they can be obscured by the bankside vegetation.

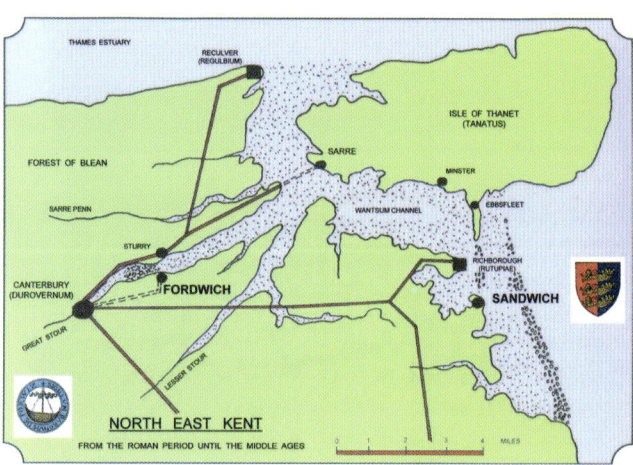

Fordwich as a historic port. *Fordwich Town Council*

Arriving at Fordwich. *Matt Oseman*

The Journey

Launching at **Grove Ferry**, a short paddle under the bridge takes you away from the road and moored craft. The river then twists and turns with lots of trees and bushes on each bank. This stretch of the valley is now a National Nature Reserve and if you paddle along quietly you will see a profusion of bird life. There are also lots of vole holes in the banks and if you are very, very quiet you may be lucky and see one of these super active creatures. The water is surprisingly clear and in the summer you can see lots of fish darting in and out of the water weed.

You can get glimpses of a couple of lakes, part of the nature reserve, on the south bank, then after some 5km the river opens out into a big tidal lake on the north bank. We saw about 40 swans on this lake and watched terns diving to catch fish.

Another 3km of quiet paddling with some very pleasant sylvan and pastoral scenery continues to **Fordwich** which is a really pretty old village – the 'smallest town in England', and well worth a short explore. There is a small landing spot just upstream of the bridge. We recommend a visit to Fordwich old Town Hall – if your crew has been mutinous then you can lock them up in the **old jail** or shackle them in the stocks. In former times scurrilous female members would be ducked in ducking stool that you can see hanging from the rafters.

If you have done your planning right then the return journey should

More information

O.S. Maps 1:50,000 – this trip is covered on sheet 179.

Kent tourist information
www.visitkent.co.uk

Canterbury tourist informantion
www.canterbury.co.uk

Historic Fordwich
www.fordwich.net

Grove Ferry Boat Club
www.homepages.rya-online.net/groveferrybc/

21 Canterbury Stour

be faster as the ebb tide is normally more powerful. Cruise along and enjoy the trip in reverse!

Extending the trip

About 600m upstream from Fordwich there is a sluice, and the river then becomes non-tidal. The river is a historic navigation from Abbot Mill in Canterbury and this section of the river has been regularly paddled but it does not appear to be that popular – mainly we suspect because it is a much pleasanter paddle downstream of Fordwich.

Other paddling trips nearby

There are sadly no other rivers of interest in this corner of Kent.

The **Rother to Bodiam Castle** is less than an hour's drive away and offers a quiet non-tidal trip – see trip no. 22.

There is a short interesting circular trip in Canterbury city centre (see description).

Downstream of Grove Ferry, the River Stour can be paddled for some 15km to Sandwich, however there is not a lot of interest as the river meanders through flat featureless marshland with high muddy banks. The river also becomes a more serious undertaking as the tidal ebb current become more powerful as you approach the sea and there is some risk of you being swept out into the English Channel!

Setting off from Grove Ferry. *Matt Oseman*

Summer day on the Stour. *Canoe Wild*

Paddle the historic Canterbury city centre

The Great Stour flows through the heart of the historic city of Canterbury and if you want a unique view of the city you can pay for a guided tour in a punt - or alternatively if you are suitably experienced and feeling adventurous why not paddle it in your own craft? On the negative side, the river splits into several narrow channels, the banks are vertical, landing is very limited and it can be busy with tourist punts - so try to avoid busy times.

The best place to park is probably at St Radigunds car park CT1 2AA, GR 149582 and then cross St Radigunds Street to put in in a small green on the site of the old Bishops mill, conveniently next to the Millers Arms. From here proceed upstream (south west) past the Marlow Theatre. Look out for the replica of the ducking stool before going under the Kings Bridge and then East Bridge Hospital (13th Century). Shortly after this while paddling alongside the Greyfriars Garden listen out for other rivers users shouting to warn of their approach to a narrow bend with limited visibility. Carry on upstream beyond the inner ring road and then turn right down a narrow channel. This will bring you to wider branch of the river and you can turn left here and continue upstream as far as you like on this the main river as it takes you out of the city. We recommend you return by the same route as the wider channel (into which you turned left) leads to mill sluices and potential danger.

Tied up at Fordwich. *John Lengthorn*

Bodiam Castle 22

Small placid river

There and back

12km return 3 hours

Very easy paddling

Parking	★★
Launching	★★
Portages?	None
Quiet?	Very few other boats

Why do this trip?

Shiver me timbers my hearties! What stout hearted sailor could resist the appeal of a stealthy boat attack on one of England's famous castles?

Special points

No permits needed.

Tell me more

Our suggested trip is to launch on the River Rother at Newenden Bridge and then to paddle upstream to the magnificent and evocative Bodiam Castle – to "assault the ramparts", climb the towers, explore, have a picnic or a pub lunch, and then a lazy return. There are several River Rothers in England: this one, the Kent and East Sussex Rother, is a public navigation from Robertsbridge upstream and no permits are required. The water level is controlled by a sluice near Rye so there is a good level year round, with hardly any current and only the possibility of wind to worry about. The river sees very few other boats and there are no roads, bridges or other signs of civilization as you paddle through the peaceful water meadows.

Canoe & SUP hire

Bodiam Boating Base is at Newenden Bridge, TN31 6FE. They have SUPs, sit on top kayaks and open canoes for rent. They also have a popular campsite and are next to the Lime Wharf Cafe. Tel: 01797 253838.

Epiclife are based at the The Hub, Quarry Farm, Bodiam, TN32 5RA. This is a lovely quiet riverside spot less than a km upstream of Bodiam Bridge. They rent sit on top kayaks, canoes and SUPs. Tel: 07377 184505.

Bodiam Castle - water approach. *Peter Knowles*

22 Bodiam Castle

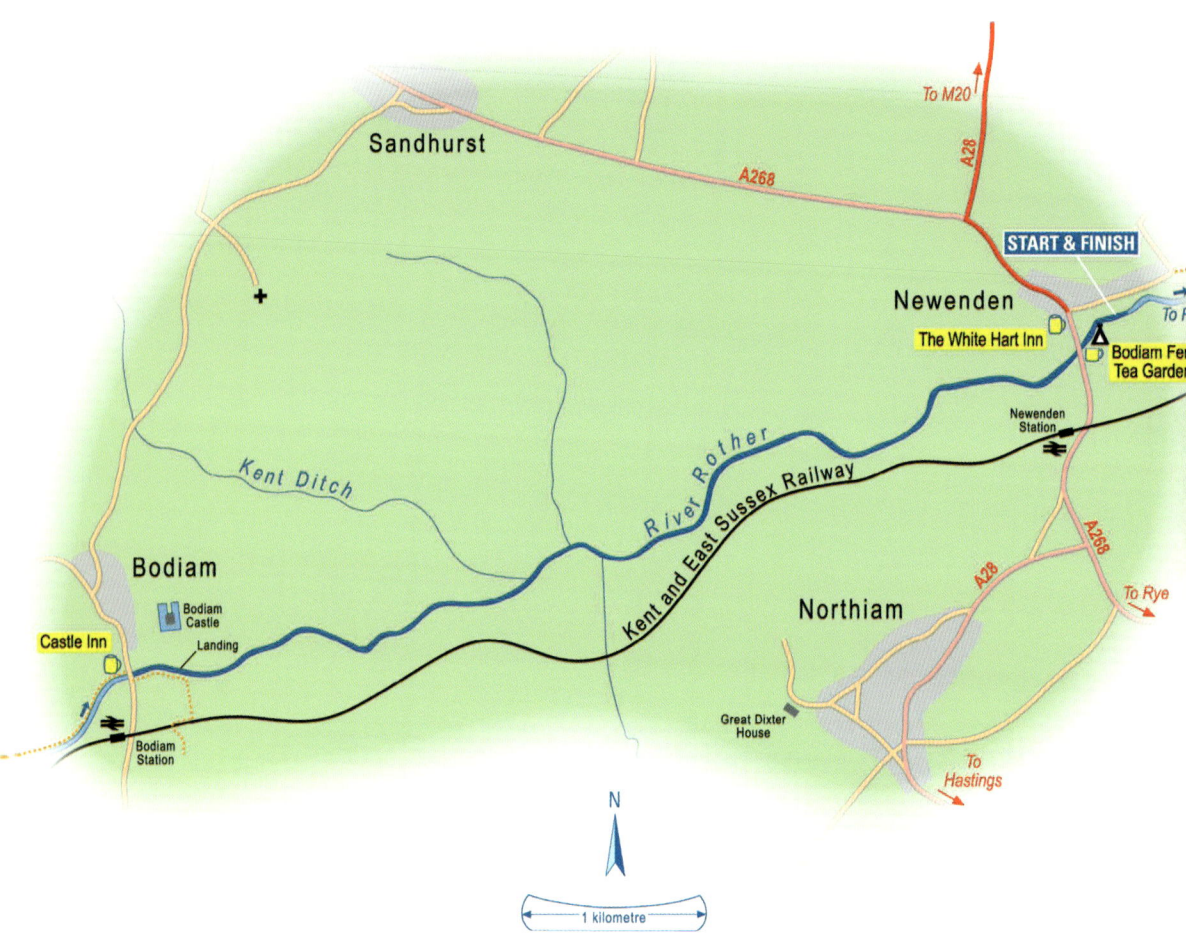

Start and Finish

Start and Finish Point   Newenden Bridge.
GR TQ837273   Post code: TN18 5PP
(No public toilets.)
From London, take the M20 and come off at exit 9, Ashford. Then follow the A28 through Tenterden and on towards Hastings. At Newenden turn left just before the cricket ground and park down this road near the play ground. Please park on the river side of the road and not in the residents' parking places on the houses side. The river and the launch spot is 70m through a gate, across the water meadow and then down a grass bank to the water.

Bodiam Castle. *Martin Sanchez*

Pubs, tea shops, etc

In **Bodiam**, the **National Trust Tea Shop** is near the bridge, whilst just over the road is the **Castle Inn** (Tel: 01580 830330) which is a friendly village local where kids are welcome. It does genuine home cooking and we gave top marks to their hearty sandwiches.

Back at **Newenden** the Lime Wharf café has an interesting menu and a campsite (Tel: 01797 253838).

Over the bridge and past the cricket ground is the **White Horse Inn** which offers more substantial fare and accommodation. (Tel: 01797 252166)

Other trips nearby

The Cuckmere and the Medway are less than an hour's drive away – see trips 20 and 23. The Royal Military Canal is another public navigation that can be paddled for most of its length although it has quite a lot of water weed in the summer. The best stretch for scenery is probably from Appledore to near Hamstreet – see www.canoedaysout.com.

More information

O.S. Maps 1:50,000 – this trip is shown on sheets 188 and 199.

Bodiam Castle
www.nationaltrust.org.uk/places/bodiamcastle

Tourist information
www.1066country.com

Kent and East Sussex Railway
www.kesr.org.uk

Historic port of Rye
www.visitrye.co.uk

22 Bodiam Castle

Upstream of Bodiam Bridge. *Fiona Firth*

Medieval fair at Bodiam. *Lisa Nicol*

Places to visit nearby

Great Dixter is a charming 15th century timber-framed manor house set in one of the most beautiful gardens in England. Just 3km south west of Newenden at Northiam. www.greatdixter.co.uk

Seddlescombe Organic Vineyards are about 12km South East near Cripps Corner.

Rye is an ancient town and port which is well worth a wander - it is about 12km away.

Go Ape have a high ropes course at Bedgebury 10km to the North West www.goape.co.uk.

Bateman's is another National Trust property which was Rudyard Kipling's home for the latter part of his life and is located about 15km west of Bodiam. It is furnished as he left it, with exotic oriental ephemera and you can also see the original illustrations for The Jungle Book.

The Journey

Newenden used to be a small port and historic ford. The village is linked with the first mention of the game of cricket in around 1300 and the game is still played at the cricket ground on your right as you set off. Head upstream under Newenden Bridge and soon the traffic noise peters out and all is quiet and peaceful. The landscape is flat and featureless with a low green grassy flood embankment that cuts off much of the view - so on a grey winter's day this could be the ultimate flat, boring paddle! However, on a sunny day in summer, what could be more perfect than gently paddling along this peaceful oasis – completely cut off from the busy world, with just an occasional water fowl, heron, kingfisher or a curious cow to keep you company? The only sound that may perhaps intrude is the whistle of a steam train on the Kent and East Sussex Railway that parallels the river.

There is absolutely nothing of note on this paddle – and that must be part of its attraction – just nature at its greenest, rushes and grasses, water lilies, the occasional swan, gulls flying overhead and perhaps a fish jumping. After about an hour of paddling you get the merest glimpse of some grey stone battlements behind trees in the distance – and that is all you will see of the castle from the water – and likewise, any defenders cannot see you, hidden by the low flood embankment - so you can creep up all unseen until you land your forces! You will see a small jetty, used by the Bodiam Ferry, and we suggest you land just past this – climb the bank and the magnificent castle hits you in the eye and an assault beckons!

Bodiam Castle is always described as the perfect example of a late medieval moated castle. It is open every day from March to October. The Ticket office is by the café close to the river – if you tell

Start point at Newenden. *Peter Knowles*

them that you came by boat and not by car you should get a reduction. There is a really good audio-visual presentation that brings to life the history of the castle and then you will probably want to explore and climb the spiral staircases to the battlements. There are sweeping views from the tops of the towers - over the valley of the Rother, but note how you cannot see the river at all. On selected days in the summer there are medieval events and you can try on armour.

For the return journey, you can of course just have a leisurely paddle back, or you have the interesting option of taking the steam railway.

Extending the trip

It is said that in the 14th Century the French attacked up the river a further 7km to Robertsbridge. This is a bit hard to believe – just upstream from Bodiam bridge the river narrows and then after the "Hub" hire base it becomes even more narrow and shallow. You can continue downstream from Newenden - the river can be paddled for some 15km past the confluence with the Royal Military Canal to Scots Float Lock (2km upstream of Rye) where there is a slipway. After this it becomes tidal.

A welcome sign! *Lisa Nicol*

Cuckmere 23

Small tidal river
There and back
13km return 3 hours
Easy paddling

Parking	★★★
Launching	★★★
Portages?	One
Quiet?	Very peaceful on the river

Why do this trip?
Cruise up with the tide through the most scenic part of the South Downs to one of England's prettiest villages.

Special points
Tidal planning advised

No permit needed.

Tell me more
The Cuckmere is a small tidal river that has cut a steep sided, sinuous, beautiful valley through the South Downs. The valley, the river mouth, and the famous Seven Sisters Cliffs make up the Severn Sisters Country Park, an area that is really popular with walkers and attracts over a million visitors a year. To explore this lovely valley by SUP or canoe is a special treat.

Canoe & SUP Hire
Buzz Active offers sit on tops and SUP hire at the Severn Sisters Country Park – but only on the Meanders Lake. Tel: 01323 463300.

Start and Finish
Seven Sisters Country Park
GR TV517994   Post code: BN25 4AD

The Waterside car park is on the south side of the A259 between Seaford and Eastbourne. **Toilets** are over the road. This is a popular car park and usual fees apply. Although large, it occasionally gets full on Sunday afternoons in the summer. There are alternative car parks close by if necessary. The **Meanders lake** at the start point is non-tidal, shallow, warm, safe and **ideal for beginners**.

Padding the flood tide up to Alfriston. *Alan Tilling*

23 Cuckmere

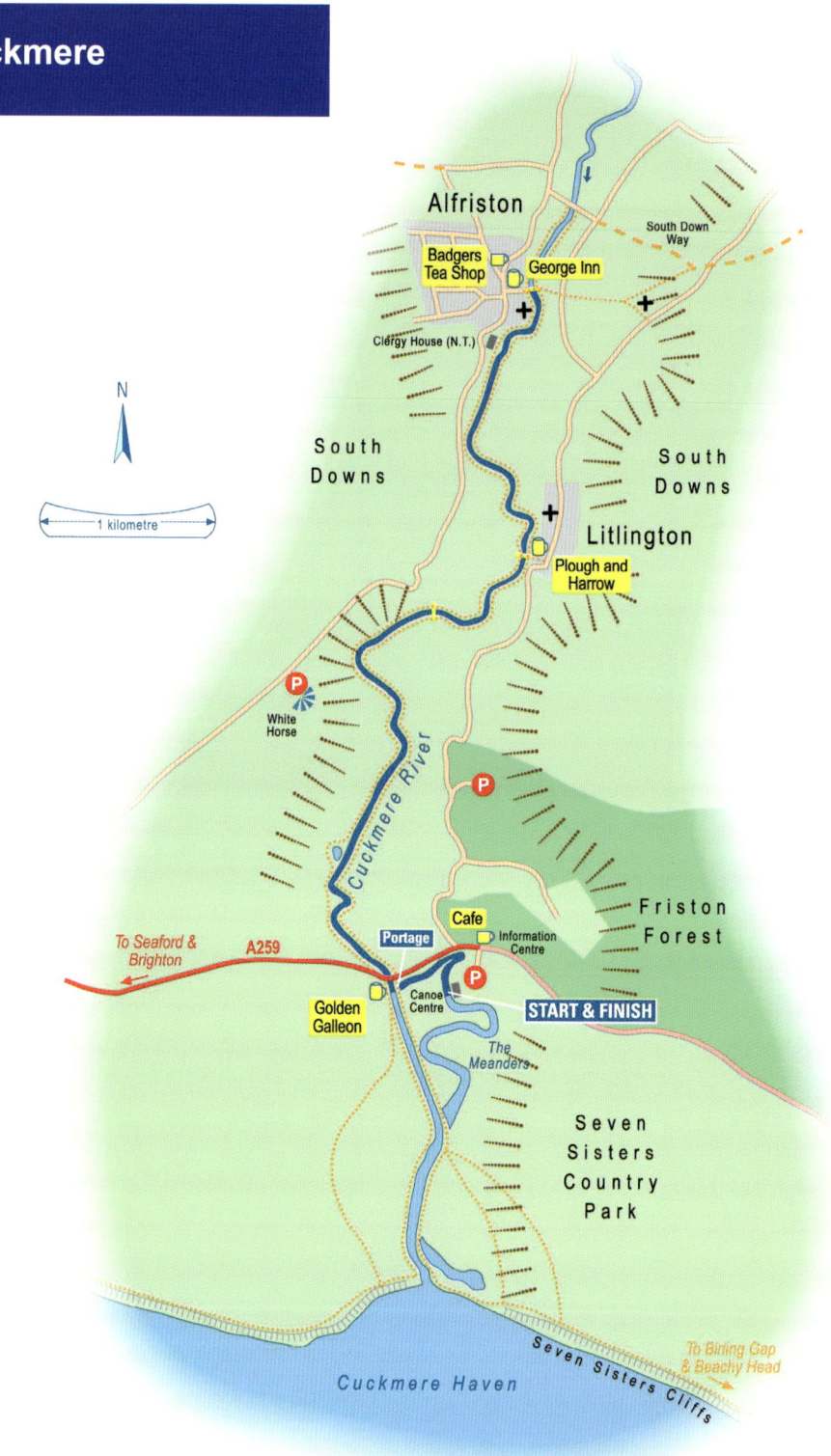

Cruising the Cuckmere past the White Horse. *Matt Oseman*

Tidal Planning

This is a fairly small river, so you need to get your timing right to arrive at Alfriston just before high water. A spring tide is best because it gives a higher tidal range – a low neap tide and you may be struggling to make the last km. We suggest that the ideal is to set off from Seven Sisters Car Park at about **one hour before High Water Eastbourne** (don't forget to allow for British Summer Time if necessary when looking up the tide tables!). You probably have up to an hour's leeway either side if you get delayed. A typical trip schedule could look like this

1200		Set off from Seven Sisters Car Park.
1300		(HW at Eastbourne)
1315		Arrive Alfriston – head for an explore and some refreshments.
1415-1430		HW at Alfriston.
1445		Set off back (start of the ebb)
1545		Arrive back at Seven Sisters Car Park.

Both the flood and the ebb flows at anywhere from 1 to 3 knots (mph) so you will have a helpful current to push you along.

More information

O.S. Maps 1:50,000 – this trip is covered on sheet 199.

Seven Sisters Country Park
www.sevensisters.org.uk

Cuckmere Valley Canoe Club
www.cvcc.org.uk/

Alfriston
www.visitsoutheastengland.com/places-to-visit/alfriston

23 Cuckmere

The Market Cross in Alfriston. *Matt Oseman*

Alfriston Clergy House

The Clergy House is remarkable as being one of the few ordinary houses to have survived from the 14th century. The house may have been built as early as 1350 and was originally built as a farmer's house. The Church acquired it but although it housed the priest it is a very modest property and not at all like the grand rectories that many Church of England clergy often occupied. It is a low-ceilinged, two-storey, timber-framed building with a thatched roof. Part of the house was rebuilt in the 17th century and it is also famous for its rare chalk and sour milk floor. Outside there is a small but well-planted cottage garden.

The house was the first property to be acquired by the National Trust and was purchased in 1896 for £10! It is now open to the public for much of the year and most weekends.

Pubs, tea shops, etc

At **Alfriston** you are spoilt for choice with several pubs and shops. Most convenient pub is the **George** which has a rear garden and passageway that comes out near the footbridge – real ale and pub food, tel: 01323 870319. Our favorite café is **Badgers Tea Shop** which is the epitome of everything a tea shop should be, and it welcomes, walkers, cyclists and even paddlers! To find it turn right along the high street, if you go right at the fork you will come to the front door. Drippy paddlers might feel more comfortable forking left and coming in the tea garden at the back.

Near the Start and Finish point is the **Saltmarsh Kitchen** behind the Information Centre. Tel: 07932 686121. Alternatively, just over the bridge is the **Cuckmere Inn** with a superb view and lots of outside tables - Tel: 01323 892 247. On most days there is also an ice cream van in the car park at the start point.

Other trips nearby

The River Rother **to Bodiam Castle** is a non-tidal paddle that is quite close and can be done anytime – see trip no. 22.

The **Sussex Ouse**, just to the north of Lewes, offers a pleasant non-tidal paddle and deserves to be better known. The **Anchor Inn** at GR TQ442161 hires touristy canoe type boats in the summer months. Whether visiting paddlers are welcome or not depends on the current landlord so if you want to park and launch at the pub, then we suggest you give them a ring - Tel: 01273 400414. Alternatively you can start at **Barcombe Mills**, 2km downstream and go upstream past the Anchor Inn as far as the weir near Isfield, another 3km, and then return. There is a small car park at Barcombe Mills, turn right out of the car park, walk some 50m, through a gate, then 50m up the public footpath to launch above the fish ladder. There is one easy portage on river right at the sluice gate downstream of the Anchor. Local paddlers seem to prefer the tidal trip from Barcombe Mills to Lewes.

Summer paddling on the Meanders. *Steve Douch*

Relaxing at Alfriston Bridge. *Matt Oseman*

The Journey

The **Seven Sisters car park** is large and busy with tourists and walkers. If you have time, we recommend that you spend a little time in the visitor centre over the road to find out more about this interesting place. There is easy launching from the concrete steps in the South Car Park (not the slipway of the hire centre) This takes you afloat on 'the Meanders' which surprise, surprise, is an old meander of the river that is now cut off from the main tidal river so it forms a nice shallow, sheltered, lagoon – ideal for a warm up paddle, or for the kids to have a mess about before or after your trip. Setting off, turn right from the slipway and 5 minutes of paddling will bring you to the upstream end of the meander – portage here up the embankment some 10m and then carry down to launch again off some **slippery** wooden steps.

Ignore the magnetic force that draws you towards the pub opposite, and glide upstream under the road bridge. The current whooshes you along, with gorgeous vistas of the South Downs opening up ahead of you as the river bends and twists under the scarp face of the downs, passing the delightfully named 'Brock Hole Bottom' (a brock is the old English term for a badger). The main road leaves the valley and all is quiet and peaceful with the occasional sheep and rabbits munching the sweet grass of the downs. A foot path follows both banks and walkers will look at you enviously and shout a

The portage into the Cuckmere river. Steve Douch

23 Cuckmere

Smuggling in Alfriston

The Smugglers Inn originally went by the name of Market Cross House. It has 21 rooms, 47 doors and 6 staircases, as well as an assortment of hiding places such as the cellars and a hiding place in the roof, all intended to confuse the enemy and allow easy escape from excise men. There were even said to be tunnels leading to other houses in Alfriston, and one going as far as the Long Man of Wilmington. The smuggler and owner of this house was one Stanton Collins who led the local smuggling gang and had a reputation for being quite ruthless.

friendly greeting. Keep looking about you, after a couple of km you will see over your shoulder the **White Horse** of Litlington carved into the hillside.

Passing under the next foot bridge the steeple of **Litlington Church** pokes up though the trees ahead. The footbridge at Litlington is a time to take stock and in the unlikely event that you want to cut the journey short then the **Plough and Harrow**, a well recommended pub, is just 100m away. Continuing on, you have another gentle 2km up to Alfriston. The river now narrows to just 3m or so wide, with tall reeds hiding you from the bank on one side. Look down and you may see grayling darting amongst the weeds, and at the right time of the year you may have wriggling hordes of eels riding the tide upriver to spawn. As we glided up on the tide, I dreamt that perhaps centuries ago, a Viking longship crept up the river through the early morning mists to raid and pillage the small saxon settlement of Alfriston. Talking later to the local historian Dr June Goodfield, she burst my dream - "of course, its very unlikely the Vikings would have raided this far inland as they could so easily have been cut off – however Alfriston was notorious for smuggling and on dark misty nights there would certainly have been sinister boats creeping up with the tide".

Places of interest nearby

1. If this gentle paddle has left you still full of energy then local friends recommend the walk along the top of the Seven Sisters cliffs – "one of the classic walks in England". If you are feeling energetic, walk to Birling Gap, then return via East Dean, where there is a great pub, the 'Tiger' on the green, and then back through Friston Forest.

2. Alternatively there is some interesting single track mountain biking, with bikes for hire, in Friston Forest. www.cuckmerecycle.co.uk.

3. For the less energetic, just walk down to the beach at Cuckmere Haven.

4. For younger families, the small zoo at Drusillas Park is recommended. www.drusillas.co.uk

5. Or, how about a stroll and fish and chips on the sea front at Seaford?

Alfriston Old Clergy House and Church. *Matt Oseman*

The Seven Sisters from Cuckmere Haven. *Steve Douch*

A little way on, and the spire of **Alfriston Church** beckons through the trees, then some roofs and the thatched roof of Alfriston Clergy house pokes up above a long thick hedge. Then the church, and just beyond here is the long footbridge where we suggest you land to explore and to take some refreshment, whilst the tide turns. Make sure you pull your boat up well above the water level – there is nothing worse than coming back and seeing your SUP or canoe disappearing off on the ebb current! Alfriston is a delightful, picturesque village to explore with some interesting shops (including one making home made chocolates....) tea shops, and pubs. If it is a fine day, you may just prefer to picnic on the village green near the church. There is no mad rush to start your return journey, as the fastest current is an hour or two after high water so plenty of time to explore.

If anything the scenery is even more beautiful on the return, with the White Horse standing out ahead of you. We surprised an otter or a mink on one of our return journeys. All too soon you will be back at the highway bridge – then make sure that you don't miss the take out at the **slippery steps** – if you are tempted to continue past here, then beware as there is no easy landing, and the river roars down past the groynes in a bouldery rapid and then out to sea.

Extending the trip

It is possible to paddle beyond the footbridge at Alfriston another 600m upstream to the next bridge and a weir – but rather featureless. For those sea kayakers with the necessary experience, the journey along the coast past the famous cliffs of the Seven Sisters makes a challenging and memorable paddle.

Alfriston was infamous for smuggling . *Peter Knowles*

185

Arun 24

Small tidal river
There and back
13km 3 hours
Easy paddling

Parking	★★
Launching	★
Portages?	None
Quiet?	Very few other boats

Why do this trip?

This tidal paddle takes you through the spectacular Arun Gap - where the river has carved its way through the South Downs with high chalk cliffs and hanging woods.

Tell me more

This is one of the most scenic of the South Coast rivers with an interesting village and good food at your destination – plus of course no shuttles needed. If you get the tides right then this is a 'whoosh' of a trip - the equivalent of riding a bicycle down hill all the way and note that in strong tidal conditions this trip could be dangerous! The river Arun has existed as a tidal navigation as far inland as Pallingham Quay, near Pulborough, since 1575. Nowadays there is no commercial traffic and only a few pleasure boats travel upstream of Amberley, so you will probably have the river to yourself.

Special points

Tidal planning essential.

Fast tidal current.

No permit needed.

Canoe & SUP Hire

Pulborough Paddles
Are close to the old Stopham Bridge, RH20 1DS
They hire SUPs, canoes and sit on top kayaks.
Tel: 07538 211071

Fluid Adventures
Have a location at Pulborough and hire canoes and sit on kayaks
Tel: 01243 942777

Paddling the Arun. *Joel King*

24 Arun

Trip description by Richard Ash

Arriving back at the Black Rabbit. *Mike Havard*

Start and Finish

Black Rabbit Pub, Ofham.
GR TQ025085   Post code: TN18 9PB

Our suggested start point is at the Black Rabbit pub at Ofham. From Arundel, head north on Mill Road, signposted to the Wildfowl Trust, and keep going until you see the pub and park in the first gravel car park. Launch from the river bank 20m along the footpath to the South. On return you may be able to land your crew at the pubs landing stage prior to a reviving pint. A long rope may be useful to recover your boat up the muddy bank at the launch point.

Tidal Planning

Tidal planning is fairly crucial for this trip and it is better to allow some leeway and take your time. Spring tides produce the strongest flow at up to 4 knots. I reckon that the high tide at Amberley will be approximately two hours after high water at Littlehampton (where the river meets the sea). Tide times are available from Admiralty Tides online - www.easytide.ukho.gov.uk. Just remember to add an hour in Summer as all tides are quoted in GMT. Mac users can also use Mr Tides.

For instance, if high tide at Littlehampton is at 11:00 - set off from the Black Rabbit at 11:00. Get carried up river and arrive at Amberley at around 12. Have a drink and a rest and wait for the tide to turn. At about 13:00, return with tide.

Pubs, tea shops, etc

You are of course duty bound to use the **Black Rabbit** pub at the start. The pub is popular on fine weekends in the summer as it has a magnificent location with fine views all around and especially south to Arundel Castle. The food is good and the staff are friendly. Tel: 01903 802638.

The **Riverside Café** and Bistro at Amberley serves home made food all day. Tel: 01798 831558. The **Bridge Inn** here is also recommended for good food and beer – tel: 01798 831619.

24 Arun

The Wey and Arun Canal – 'London's lost route to the sea'

In the 19th century it was possible to travel by river and canal from London to the south coast of England. The route was via a 23 mile canal that linked the river Wey at Shalford in Surrey (see trip no. 5.) and the Arun at Pallingham in Sussex. The canal formed a vital link, the only one like it, and it meant that in the Napoleonic wars barges could travel safely between London and Portsmouth.

The canal was authorised by an Act of Parliament in 1813 and it was built to accommodate large barges about 11 feet wide and approx 67 feet long. There were 3 aqueducts, 26 locks and many bridges. Following the Industrial Revolution, commercial trade on the canal gradually increased, with 23,000 tons carried at its peak in 1839. However, the railways took over as the new form of transport and the canal could not compete with them for speed and convenience so that by 1868 canal traffic had virtually ceased.

For almost a century the canal remained disused and largely forgotten until 1970 when a group of enthusiasts formed the Wey & Arun Canal Trust. Restoration is now progressing well - see www.weyandarun.co.uk

Other paddling trips nearby

For those looking for a friendly non-tidal place to paddle or potter we recommend the 6 acre lake at **Southwater**, just south of Horsham –this has canoe and SUP hire, tuition, nature centre and café. Another safe venue that welcomes the casual user is the **Wey and Arun Canal** at Loxwood – free to members of Paddle UK.

The **Sussex Adur** offers a paddling trip which is similar in character to the Arun, but is in our opinion less interesting and not as scenic.

The **Arun upstream from Pulborough** is an interesting 12km round trip and normally done as a separate trip in its own right. Note that spring tides are necessary to reach Pallingham comfortably. You need to launch at Pulborough about 2 and a half hours after high tide at Littlehampton – there is a public slipway on the north bank next to the tea rooms and there is parking just south of the old bridge and at the station nearby. The river is quite scenic as it turns north to cut through the Greensand Ridge near Stopham. There are then hills on either side, and eventually the river narrows and becomes overgrown until you reach the head of navigation at the disused Pallingham Quay, the start of the Wey and Arun canal. This is now a private residence and there is no landing. On the way back, the White Hart at Stopham has a pleasant garden and makes a convenient refreshment stop.

Places of interest nearby

Arundel Wetland Centre is one of the top ones in the country and has lots of hands on exhibits to explore - www.wwt.org.uk.

Amberley museum is a working museum located in an old chalk quarry with many practical working exhibits and things to see and do for the family - www.amberleymuseum.co.uk.

Paddling past the Black Rabbit. *Luke Smallman*

South Stoke church. *Mike Havard*

Arundel Castle is one of the great castles of England and still lived in by the Duke of Norfolk - www.arundelcastle.org. Arundel town is an interesting old town for a stroll - www.arundel.org.uk.

The **Weald and Downland open air museum** has Britain's finest collection of ancient buildings and is 6 miles north of Chichester – www.wealddown.co.uk

Why not relax at the **seaside** after your paddle? Littlehampton has a good beach and convenient parking.

More information
O.S. Maps 1:50,000 – this trip is covered on sheet 197.
www.southwatersports.co.uk
www.easytide.ukho.gov.uk

The Journey

Take a few minutes to admire the view downstream to **Arundel Castle** before launching. Set off from the pub and marvel at the speed travelled without putting any effort in. Oddly, after a while, this soon feels somewhat normal, and one ends up paddling at the "normal" rate for short spells. Soon after the start, you pass a few wooden jetties with some craft tied up that seldom appear to move. The river soon splits after leaving the steep West bank, with the main flow going to the left (N), and the fork going off to the right. This will be where you come out on the return. You continue past some lightly wooded stretches, with a bank on the left which interferes with the Westward view a little. Some distance further there is another fork to the right that goes under a low railway bridge (this is taken on the return leg).

Comfy cruising on the Arun. *Luke Smallbone*

24 Arun

A sweeping bend to the left brings **South Stoke church** into view. Things are looking up from a scenic point of view from hereon. The river, (still pushing you along nicely) now skirts to the right side of the church, and bends to the West within a hundred metres or so. Here you meet a footbridge, and this is one of the places that it is possible to become involved in conversations about "that looks really good fun", "where can I hire one of those" and suchlike. Immediately after passing under this bridge, one is presented with a fantastic view of the South Downs, a sweeping river valley, wooded and steep on the left, and less steep rolling arable land to the East. This is a great spot, and I look forward to entering this section of river.

All too soon you enter a meandering stretch of river, overhung on its (mainly West) banks by trees. Take care and do not do as I did, I lay in my canoe, drifting in the current without a care, only to nearly drift into a tree strainer and almost capsized!

A chalk cliff comes into view ahead, and as this is passed, the distant and unwelcome noise of a road can be heard. This is not a very busy road, but its presence is felt due to the comparison of what has passed before. A turn right and then the bridge at **Amberley** is in sight. Go under this, turn right, and go under the last archway.

Paddling past the chalk cliffs. *Mike Havard*

Cruising through the South Downs. *Richard Ash*

Paddling the Burpham loop. *Joel King*

Observe here the anchored plastic ducks!?! The cafe will be found a little way on the right after this, and this is an excellent place to tie up. Here is the time to drink tea or coffee, watch the ducks, read the papers, and wait for the tide to turn. Those more active can practice ferrying in the fast moving water by the bridge. Or why not consider the idea of locking the boat up and walking up New Barn Road to the **Amberley Working Musuem** – a museum of outdoor working crafts, with a narrow gauge railway for the kids to ride.

When the flow of water has stopped, off we go on the return journey. Due to the tide being on the stand, it will all seem a little slower at first, but worry not, it will soon pick up and carry you home. On the return journey, we suggest you take the left fork and go under the railway bridge. One day I will be under this when a train passes, it's got to be a great noise. The river is quite narrow here and becomes reedy either side. Look out for kingfishers - I once followed one for about half a mile. This loop takes you under another little railway bridge, after which you turn left and find yourself close to the pub. Take care not to miss the take out as duty calls and a beer beckons!

Extending the trip

Extending the trip is very easy by leaving earlier, and drifting further upriver. Perhaps raft up and eat a packed lunch on the move, or tie up river to a tree? However, it has to be said that the river and scenery after Amberley is not as interesting. The next good access point is at Pulborough some 11km upstream where there is a slipway by the bridge. See 'Other paddling trips nearby' for information on the river upstream of here .

Going the other way, you can continue downstream past Arundel to Littlehampton but you need to plan for strong tidal flows and there is less to see as the river is constrained by high flood banks.

Hamble 25

Wide tidal river

There and back

11km return 3 hours

Easy paddling

Parking	★★
Launching	★★★
Portages?	None
Quiet?	Some other boats

Why do this trip?

This is a beautiful and diverse paddle that takes you from the maritime world of yachts and marinas, through unspoilt riverine landscape to a fine English pub

Tell me more

The Hamble is famous as a busy yachting river full of expensive yachts, marinas and boat yards, but few people know about the upper river which is quite different – quiet and beautifully rural - tidal flats, wooded banks, fields and wildlife. This is an excellent paddle but you do need to plan your trip to use the tides so that you travel with the tide upstream to arrive at the Horse and Jockey at, or around High Tide in time for a leisurely break and then to return with the ebb.

In the first kilometer of the trip you will be passing close to some expensive yachts so we suggest you consider our alternative starting point if you have many beginners in your group.

Special points

Exposed on windy days.

Tidal planning needed.

No permit needed.

Canoe & SUP Hire

The Paddle Centre

Is next to Swanwick Hard and has SUPs and sit on top kayaks for hire. Tel: 01489 536151.

Paddling the Hamble River. *Peter Knowles*

25 Hamble

Start and Finish

Swanwick Hard.

GR SU495993   Post code: SO31 7FN

Take junctions 8 or 9 off the M27 and then follow the A27 to Lower Swanick. Look out for the Old Ship Inn and a small sign to 'Swanwick Hard' where there is parking and a public slipway to launch from – but no toilets. This is now a popular launch spot for SUP's and parking may be difficult. So after launching you may need to park elsewhere. A Possible spot is Swanwick Marina near the Boathouse Café (£10 a day in 2023).

Upper Hamble. *The Paddle Centre*

Alternative Start Points

Botley Quay. GR SU514127   Post code: SO30 2UG
Church lane is the first lane off the main A334 west of the bridge in Botley. Continue along this to the bottom of the hill. The large old building here on your left is the Bark Store and the grassy public quay can be accessed through a pedestrian gateway. There is limited roadside parking just past the building. You can launch here from a slipway about an hour before high water, and then it is a relatively safe and very easy paddle around to the Horse and Jockey at Curbridge. Don't leave the return too late though! This also makes a really fine memorable evening paddle.

River Hamble Country Park.
GR SU494110   Post code: SO31 1BH
This is very handy for junction 8 of the M27 and has a good car park, toilets and café. At the time of writing launching was allowed but not publicised. There is a pleasant beach for launching but be warned, there is a long walk from the car park!

Setting off from Swanwick Hard. *Kazbunny*

More information

O.S. Maps 1:50,000 – this trip is covered on sheet 196.

Tidal planning
www.easytide.co.uk

Tourist guide
www.visit-hampshire.co.uk

Upper Hamble Canoe Club
www.upperhamblecc.co.uk

Curbridge Nature Reserve
www.nationaltrust.org.uk/visit/hampshire/curbridge-nature-reserve

River Hamble Country Park
www.hants.gov.uk/thingstodo/countryparks/rhcp

25 Hamble

Pubs and tea shops

The **Horse and Jockey at Curbridge** makes a great destination and welcomes paddlers – it is a riverside pub with a large garden, lots of tables, good food and real ale. Tel: 01489 78654.

Just across the river from Swanwick Hard, the **Jolly Sailor** at Bursledon has a mooring pontoon and is popular with yachties for its meals.

Feebs floating café is just before the motorway bridge – great for a coffee as you float. Back at Swanwick Hard, the **Old Ship Inn** is more of a local's pub and a convenient place for a quick pint after paddling.

500m upstream in Swanwick Marina and overlooking the river is the **Boathouse Café**, Tel 01489 895745.

The **Botley Brewery and Hidden Tap** is just upstream of Botley Bridge next to the mill pool.

Tidal planning

We recommend ideally **departing Swanwick Hard one hour before high water at Southampton**. This will give you the last of the flood tide, maybe a knot or so to help you paddle the 5km to Curbridge, your destination (the HW here is approximately 20 minutes after Southampton). The Southampton area has a 'double tide' caused by a second push around the Isle of Wight – this means that you have a long period of about two and a half hours of slack water at high tide so you have plenty of time to have lunch and explore before catching the first of the ebb to return.

The ideal is probably to depart one hour before high water, however there is quite a bit of flexibility - Local experts reckon that you are O.K. to set off from Swanwick anywhere from 3 hours before Southampton High Water up to H.W. itself. Then you can return anytime up to 3 hours after Southampton HW. Note though that starting early or returning late means that you will have a more powerful tide to sweep you past the yacht moorings, and it is worth remembering that the ebb flow is always a lot faster than the flood and on a Spring tide might be as much as 4 knots at half tide.

The ideal day! High water Southampton is 1230 and it's a lovely calm sunny summer day!

> 1100 arrive Swanwick Hard, unload and get ready.
> 1130 depart Swanwick Hard and gently paddle upstream with the help of the last of the flood tide.
> 1230 arrive at Curbridge, the Horse and Jockey - in good time to beat the lunch time rush.
> 1400 depart and paddle round to explore Botley Quay
> 1445 depart Botley Quay (tide starts ebbing around. 1500)
> 1530 arrive back at Swanwick Hard.

Horse and Jockey at High Tide

and at Low Tide! *Kazbunny*

Resting for lunch amidst ancient woodland.   *Tom Mace*

The Journey

Setting off from the slipway at **Swanwick Hard** you are in the heart of the yachting world and surrounded by millions of pounds of beautiful prestige boats. As you paddle past in your little cheap plastic canoe and admire these magnificent boats just remember my Yachtmaster friend Mike's saying "the smaller the boat – the more the fun". Revel in the feel of your small but superior craft - however keep to the right of the channel and take care – yachties really don't like plastic smears along their expensive gleaming white paintwork! For this reason we don't recommend this as a paddle for beginners – see our *'Alternative start'*.

25 Hamble

Upstream from Botley Quay. *Peter Knowles*

Passing the marinas and moorings, look out for strong currents under the road bridge; then you pass under the railway bridge and then the motorway. Now everything changes – there are no more moorings, just a wide empty river with grassy saltings either side and the valley opens up with wide vistas of rolling fields and woods which are little changed from the 18th century. All is space, water and sky. The mudflats along the tidal river attract waders such as curlew and redshank, together with a variety of wildfowl and gulls. You may also see egrets, recently arrived on these shores from the continent, together with cormorants, black-headed gulls and grey herons. All is fairly peaceful - however on a fine day you may meet other paddlers on their way up to the pub. Note though that there is a speed limit of 6 mph so motor boats are not a problem.

On both shores are remains of old wooden wrecks and there are also some small muddy side creeks that you can explore. About 2km up from the bridge a wood comes down to the south shore and there is a gravel beach here that makes a good landing spot to stretch your legs – also a fine picnic and bivy site. Another 2km of gentle paddling brings you to the confluence and you may see some sailing dinghies here from **Fairthorne Manor**, the YMCA centre.

The river now narrows and is even more delightful with ancient deciduous woodland on either bank. This used to be managed to produce oak and other timber for ship building – felled and then floated down to shipyards on the lower Hamble. The woods are now owned by the National Trust and protected as a nature reserve. With luck you will probably see the electric-blue flash of a kingfisher; local

Other trips nearby

The **Itchen** at Woodmill offers the option of a very easy non-tidal paddle or another tidal trip – see trip no. 26.

Places of interest nearby

River Hamble Country Park

Bursledon Windmill 023 8040 4999

Bursledon brickworks museum
www.bursledonbrickworks.co.uk

"We made it!" *Peter Knowles*

Setting off from Botley Quay. *Peter Knowles*

paddlers have seen mink, turtles, and deer swimming in the river. Round a bend, and there is the bridge ahead of you and the pub on the right. We suggest hauling your SUPs or canoes up well clear of the river and any other arriving boats.

River Hamble Country Park

Extending the trip

We recommend extending the trip with a paddle round to **Botley Quay**, our alternative start point. On the north shore you will see the boat house for Fairthorne Manor YMCA building then a further km of delightfully rural paddling brings you to a grassy area with an old slipway – this is Botley Quay and a public hard where you can land to stretch your legs – the Upper Hamble Canoe Club (a friendly, thriving club) have their base here and make good use of the restored old Bark Store. You can then explore further upstream if you wish, a spooky tunnel takes you under the main road and into the old mill pool.

Local experts suggest that if you are a more experienced paddler and looking for a longer paddle, then you should consider starting and finishing at the public hard at **Warsash** about 3.5km downstream, where there is convenient parking and launching.

Itchen 26

Narrow river
There and back
3km return 1 hour
Very Easy paddling

Parking	★★★
Launching	★★★
Portages?	None
Quiet?	Only a few other paddlers

Why do this trip?

A short trip on easy, non-tidal water, conveniently close to Southampton.

Special points

No permit needed.

Tell me more

This is such a short paddle that we wondered at first whether to include it in the book - however, size is not everything - this is a super clean, clear, running river and very convenient for a quick paddle. An easy tarmac path runs immediately alongside the river so friends can accompany you along the shore, with perhaps the push chair and the dog. There are normally lots of people walking along the riverside path, but only a few canoes or SUPs on the water and no power boats, so this is a friendly and **ideal venue for beginners**.

The Itchen here flows at about 1 mph and is roughly 10m wide at the put in. It's a lovely clean chalk stream with a chalk and gravel bottom and fish darting in and out of the water weeds waving in the current. The whole of the Itchen has been designated a SSSI because of its fine example as a chalk stream habitat – there are crayfish, otter, salmon, and lamprey besides trout, water fowl, and voles.

As an alternative, or in addition to this paddle above, there is also a **well recommended tidal paddle** extending downstream and to further tickle your interest there is the popular WoodMill Playwave.

Gaytor's Mill. *Mick Coyne*

Canoe & SUP hire

Woodmill Boathouse is a well-established centre that hires SUPs, open canoes and sit on top kayaks. Tel: 023 8043 9185

The SUP Company has a shop for sales and demos next to Woodmill Boathouse. Tel: 01489 536151

Notes

26 Itchen

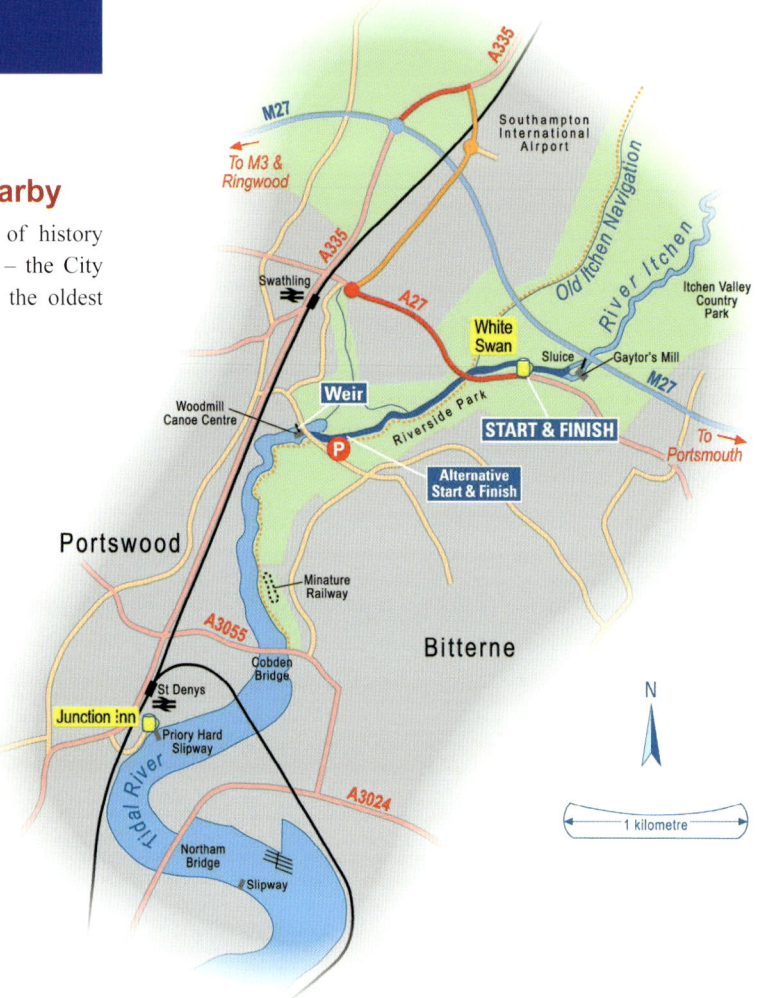

Places of interest nearby

Southampton itself has a lot of history which is best explored on foot – the City Wall Walk, Museums, Bargate, the oldest Bowling Green, etc.

Bursledon Windmill
www3.hants.gov.uk/windmill
tel 02380 404999

Solent Sky Museum
www.spitfireonline.co.uk
tel 02380 635830

Other paddling trips nearby

The trip on the **Hamble** is undoubtedly the star in this area – see trip number 25. Another pretty tidal paddle to consider is the **Beaulieu river** see - www.newforestactivities.co.uk. The **Avon** is quite close and a beautiful river for padding but the historical right of navigation is contested by some riparian owners and fishing interests, so if you choose to paddle this river you may encounter threats or abuse. The most convenient trip is probably the 12km paddle from Fordingbridge to Ringwood. See www.theriveravon.blogspot.com.

Start and Finish

White Swan Pub
GR SU450156   Post code SO18 3HW

Exit off the M27 at junction 5 and follow signs for the Airport. At the Airport roundabout continue on past the Ford car showroom and then turn left at the next roundabout signed 'West End'. The White Swan pub is on the left after a km. Drive past the pub, turn left and then right to park in the cul de sac lane next to the river and upstream of the pub. At the time of writing parking here was free and unrestricted.

An alternative Start is the large public car park at Riverside Park on Woodmill lane, GR441152. This is busier and more public. It has a height restriction, will cost you good money, but is more convenient if you are considering the tidal paddle. The idea of a pint after paddling may tip the balance for some paddlers!

Paddling next to Riverside Park. *Woodmill Centre*

The Journey

Launching is quite easy at either start point from the low concrete bank. We suggest that you set off upstream to begin with – about 300m from the White Swan will bring you to the old brick 18th century **Gaters Mill**. There are vistas of woodland and water meadows on the far side of the river and the only thing that tells you that you are close to Southampton is the traffic noise – that and the sudden whoosh as a plane landing at Southampton Airport swoops low over your head. Grazing cattle, swans, ducks, and other water fowl, all blithely ignore the aircraft. At the mill, there are signs headed "Private" so sensible people will take the hint, turn round, and paddle back downstream.

Returning to the pub, ignore that dry tickle in the back of your throat and carry on downstream - in about 300m you will come to the new concrete road bridge, and then the old **'Mans Bridge'** that carries the 'Itchen Way' footpath over the river. The current runs fast through the arch and the gentle eddy below is a favourite place for beginners to get their first feel of breaking in and out of the current. When the rivers was used as a commercial navigation this old bridge was a real bottle neck and you can imagine the bargees cursing as

More information

O.S. Maps 1:50,000 – this trip is covered on sheet 196.

Woodmill Outdoor Activities Centre and Hire Shop,
tel: 023809 15740
www.activenation.org.uk

Southampton Tourist Information
www.visitsouthampton.co.uk

Itchen Navigation
www.sotoncs.org.uk/itchen

Itchen Valley Country Park
www.itchenvalley.co.uk

Southampton Canoe Club
www.southamptoncc.org.uk

26 Itchen

Woodmill Weir playwave

On the other side of the Mill building is a weir that creates a 'playwave' that is popular with local kayakers for freestyle practice. This normally works for two hours either side of Low Tide and at weekends it can get quite busy. **All weirs are dangerous** and if it is your first time here, then we recommend you check with the hire shop for up to date information and any special hazards. There is no public access to view the weir or the wave – you need to park and launch from the Riverside Park and paddle around to the other side of the Mill building. Enjoy but take care!

Woodmill play wave. *Chris Vian*

they heaved and sweated to winch their heavy craft up against the current through the narrow arch.

The **Riverside Park** starts below the bridge and on your left bank there are nicely manicured grass and parkland, whilst in contrast on the right bank it is all dense, wild jungle of shrubs and trees. The river bends and turns and in less than a km you come to **Woodmill** – the old mill at the end of the tidal limit which is now a very active outdoor centre run by Southampton City Council. The road is built over the site of the old Woodmill Lock where barges used to transfer from the Itchen Navigation to the tidal river. We suggest that you land here for a run ashore to perhaps –

- Have an ice cream from the van in the main car park?
- Dip your toe in the salt water of the tidal Itchen?
- Just lie on the grass and stretch out?
- Have a ride on the model railway in Riverside Park – this is about 1km downstream from Woodmill and usually runs at weekends in the summer.

Paddling back upstream reveals fresh vistas and will seem to take a lot longer as you have to paddle against the current. –probably you will feel that you deserve a pint after all that exercise!

Special thanks to Steph Coyne

Extending the trip

Downstream on the Tidal Itchen

The trip downstream from Woodmill is popular with local paddlers. This is tidal water so you need to plan your journey. Local experts suggest putting on 2-3 hrs before the First high water and if planning a return run to be off the water by the Second High Tide. (Southampton has two high tides, caused by the flow around the Isle of Wight – the second one an hour or two after the first, so it's almost like a long period of slack water at High Tide with just a bit of ebb and flow. After the second High Tide there is a strong, fast tidal stream on the ebb, which most people would have a problem paddling against - especially on a high spring tide.

Setting off from Woodmill, initially the river is reed lined and very pleasant before it opens out to Bitterne Park. Cobden Bridge is followed by the railway bridge and just beyond here you can land on the river right at **Priory Hard**, which has its own car park and about 100m away is the well recommended **Junction Inn**. The next bridge is **Northam** and there is a landing just downstream on the right at the public quay, also with car parking. This is about 3.5km by river from Woodmill and for many paddlers makes a convenient turn round point - beyond this point the river is used by a lot of commercial and pleasure craft and there are several wharves and marinas.

Warming up for a marathon race on the tidal Itchen. *Caroline Barnes*

Continuing on, Itchen Bridge is about 7km from Woodmill - there is a pubic landing and parking here at Crosshouse Hard, just under the bridge on river right. For the experienced paddler, it is possible in the right conditions to continue beyond here, staying river left and following the shore line to Weston shore (car parking), or onto Netley Country Park. Another idea for a full day trip is to plan to arrive at the entrance to the Hamble river, to go upstream with the tide to arrive at the Upper Hamble (see trip number 25.).

Upstream on the River Itchen
Some 100m past Gayter Mill is a sluice under the motorway bridge that can be easily portaged and then there is about 3km of easy paddling bordering the Itchen Valley Country Park. There is supposed to be a historical right of navigation all the way from Winchester however this may be disputed by some of those who lease the expensive fishing rights. If you choose to paddle on the river upstream then you should bear this in mind and perhaps plan to avoid popular angling times.

The Itchen Navigation

The Itchen Navigation was built in the late seventeenth century to link the historic city of Winchester with the coastal port of Southampton. It fell into disuse over a century ago and although it is still a navigation, much of it has insufficient water for SUPs or canoes.
The old tow path is well maintained and is now a popular public footpath, called the Itchen Way, 17km from Woodmill to Winchester. You can still see many of the old locks, bridges and sluices.

London

Regents Canal *Paddleboarding London*

Introduction to paddling in London

Wherever you live in London you are normally within walking distance of some kind of water that will float a canoe or paddle board - but we feel that there are no trips in Central London that satisfy our 'family friendly' selection criteria. That being said, if you don't mind a challenge then we suggest that the Regents Canal and the Thames Tideway are worth considering - see the following.

Hire & Clubs

Paddleboarding London have a base at the Pirate Castle on Regents canal and offer SUP tuition, board hire and a friendly club. Tel: 07568 157300.

Regents Canoe Club is a well-established, recreational canoe club for adults. It meets twice a week at the Islington Basin, further east along the canal and has a full programme of trips, courses and events for its members.

Inner London – Regents Canal

The Regents Canal has been described as one of the finest stretches of urban canal in the UK and it makes an easy, scenic and memorable paddle - best early morning when it is less crowded. We suggest you start at the north side of **Regents Park** near Primrose Hill Bridge. There is parking on the Outer Circle of Regents Park, access to the canal towpath and launching at several points.

Our suggested trip is about 2km long to the **London Canal Museum** and takes you east past London Zoo - observe the animals and birds whilst gently paddling past. There are then four locks to portage, including the Camden Locks which are famous for Caribbean parties. This popular stretch of the canal has seen a redevelopment programme - it is busy and popular with walkers and cyclists, and there is a good choice of cafes and pubs.

Note that you cannot extend this trip as there is a **canal tunnel** close to each end - narrow, dark, forbidding and you are not allowed to paddle. However if this trip has inspired you, there are over 80km of canals through London.

Paddling past Regents Park. *Thames River Adventures*

We'll look after your sandwiches to make sure they don't get wet. *Ella Young*

The Tower of London. *Chris Wheeler*

London

Further information

www.canoelondon.com is a useful website that focuses on information needed by paddlers.

www.pla.co.uk is the website for the **Port of London Authority** – download the **Tideway Code** for essential navigation advice.

www.thames.me.uk is a great guide to riverside landmarks, history, and buildings.

Canoe Clubs & Providers

Several canoe clubs and commercial providers operate on the Thames Tideway. Most meet for regular mid-week paddles and offer coaching and trips further afield. If you live or work in London and want to paddle regularly and meet like-minded people then we highly recommend you join a club - paddlers are a friendly bunch!

London Kayak School offer tuition, guided trips on the Tideway and a kayak club.

Active360 offers paddle board tuition and guided trips on the Tideway.

Chiswick Canoe Club runs from Chiswick Pier.

Putney Bridge Canoe Club runs from Putney

Battersea Canoe Club is based at Barn Elms.

Westminster Boating Base is on the river upstream of Westminster.

Regents Canoe Club is a very active club based on the Regents Canal.

Tower Hamlets Canoe Club has a base at Shadwell Basin on the lower Tideway.

London Kayak Company offer guided Sea Kayak trips from their Greenwich base.

The River Thames through London

Paddling the 'Thames Tideway' through the heart of London is an exhilarating and unique way to experience this historic city. However the snag is that this is a **busy commercial waterway** with strong tidal currents. A safe trip demands good planning, awareness and skill - so this trip is for teams of **experienced paddlers**.

Planning a safe Trip

• No matter your experience level, we recommend paddling with a **local qualified guide**.

• If you want a stress-free trip, consider booking a guided tour with a commercial provider.

• Proper planning and awareness of the tides are essential - see www.pla.co.uk. for tide tables.

• Choose a day when you will have a **Neap Tide = quieter currents** and more exposed beaches.

• Plan to use the ebb and flood tides to help carry you along.

In the past our favourite Thames Tideway trip was from Putney to Greenwich on the ebb tide, stopping for a relaxed lunch while the tide turned, then riding the flood tide back upstream. While this is still possible, it is a committing trip for the well experienced paddler and if you have any doubts then a safer option is to avoid paddling the busier central section altogether.

Recommended trip from Tower Bridge

Launch at Horsleydown Old Stairs on the south side of the river (this may be awkward on a very high tide) and then head east on the ebb tide. You can stop at a historic riverside pub like The Prospect of Whitby or The Grapes, then either return or continue down to Greenwich. If you prefer a shorter journey then you can take out before Greenwich at Greenland Dock where there's plenty of parking. This route is easy to manage as a one-ended shuttle—simply take the Tube from Canada Water to Bermondsey or hop on a bus from Surrey Quays to Tower Bridge.

A cleaner, pleasanter River Thames!

The good news is that river is much cleaner than in the past and the water quality has improved significantly since the Thames Super Sewer was built. Paddlers often spot seals up and down the Thames and one individual became a regular weekly visitor to Tower Bridge!

An iconic trip. *London Kayak School*

Rules & Regulations

The Thames Tideway is a public navigation: no permit is required but it is regulated by the Port of London Authority. Just like driving on the road, you must follow the rules and a fine can be as high as £5,000. We strongly recommend reading the **Tideway Code**, which can be downloaded from the Port of London Authority website. Note that **SUPs were banned until recently** and are now only allowed subject to strict regulation - see the 'Tideway Code' and www.active360.com

Pubs and tea shops

There are many historic riverside pubs along the Thames that once catered to sailors and dockworkers. However landing can be tricky - often requiring the correct tide and then climbing a ladder or slippery stairs—so plan accordingly.

The best pubs are reserved for East London. The **Prospect of Whitby** is a favoured haunt of Tower Hamlets Canoe Club and is said to be the oldest riverside pub on the Thames. The **Grapes** in Wapping, extends over the river and once had a trapdoor in the bar - Just be careful you're not 'shanghaied' as in years past after a heavy night many an unsuspecting sailor would awaken at sea to find they'd signed on for a year-long voyage to China!

Special thanks to Michael Shaw

> **Special points**
>
> **The central stretch of the Tideway, from Westminster to Tower Bridge, is especially busy and dangerous.**
>
> Throughout London's history, the River Thames has been a vital and bustling waterway and today it is no different. Tugs and barges transport construction materials, Thames Clippers ferry commuters, and high-speed tourist RIBs - this equals lots of boats to avoid!
>
> The tidal range between high and low water can be up to seven meters, so we recommend you avoid high spring tides when currents can be extremely strong with surging eddies forming behind bridge piers. Even on calm days, the wake from frequent boat traffic can create rough and unpredictable waters and if you do get into trouble the high embankment walls provide few exit points.

Where next?

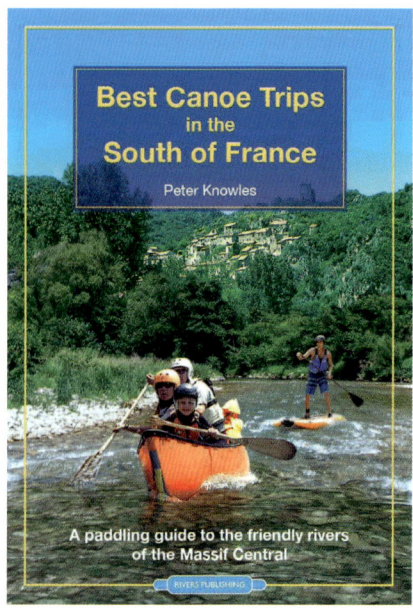

Longer trips

Most of the trips in this book can easily be extended or combined. A word of caution when planning your trip – it's easy to get too enthusiastic and plan too long a distance. We recommend that especially with children, you think in terms of 10km rather than 20km - remember it is easy to explore past your planned finish - much harder to shorten it!

River Thames

There are several small, pleasant campsites on the River Thames at some of the locks, intended for paddlers arriving by river - see www.visithames.co.uk. One popular weekend trip is to combine trip numbers 8 and 9, camping at Hurley lock overnight. The Upper Thames above Oxford offers a quiet 2 day trip from Lechlade.

East Anglia

We recommend Constable's Stour (trip no. 19) which makes a fine weekend trip, albeit with a lot of portages. Also in East Anglia, the Waveney is another pleasant river to consider.

Kent

A pleasant weekend camping trip is possible on the Medway – see trip no.20.

River Wye

This is our top choice for a weekend get away from London as it is only 3 hour's drive and it has a good selection of camp sites, pubs and hire companies. It is a beautiful natural flowing river with 150km of paddling. The 22km from Kerne Bridge to Symonds Yat and then on to Monmouth is deservedly popular but can get very busy. Our own favourite with young nephews and nieces is Hay on Wye to Bycross as a leisurely two day trip. This is shown on our 'River Wye Canoe Map 1' which is of course a Must Buy as it is waterproof and floats!

Scotland

This is a great country for more adventurous multi-day trips. Our favourites are the River Tay and the River Spey, both of which hold their water levels through the summer. See the *SCA guidebook 'Paddle Scotland'*.

South of France

The Massif Central region has several beautiful, natural flowing rivers like the Dordogne, Tarn, Allier, and the Ardeche. These are fun rivers, with spectacular gorges and ideal for canoe camping. They are detailed in our popular guidebook – *'Best Canoe Trips in the South of France'*.

Paddling in England and Wales - the legal position

Most river users are friendly folk and we think that it is extremely unlikely that you will be challenged or encounter problems paddling the trips in this book, as most are on statutory navigations or tidal waters. However we are often asked "what is the legal position on other rivers?" These notes are our personal understanding of the opinions at the time of writing in April 2025 and are written without prejudice.

Other non-tidal rivers are normally covered by Common Law which goes back to the Magna Carta. In the last 20 years, attitudes and legal opinions about access on these rivers have changed dramatically in the light of the legal work of the Rev. Douglas Caffyn, LLD. Our impression is that most outdoor experts now agree with England's National Governing body - who stated in 2021 that -

> "British Canoeing believes on a wealth of historical evidence, that there is at common law, a public right of navigation on all rivers which are physically capable of navigation".

The alternative legal opinion, still quoted by some landowners, goes back to a book written in Victorian times that asserted that if a person owned the bed of the river so anyone navigating on that river was "trespassing". To the best of our knowledge no paddler has been taken to court in modern times for such "trespassing" on a river. Of course it is your decision where and when you choose to paddle and we urge you to paddle responsibly and with consideration for other river users - research and check the internet so as to avoid rowing regattas, fishing matches, raft races, etc.

River Access Notes

Note well that if you have to **cross private land to access the water** then you should have the consent of the landowner or you are committing the civil offence of trespass (unless there is a public right of way to the river).

For more information see

www.clearaccessclearwaters.org.uk

www.riveraccessforall.co.uk.

Canoe-Camping Club

This is a national club for those who like to combine canoeing/kayaking and camping. The Club caters for everyone, with a variety of meets around the country. All ages are welcome, and in particular the Club likes to encourage families.
www.canoecampingclub.co.uk

DISCOVER THE REST OF BRITAIN'S PUBS AND PADDLES

"A kayak and canoeist dream pin up! A great wall map of Britain's water ways, both sides of map, with website links and info of the area's canoe sites and shops, canoe trails, guide books and info on rules and regulations with further links! Brilliant buy for all levels. 5 stars!" **Independent review on Amazon**

Index

Abbey Meadows 11
Abbey Stream 3
Adur River 24
Aldershot 6
Alfriston 23
Allington 20
Amberley 24
Arun Gap 24
Arun River 24
Arundel 24
Ash Vale 6
Aston 9
Avon (Hampshire) 26
Aylesbury Arm 14

Barcombe Mills 23
Basildon House 11
Basingstoke Canal 6, 7
Bateman's 22
Beachy Head 23
Beale Park 11
Beaulieu River 26
Beeleigh Falls 18
Betchworth 4
Beult River 20
Bishops Stortford 15
Bitterne 26
Blackwater (Essex) 18
Blackwater Valley 6
Blenheim Palace 12
Bodiam 22
Botley Quay 25
Boulters Lock 8
Bourne End 8
Box Hill 4
Branbridges 20
Bray 8
Broad Oak 7
Brockham 4
Brookwood Cemetery 6
Broxbourne 15
Bulbourne 14
Marsworth 14
Bures 19
Burlesdon 25
Burnt Mill 15
Burpham 5
Burridge 25
Bushy Park 2
Byron's Pool 16

Cam River 16
Cambridge 16
Canterbury 21
Cattawade 19
Caversham Bridge 11
Chelmer Navigation 18
Chelmsford 18
Chertsey 3
Cherwell 13
Cherwell Boat House 13

Chesterton 16
Chichester Ship Canal 24
Chiltern Hills 14
Chilterns 11
Christ Church Meadows 13
Cliveden House 8
Cobden Bridge 26
Colt Hill Wharf 7
Constable's Stour 19
Cookham 8
Cow Roast 14
Cuckmere River 23
Curbridge 25

Dapdune Wharf 5
Dedham 19
Deepcut 6
Denbies Wine Estate 4
Desborough Cut 3
Dinton Pastures Park 10
Donnington Bridge 13
Dorking 4
D'Oyly Carte Island 3
Dukes Cut 12

East Bergholt 19
East Bergholt 19
Eastbourne 23
Eels 5
Eton 8

Fairthorne Manor 25
Flatford Mill 19
Fordwich 21
Frimley Green 6
Frimley Lodge Park 6
Friston Forest 23

Gade River 14
Garrick Temple 2
Gibberd Garden 15
Godalming 5
Godmanchester 17
Godstow Lock 12
Goring 11
Goring Gap 11
Grand Union Canal 14
Grantchester 16
Great Dixter House 22
Great Ouse 14
Great Ouse 17
Great Stour 21
Greenwich 27
Greywell 7
Greywell Tunnel 7
Grove Ferry 21
Guildford 5

Ham House 1
Hamble River 25
Hambledon Lock 9

Hampton 2
Hampton Court Palace 2
Harlow 15
Harlow 15
Hatfield Peverel 18
Hedsor Backwater 8
Hemingford Abbots 17
Hemingford Grey 17
Henley upon Thames 9
Hennerton Backwater 9, 10
Hertford 15
Heybridge Basin 18
Hogsmill Stream 1
Hop Farm Park 20
Houghton Mill 17
Hurley 8
Hurst Park 2

Isis 13
Isis lock 12
Islip 13
Itchen River 26

Jesus Lock 16
John Constable 19
Jubilee River 8

Kennet 11
Kew Gardens 1
Kingston upon Thames 1

Langford 18
Lea Navigation 15
Lea Valley Park 15
Leatherhead 4
Lees Car Park 20
Leighton Buzzard 14
Lewes 23
Litlington 23
Little Baddow 18
Little Ouse 17
Little Tring 14
Littlehampton 24
Loddon River 10
London 27
London Canal Museum 27
Longridge 8
Lower Swanwick 25

Magdalen Tower 13
Maidenhead 8
Maidstone 20
Maldon 18
Manningtree 19
Mapledurham 11
Marble Hill Park 1
Marlow 8
Marsworth 14
Meanders Lake 23
Medway River 20
Mickleham 4
Milton Keynes 14
Mole River 2, 4
Molesey 2
Mychett 6

Newenden 22
Newnham 16
Norbury Park 4

North Downs 4, 5
North Warnborough 7
Northam Bridge 26
Northiam 22

Oak Weir 20
Odiham 7
Odiham Castle 7
Offham 24
Old Marston 13
Old Town Hall 21
Ouse 17
Ouse (Sussex) 23
Ouse River 16
Ouzel River 14
Oxford 12, 13
Oxford Canal 12

Pallingham Quay 24
Pangbourne 11
Paper Mill Canal Centre 18
Parndon Mill 15
Parsons Pleasure 13
Petersfield 24
Petersfield Heath 25
Pitstone Windmill 14
PLA 27
Polesden Lacey 4
Port Meadow 12
Portswood 26
Priory Hard 26
Pudding Stones 18
Pulborough 24
Punts 13
Putney 27
Pyrford Lock 5

Reading 11
Reading 9
Regents Canal 27
Richmond 1
River and Rowing Museum 9
Riverside Centre 13
Robertsbridge 22
Rother River 22
Royal Canoe Club 1
Royal Military Canal 22
Rye 22

Sawbridgeworth 15
Seaford 23
Seven Sisters Cliffs 23
Seven Sisters Park 23
Shalford 5
Shepperton 3
Shepperton Marina 3
Shiplake 10
Solent 25
Solent 26
Sonning 9, 10
South Downs 23
South Downs 24
South Stoke 24
Southampton Airport 26
Southwater Lake 24
Spade Oak 8
St Denys 26
St Ives 17
St Patrick's Stream 9, 10

Stanborough Lakes 15
Stodmarsh 21
Stodmarsh Nature Res. 21
Stonebridge Wharf 5
Stort Navigation 15
Stour River (Kent) 21
Stour River (Suffolk) 19
Stratford St Mary 19
Streatley 11
Sturry 21
Sudbury 19
Sunbury Lock 3
Swan Upping 8
Swanwick 25
Swanwick Hard 25
Swaythling 26

Teapot Island 20
Teddington Lock 1
Teston 20
Thames Ditton 2
Thames Tideway 27
Thrupp 13
Tonbridge 20
Tottenham 15
Tower Bridge 27
Tring 14
Trumpington 16
Twyford Bridge 20
Twyford Bridge 20
Twyford Mill 10

Ulting Church 18
Upstreet 21

Victoria Arms 13

Walton Bridge 3
Wargrave 9, 10
Warwash 25
Waterside Centre 5
Waveney River 16
Welwyn Garden City 15
Wendover Arm 14
West Green House 7
Westbere 21
Westminster 27
Wey & Arun Canal 24
Wey and Arun Canal 5
Wey River 3, 5
Weybridge 3
Whipsnade 14
Whitchurch 11
Willow 18
Winchester 26
Winchfield 7
Windsor Castle 8
Winnersh 10
Wisley 5
Wissey River 16
Woking 6
Wokingham 9
Wolvercote 12
Woodbridge Meadows 5
Woodmill 26
Wytham 12

Yalding 20

LONDON KAYAK SCHOOL
Your Adventures Start Here!

LONDON KAYAK SCHOOL
Paddling for All Ages & Abilities

Join Our Youth Or Adult Canoe Club
Weekly Coached Sessions in London
All Gear Provided • Beginners Welcome

Level Up Your Skills
Pool Sessions • Rolling Clinics
British Canoeing Awarding Body Courses

Adventure Beyond London
Monthly White Water Trips • Wild Camping • International Kayaking Getaways

From calm rivers to wild rapids – find your next challenge!

www.londonkayakschool.com

 info@londonkayakschool.com   @londonkayakschool

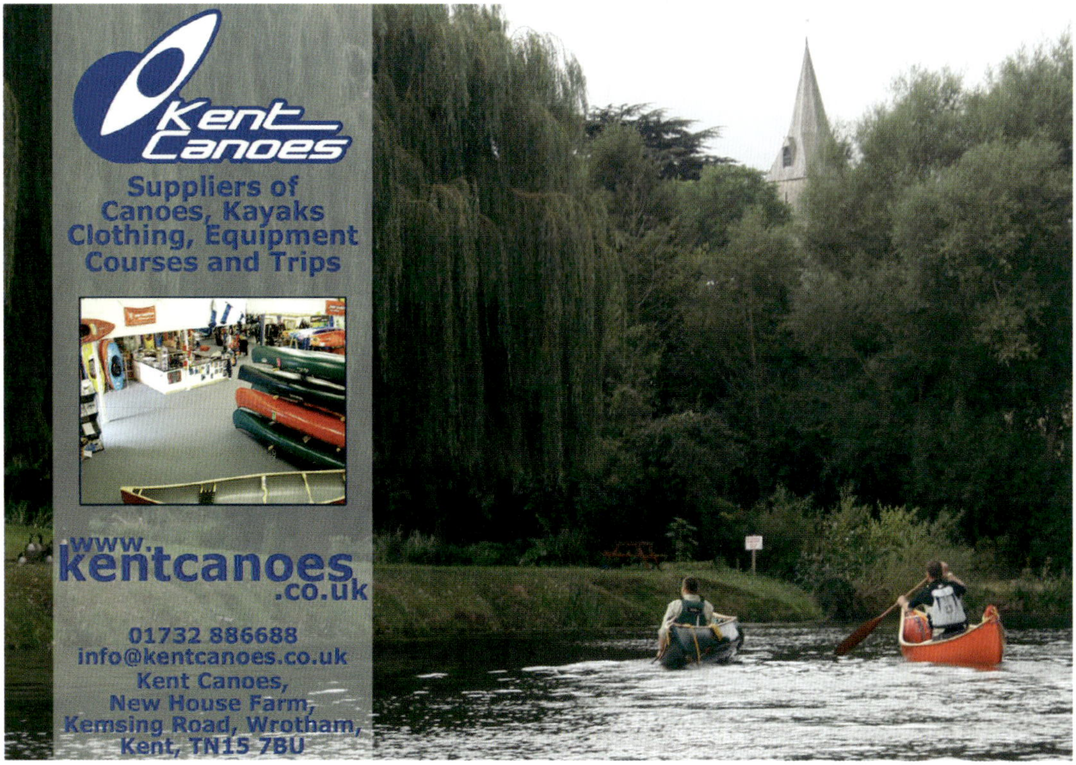

Kent Canoes

Suppliers of Canoes, Kayaks Clothing, Equipment Courses and Trips

www.kentcanoes.co.uk

01732 886688
info@kentcanoes.co.uk
Kent Canoes,
New House Farm,
Kemsing Road, Wrotham,
Kent, TN15 7BU

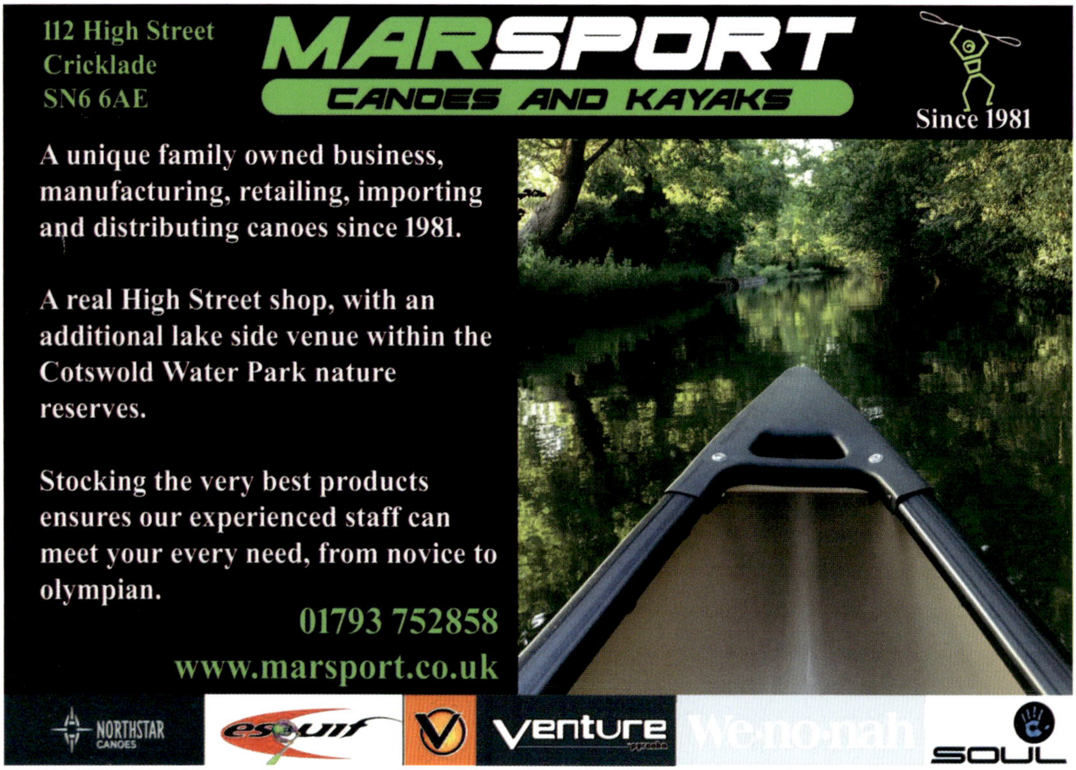

MARSPORT
CANOES AND KAYAKS

112 High Street
Cricklade
SN6 6AE

Since 1981

A unique family owned business, manufacturing, retailing, importing and distributing canoes since 1981.

A real High Street shop, with an additional lake side venue within the Cotswold Water Park nature reserves.

Stocking the very best products ensures our experienced staff can meet your every need, from novice to olympian.

01793 752858
www.marsport.co.uk